BRITAIN AND THE PEOPLE'S REPUBLIC
OF CHINA 1949—74

Britain and the People's Republic of China 1949—74

ROBERT BOARDMAN

Dalhousie University

BOOKS

10 East 53d St. New York 10022

(a division of Harper & Row Publishers. Inc.)

First published 1976 by
THE MACMILLAN PRESS LTD
London and Basingstoke

Published in the U.S.A. 1976 by
HARPER & ROW PUBLISHERS, INC.
BARNES & NOBLE IMPORT DIVISION

ISBN 0-06-490514-4

Printed in Great Britain

For my parents

Contents

Preface

This short study of British attitudes and policies towards the People's Republic of China ostensibly covers a long period of time. A few preliminary observations are therefore necessary. It has not been my objective to provide a comprehensive account of Sino-British relations in the quarter-century since 1949. I have tried rather to obtain an impression of the British side by looking in some depth at several aspects and periods, in the belief that this would throw light on the whole. It seemed important at least to try to tackle a large number of questions. Was Britain's China policy, as Republicans in the United States Congress tended to argue during the Korean War, simply the product of the cynical pursuit of material self-interest? Was it, alternatively, as Labour MPs in the House of Commons often maintained, the outcome of pressures from, and constraints imposed by, Washington? Did China policy originate entirely within the confines of the Foreign Office, as a public opinion indignant at the apparent passivity of the government in the face of the treatment of British subjects during the Cultural Revolution was inclined to suspect? Why did negotiations on the exchange of ambassadors fail in 1950 and succeed in 1972? How, in their turn, have the Chinese viewed Britain?

In the event, many questions (such as the last) had to be discarded; though a few husks remain. Relatively greater emphasis has been placed on the earlier part of the period since 1949, and in particular on the period from then until 1955. It was during these years that the main contours of policy were etched. After a brief historical glance, Chapters 2 and 3 examine official and public attitudes towards the Communist regime established in October 1949 and the sequence of events leading up to British diplomatic recognition of it early in 1950, together with the collapse of the negotiations on an exchange of ambassadors in the months following. British views of China within the broader perspective of nationalism and Communism in Asia are discussed in Chapter 4, which centres on the debate in Britain on the creation of the South-East Asia Treaty Organisation (SEATO) in 1954. Trade is the focus of the next two chapters. The first of these is an account and assessment of the changes that took place in Sino-British trading relations in 1949—54, including the virtual disappearance of British enterprise within China, and the setting up of new channels for the negotiation of contracts between British traders and Chinese officials. Chapter 6 then turns to issues connected with the strategic controls on Sino-British trade. The origins of the control system from 1949 are investigated; particular attention is paid to the arguments and events which led the government in 1957 unilaterally, against strong American objections, to revise the regulations in such a way that Britain's China trade was brought into line with Soviet and East European trade. It has been a recurrent British argument that London could in the right circumstances play a useful mediatory role between Washington and Peking. The government's attempt to do this in the Quemoy and Matsu crises of 1954—5 and 1958 are the subject of Chapter 7. These were also important for clarifying the government's view of the legal status of Taiwan and the various Nationalist-held islands close to the coast of the mainland. Chapter 8 is a study of the period 1967—74: from the low point in relations brought about by the Cultural Revolution in China, the two governments proceeded to enter official talks which led to an agreement to exchange ambassadors in 1972, and during which delegates from Peking, with British support, finally took China's seat in the United Nations. The choice of the year 1974 as a finishing point is partly aesthetic: it rounds off the first twenty-five years of the People's Republic. It also allowed me to discuss something of the immediate aftermath of the 1972 agreement, which included official exchanges at foreign minister level, and which — but for the intervention of the first 1974 general election — would have culminated in the first visit of a British prime minister to Peking.

Footnotes have been kept to a minimum. A bibliographical note at the end lists further secondary sources. No effort has been made to achieve consistency in the citing of Chinese terms or names; any glaring howlers that may remain are entirely my own responsibility.

There is space for only a few of the many acknowledgements that ought properly to be noted. My primary indebtedness it to Dr John W. Burton, of University College, London, and to Dr Peter Lyon, of London University's Institute of Commonwealth Studies. Professor Sven Lindman, of Abo University, kindly supplied a copy of Pekka Laine's thesis on British and American China policies, which was translated for me by Martin Latham. Others who lent assistance through conversations and correspondence included Dr Audrey Donnithorne, Professor Richard Rose, Dr Joseph Needham, Lord Lindsay of Birker, Sir William Teeling, Nicholas Deakin, Sir Cecil Parrott and Sir Esler Dening. I am grateful to Dr Kao Hsin, of the Overseas Chinese Affairs Commission, Taipeh for information on the Chinese community in Britain. The staffs of the libraries of University College, London, the University of London, London University's School of Oriental and African Studies, and the Royal Institute of International Affairs, among others, provided invaluable help. The book could not have been written in anything like its present form without the assistance I received from officials and members of a number of organisations, including the China Association, the Hongkong and Shanghai Banking Corporation, the Sino-British Trade Council, the British Council for the Promotion of International Trade, the Society for Anglo-Chinese Understanding, and the Great Britain—China Centre. To all these I should like to express particular thanks. I am grateful to the Social Science Research Council for a grant with which to carry out research for the bulk of the study.

My friend and colleague Roger Dial has added greatly to my knowledge both of China and of my ignorance of China.

My son tolerated his father's puzzling habit of typing when more important things needed doing. My wife, who has known the manuscript in one form or another for as long as she has known its author, showed patience and understanding when it was most needed. To them both go my love and gratitude.

R.B.

Chester Basin
May 1975

1 Empires in Flux

It was a self-contemplative land, beset by buzzing impor-
tunities ... The charm of the Flowery Kingdom lies in its
dreaming, through thirty centuries, in one mood, or one
landscape of moods melting into one another with an
incomparable harmony, as perfect as that of a Chinese
painting on silk, or of the image called up in half a dozen
phrases of a Chinese poem .... It was an existence of a
palace garden, a world of subtle experiences deposited
century by century, and which embodied the culture, the
thoughts, of a nation; for there were no rival philosophies,
and some flavour at least of it touched the whole people ...
There was nothing left to learn — least of all from the cruder
uses of peoples in the outer space which the sun of Peking
did not warm ... Beyond China was nothing, as though the
world-surrounding river of the ancients had flowed at the
foot of the Great Wall.

E.V.G. Kiernan, *British Diplomacy in China, 1880 to 1885*
(Cambridge University Press, 1939) pp 1—2.

Western veneration for the fruits of the Chinese tradition has
often been shared by British scholars. One has written:

If our Universities had devoted to China a fraction of the
learning that has been lavished on Greece, not only would
our art and literature have been enriched but we might also
have learned much from a political system which has enabled
Chinese civilisation to continue without a break from the
Stone Age period and span what in the West are regarded as
separate epochs. Had Chinese thought been understood,
western civilisation might have been helped to avoid the
catastrophes of the past and to surmount the still graver
dangers that threaten us today.[1]

It is a fascination that has long since broken through academic doors. Through his translations and commentaries, Arthur Waley was foremost among those who forged links between the scholarly and the public worlds. Age and changelessness were virtues with peculiar attraction for the citizens of an urbanised, industrial society. Thousands visited the great exhibitions of Chinese art and antiquities held in London in 1935 and 1973. The emergence in the interim of a Communist regime in China prompted disquiet, but gave rise to no widespread call for its shunning.

Their own different histories may have fed the divergent British and American responses to the idea that fundamental political change could take place in a country without its roots in the past being ripped up and discarded. On balance, the American disposition was to deny this. A Communist China was almost a contradiction in terms. Either Communism had been successful, in which case the past had been obliterated; or it had been only partly so, in which case tradition would eventually reassert itself, and Communism would wither away. British opinion did not underestimate the magnitude of the change. One observer in Shanghai wrote in 1949: 'What has happened here, the coming of Communism to this hopeless people, is one of the greatest climacterics of human history, which will change its course as surely and perhaps as deeply as the coming of Christ changed Europe, and the conquests of Mohammed the Middle East'.[2] But there was also present some tendency to see in Communism at least something resonant with Chinese tradition. Communism there was home-grown: it seemed to be identified with the nationalist and reformist aspirations of the Chinese people. China had started off in a new direction. To the extent that she could be wrenched by her new leaders out of the violence, corruption and poverty of the Kuomintang years, then this route was felt to have much to commend it.

The difference between American and British views cannot, however, be characterised as simply as this. The naiver excesses of sympathisers — manifested in the assertion that Chinese Communists were really only 'agrarian reformers' — had already disappeared from British as well as from American thinking by 1949. Anxiety about Soviet intentions and policy in the Far East was as prominent in British as in United States assessments. Few in Britain in 1949 entertained hopes that the People's

Republic of China would not pose huge problems for British and for Western interests in Asia. In the United States, an idealisation of the cultural virtues of the imperial past, and of the political virtues of the Republican, led to a revulsion against the China of Mao Tse-tung. But neither the repugnance itself, nor the uniformity of American opinion, crystallised until after the start of the Korean War, or even until after Chinese intervention in that war. Before then, as in Britain, opinion was divided. In Britain, the balance of legal and political argument came down on the side of recognition of the Communist government, trade, and support of its credentials in the United Nations. While the scale tipped the other way in Washington, however, the option of taking the British route was kept alive until well into 1950. During the previous year, many American officials expressed serious misgivings about Chiang Kai-shek's military ineptitude. But a significant number also took the additional, and more distinctively British, step of arguing that Communism in China was unshakeably Chinese, and not some Far Eastern instrument of the Kremlin. After 1950, American argument drifted on the surface of a larger number of accepted truths. Debate came to be restricted to an evaluation of the means of opposing what appeared to be an implacably hostile enemy.

In Britain, by contrast, the clash of ideas flourished. The government, whether Labour or Conservative, was attacked from the left for kowtowing to American imperialism, from the centre for failing to communicate its views effectively to Washington, and from the right for indulging in a brand of appeasement the disastrous consequences of which would far outweigh those of the 1930s. Yet British policy after 1949 retained a high degree of consistency.

The historical roots of this policy lay in the nineteenth century. Events such as the destruction of the summer palace in Peking in 1860 indicate that Britain's actions, whatever the thoughts of her scholars, were not always shaped by men of leisure who found delight in contemplating the calm infinity of Chinese civilisation. Westerners 'did not come in search of verses, and much of what they saw repelled them as sordid ... The Chinese, like the Irish, were turned into derision; the Chinaman was impervious to pain, he could sleep upside down, and he was, in the time-honoured word, inscrutable — much as women, also from not being treated as equals came to be seen as insoluble riddles.'[3] The background is important for our purposes insofar as it sheds light on British policy in the middle of the following century. It recurred in Chinese Communist interpretations of the causes of China's discontents. It has played a large role in shaping Labour Party thinking on China.[4]

The first trading contacts date from the 1630s. Following agreement between Britain and Portugal, Captain Wedell arrived at Canton with four ships. He met with some hostility; but was allowed to leave China with some cargo after having signed a declaration to the effect that his action was due to ignorance of Chinese customs, and that in future, 'if we should act in any way contrary thereto, we will submit to any punishments the Mandarins and the City of Macao shall order.'[5] Trade was later carried on by agents of the East India Company at Amoy, and then at Canton, following a relaxation of Chinese regulations. Relations between Britain and China remained on an unofficial footing; both governments, for differing reasons, stayed aloof. Pressure to alter this state of affairs came from the British side. In 1784, an Englishman who had accidentally killed a Chinese during the firing of a ceremonial salute was tried by the Chinese authorities and executed by strangulation. This brought to a head the Company's grievances. It drew up plans for extra-territoriality in China, and recognition by the Chinese of exclusive British jurisdiction over British subjects. A mission of 1788 under Lord Cathcart was interrupted by his death en route for China. It came to fruition in Lord Macartney's audience with the Emperor Ch'ien Lung in 1793.

Like British diplomatic recognition of Communist China in 1950, the event did not mark the commencement of regular official contacts between the two governments. George III was informed that 'Our Celestial Empire possesses all things in prolific abundance and lacks no product within its border. We do not need to import the manufactures of outside barbarians in exchange for our own produce.' The collapse of the Middle Kingdom's protective shell did not come about suddenly in the following century. The Treaty of Nanking, signed in 1842 following hostilities, opened up Canton, Amoy, Foochow, Ningpo and Shanghai for trade. The Chinese ceded Hongkong to Britain in perpetuity; acknowledged that officials of the two governments of equal status were to have the right of corresponding as equals, rather than as mandarins or barbarians; and abolished the Hong system, until then the Empire's method of trading with foreign powers, and long criticised by British merchants, especially by the newer breed of more aggressive traders that had arisen after the ending of the East India Company's monopoly eight years earlier. Closer study of the rest of the century is outside the scope of the present book. By its close, the last of the imperial restrictions on the activities of foreign traders and businessmen had been removed. Despite increasing competition, Britain kept up its early lead as the major power with interests in China.

However, whereas the British government had first approached the Chinese in response to the demands of traders frustrated at the capriciousness and obstructiveness of imperial bureaucracies, this pattern was not always characteristic of the later period of encounters. Many traders, and those sympathetic to their cause in parliament, were highly critical of the government's apparent lack of *any* policy in relation to China. Making the point in 1899, Curzon continued: 'But of course the supreme lesson of the Foreign Office is that there is no predetermined policy about anything.'[6] Some traders at any rate had few doubts about where London's duty lay. 'The truth is that, like all oriental peoples, the Chinese can only be impressed by the display of power. So long as we thrashed them at intervals, they accorded us their respect.'[7] Ministers had other factors to keep in mind. A potential ally, even one on the face of it so weak as was China, could not lightly be snubbed by too frequent a resort to gunboat diplomacy. And, for their part, the growing body of British industrialists with connections in China were not eager to lend their support, and defend it to their shareholders, to schemes for the prosecution of British interests in China by force of arms. Partly because of circumstances in Europe, it remained a British interest that China not be Balkanised.

By the early years of the twentieth century, the dictates of balance-of-power diplomacy had begun to take precedence over the wishes of traders and entrepreneurs. An alliance was made with Japan; after World War I, however, British fears of Japanese intentions grew, following Tokyo's expansion of influence in China while Britain was preoccupied with Europe, and following also representations from Canada and the United States against renewal of the link. At the same time, the growth of nationalism in China clearly had far-reaching implications for Britain. In a famous memorandum of 1926, the British government went a considerable way towards recognising the validity of Chinese demands for treaty revision. In 1930, Britain's response to the nationalist upsurge in China was described as being 'an enforced retreat, necessitating endless rearguard actions, and in which our main effort was directed towards preventing it from being turned into a rout.' Accommodation was reached on some points. But the Foreign Office determined that there were limits beyond which Britain should not be pushed: British interests in Shanghai, 'both economic and political, are so great that British troops must be sent to protect the settlement, just as though it were a British possession.'[8]

The international settlement there was governed at the time by a Municipal Council of fourteen members under a British chairman, which included five British, five Chinese, two Japanese, and two American members. Until well into the post-1945 period, Conservative MPs in particular tended to rank Shanghai on a level almost equivalent to Hongkong and Kowloon when enumerating British interests in China. Extraterritorial rights obtained by Britain and other foreign powers had eaten deeply into Chinese jurisdiction. The governments concerned exercised full jurisdiction in civil and criminal cases over their own nationals within the defined territorial limits. Other rights included navigation of the coastal and inland waters of China by merchant ships and the policing of these with warships if necessary; the maintenance of military garrisons in China; and engaging in missionary activity.[9] All of this entailed a large British presence. In 1946, a diminution from its height, Foreign Office staff numbered 105 in various provinces, and included a judicial establishment.[10] In the 1890s, moreover, foreigners acquired the right to set up large-scale manufacturing enterprises in the concessions, in addition to engaging in the traditional triangular commerce linking China, India and Europe. There was heavy British investment in the textile industry, in primary industries, most notably in the Kailan Mining Administration, and considerable enterprise in banking and financial institutions, and inland and coastal trade. At the

beginning of the Communist period, in 1949, British entrepreneurs were still actively engaged — or to the extent that
prevailing circumstances would allow — in processing raw
materials and in manufacturing products with the aid of Chinese
labour. One of the first issues to arise in relations between the
new authorities and local British officials concerned Chinese
trade union demands relating to the pay and working conditions
of those of their members employed by British enterprises. Yet
the policies adopted by Peking towards foreign capital had
already been foreshadowed in the measures taken earlier by the
Nationalist Government.

The rise of nationalism in China coincided with a decline in
British power. Indeed it has been argued that Britain's difficulties in the region after 1933 'were compounded by the very
success of her confidence trick in the past. She was herself the
victim of a false image, the British public on the one hand and
the community of nations on the other, having an entirely
inflated idea of the role that Britain had the capacity to play in
the far eastern area.'[11] A readiness to meet nationalism half way
led to some degree of Sino-British harmony in the late 1920s,
but it could not long survive British reactions to Japanese
encroachments in the following decade. Britain's relations with
the Nationalists during the 1930s and 1940s were not good, and
were often virtually non-existent. In 1943, the British government relinquished all special privileges in China.

Before the establishment of the People's Republic of China,
then, a number of features were already prominent in the
British approach to questions of China policy: some willingness
to bend before the wind of anti-foreign sentiment in China; the
beginnings of a disillusionment with the capacity of the
Kuomintang to effect the kinds of changes needed to modernise
China, and of a concomitant sympathy with the more moderate
exponents of Communism as an alternative; a desire to continue
trade and enterprise once the struggle for power had been
resolved, within the limits expected to be set by any Chinese
government, whether Nationalist or Communist or a coalition;
anxiety over the actual or potential policies of other powers,
particularly the USSR and Japan; an appreciation of Britain's
own changing role in international politics, and more especially
of her inability to exert any decisive influence over the course
of events in China; concern for the impact of Chinese

nationalism, whether or not it took a Communist form, on the Chinese communities in Hongkong and Malaya; and, finally, a realisation that Britain's global priorities lay elsewhere than China. Each played a part in shaping the British response to China under Communist rule.

2 Tyrants or Liberators

At the end of World War II, British opinion would probably have viewed a forecast that China would have a Communist government by the end of the decade as a flight of fancy, or as at best a misjudgement of conditions in that country. China's internal weaknesses seemed endemic. The bases of Communist support had grown considerably in the previous quarter-century, but hardly appeared adequate for a final takeover. Some kind of coalition regime, of dubious stability, seemed the most likely long-term outcome of the conflict between the Communists and the Kuomintang. In this situation, Britain's new Labour government found little difficulty in reaching common ground with both the United States and the Soviet Union. The Moscow Declaration, signed by the Foreign Ministers of the three governments at the end of 1945, stated that they were 'in agreement as ·to the need for a unified and democratic China under the Nationalist Government, for broad participation by democratic elements in all branches of the Nationalist government, and for a cessation of civil strife.' It also stated that they 'reaffirmed their adherence to the policy of non-interference in China's internal affairs.'[1] Chinese affairs were for Attlee's government too distant to demand close attention by the Cabinet. British interests were involved, most obviously in Hongkong and in the British commercial and industrial presence in China. But issues of Western European security and reconstruction had priority. Asia meant India and her neighbours, and also Malaya; China was a secondary Asian concern.

Yet Britain, though studiedly neutral, was not indifferent to the course of events in China. Her stance was in part grounded in expediency. Neutrality towards the two main warring factions may have been seen as a means of deflecting animosity from Britain in the event of a clear victory by one or the other side.[2] However, as one Labour Minister wrote later, the government's knowledge of the old China did not lead it to expect anything other than a wave of anti-Western xenophobia from whatever government might be in power in the post-war period.[3] And by the middle and late 1940s, British disaffection with the corruption and incompetence of Chiang Kai-shek's Nationalist government was such as to bar active measures to preserve it. London supported American mediation efforts in China, without taking a more positive role in them. While sensitive and sympathetic to American feelings on the subject of China, Attlee viewed Washington's preoccupation with some reserve; it was 'absurd of course' to have China as a Permanent Member of the Security Council in 1945. China 'wasn't a Great Power then: hopelessly divided and in odd bits and pieces.'[4] Because of the British presence in China and the ramifications of the cold war in Europe, however, the government was in no position to wash its hands of the Far East entirely. Increasingly towards the end of the 1940s, the European and Asian policies of the Soviet Union were being seen as closely intertwined. The Moscow Declaration thus had the advantage of binding the Soviet Union, at least on paper, to a policy of non-intervention in China. As Communist successes grew in the civil war, opinion in Britain — particularly, though not exclusively, on the Conservative side — came to regret the agreements entered into at Yalta in February 1945 by which the Soviets gained Far Eastern concessions in exchange for entering the war against Japan.

At the same time, some minor forms of assistance were given to the Nationalist government. These were on nothing like the scale even of the 1930s. In particular, some British warships were lent to assist in the post-war reconstruction of the Chinese Navy; a number of sales of naval equipment took place; and the Royal Navy was engaged in a programme of training of Chinese officers and ratings.[5] The 1935 economic mission had its counterpart in a mission sent by the Board of Trade in 1946, which returned with a gloomy picture of the prospects for the Chinese economy. The Aid to China movement, which for a time had stimulated a flurry of private fund-raising activity for humanitarian purposes, continued in existence, but its role was small by 1949. Only a few Conservative back-benchers departed from the party's line and called for more direct intervention against Communist forces in China. Economic aid for reconstruction was, for the government, a matter for the distant future. In 1948, Britain explained to the Nationalist government that 'our financial and economic position precluded us from doing anything very material for China.'[6]

Predictions of continued civil war for the indefinite future, or of a functioning coalition government, proved false. Events moved quickly. In the winter of 1948–49, units of the People's Liberation Army occupied the northern cities of Peking, Mukden and Tientsin. As early as December 1948, some Labour MPs foresaw the early establishment of a Communist regime for all of China, and began calling for British recognition of those areas already under Communist control. The crossing of the Yangtse in April 1949, was widely regarded as the major turning-point in the war. It brought China once more to the forefront of British public attention because of the related incident involving HMS *Amethyst*. Grounded by Communist fire on April 19, the ship was held until her dramatic, and much publicised, escape at the end of July.[7] As the summer progressed, it became clear that the Communists were consolidating their position throughout large areas of China, so much so that in early August *The Times* referred to 'China's new masters.' Mao Tse-tung formally proclaimed the inauguration of the new regime on 1 October.

The situation arose with an alarming suddenness. 'Few had foreseen it,' Eden comments in his memoirs, 'not even the Russians.'[8] The question was approached on two levels. The first was matter-of-fact: British nationals and property were at stake, and Hongkong's interests were affected. If the Communist authorities were unequivocally in charge, then common sense as well as international law directed that some accommodation be reached with them. And with the Administration in Washington struggling during 1949 to extricate the United States from internal Chinese politics, the initiative for coming to terms with the new situation was seen to rest squarely with Britain. Secondly, however, there was the broader international political perspective. It is perhaps more accurate to speak of *two* such contexts: that of the cold war in Europe, and that of the rising tide of nationalism in Asia. The choice of the pertinent context for interpreting developments in China was important. From it followed logically the divergent views taken by observers in Britain about the nature of Chinese Communism, the likely future domestic and external policies of the People's Republic of China, and recommendations to the British government on the best course of action to take in the circumstances. Thus at the extremes, the new Chinese leadership could be seen either as genuinely nationalist and reformist, though there were divided opinions as to what these terms meant; or it could be viewed simply as an instrument of Moscow's policy. At least in 1949, one can see British officials, politicians, newspaper editorial writers, representatives of interest groups, and others, taking a variety of positions along a spectrum between these two points. The present chapter will explore these attitudes more fully, while the next will examine the evolution of policy.

Few problems were posed for British nationals by the Communist advance. In May and June 1949, Bevin and other Ministers informed the Commons that there had been no molestation of British subject in the Communist areas, and that 'considerable discipline' had been shown in the taking over of Shanghai. What damage there had been to British residential property had been at the hands of Nationalist troops. Even so, evacuation of nationals proceeded during the summer, though many businessmen remained. A similar account of the orderly transfer of authority in many areas of China was given by the Canadian ambassador upon his return to Vancouver in October.[9]

Complications did arise, however, on the question of British assets in China. In the 1943 agreements, the Nationalist government had assumed responsibility for the official obligations and liabilities of the foreign settlements. Two immediate issues came up in 1949: British private investments, and the position of British ex-employees of the former concerns, particularly the Shanghai Municipal Council. British officials tried during the civil war to secure reasonable redress on behalf of the individuals in question, but without success. The government smoothed over the hardships of redundant officials by financial and other means, and in doing so operated on the assumption that the losses incurred would be made good at a later date by the Chinese authorities. The China Association was especially active in securing official action on the problem.[10] It was a more frequent source of complaint in parliament that the Nationalists had enjoyed full possession of the assets of the occupied municipalities and other properties, without having met their liabilities to British investors. Taking the picture as a whole, the value of British capital sunk in China was often exaggerated in the course of political argument. Even so, a 1947 estimate of the 1941 value put British investments in China at £177m. Shanghai alone accounted for some £107m. of this total. Further, the Chinese government had obtained sterling loans on the London market. In 1946, there was approximately £18m. of the principal of loans issued in sterling outstanding. Many instalments of interest payments were overdue. In addition, there were loans of over £12m. outstanding from the British government itself. Still another liability, from Britain's point of view, was compensation for damage done to British property at Canton in riots during the civil war. A claim of £300,000 had been lodged with the Nationalist authorities.[11]

On none of these questions was British official opinion optimistic about the outcome of any future negotiations with the Communist regime; but their existence added weight to the argument that an official relationship with it would serve British interests. The same conclusion followed from consideration of British commercial and industrial interests in China. Difficulties being faced by businessmen during this period, partly as a result of general conditions in China, and partly of pressures from local Communist authorities, are taken up in a later chapter. In 1949, the Nationalist blockade of Communist-held areas constituted a still more urgent problem. It was instituted in June by the Nationalist authorities, then based in Canton. Both the British and United States governments reacted immediately and declared the closure order illegal. The grounds cited were that, to be internationally recognised, a blockade must be effective; it must be maintained in accordance with the rules of war; and both parties must be recognised as having belligerent status.[13] In fact, the blockade turned out to be more effective than had been anticipated. From June onwards, there was a growing number of incidents involving British vessels and units of the Nationalist armed forces. According to figures presented in parliament, British ships were interfered with on sixteen occasions by Nationalist warships, gunboats, or planes, between 1 September 1949 and British recognition of the Communist government the following January.[13] The situation became much worse towards the end of the year, with the mining of the Yangtse, and Nationalist threats to bomb any British ships found in Communist ports. With Shanghai and the central Chinese ports thus out of commission, British traders sought other routes into the country. This was not easy. Even if Canton could be reached — the rail link between Canton and Kowloon was not operative for much of 1949 — there were serious transportation and communications difficulties inside China, not least because of Nationalist air raids.

Hongkong was badly hit by the disruptions. Its economy suffered 'an unprecedented congestion', the Hongkong and Shanghai Banking Corporation reported, as goods waiting for delivery to or from China mounted in its warehouses.[14] During the year, Hongkong became almost a symbol. Macmillan referred to it as 'the Gibraltar of the East' in May, while the *Round Table* in December described it as 'the Berlin of the East.' A clear consensus existed across party lines that the area needed to be defended. The Minister of Defence, Alexander, took a series of measures in the second half of the year aimed at strengthening Hongkong's internal and external security forces. But a large measure of disagreement emerged over methods. Some reports appeared in the press that the Service chiefs were reluctant to sanction the sending of reinforcements to the colony, on the grounds that the area was generally recognised to be militarily untenable against an attack from forces commanding the land approaches to Hongkong. These reports the government denied. Care was taken, however, to avoid provocation while defensive precautions went ahead. Replying in May to a Conservative critic who had demanded a more strenuous programme, Attlee said that that approach 'seemed to me to be offering a general invitation to people to go and attack.'[15] The China Assocation also expressed its regret at the tone of much public discussion of Hongkong's position. Britain, it argued, was being made to appear in Chinese eyes as if it were 'spoiling for a fight.'[16] The main danger was viewed as subversion; it was on the internal security of Hongkong that the government's attention was focused. The Communist-controlled Hongkong and Kowloon Federation of Trade Unions, in particular, was a potential fifth column. But this in turn implied that the problem was as much economic and social as military.

The point was readily seized on by Labour back-benchers in the Commons: for Hongkong's defence to be a viable proposition, there would have to be economic and social programmes aimed at removing the sources of discontent of local Chinese, and constitutional and political measures designed to give them a greater say in government.

Behind all this lay a more difficult, but ultimately a more crucial, question. More was involved in China than simply a change of government in a country in which Britain had traditional interests. Longer-term policy would have to turn on the question of whether Mao Tse-tung and the Communist leaders ought properly to be regarded as little better than agents of the Kremlin, or whether on the other hand they should be seen as part and parcel of the upsurge of reforming nationalism that had swept Asia in the post-war years. Opinion in Britain was divided on this issue. One problem, as one of the more active supporters of British recognition of the Communists put it, was that the Peking regime did not 'fit into any of the ordinary mental pigeon-holes.'[17] The two obvious pigeon-holes were 'nationalist' and 'Communist', conceived as mutually exclusive categories. But Labour MPs in particular were quick to point out that the latter term had no clear-cut definition in the Asian, as opposed to the European, context. Even doctrine was not necessarily decisive. The varying expositions by Chinese Communists of Marxism-Leninism gave scope for conflicting interpretations of the nature of the new regime. And British pragmatism tended to inspire scepticism as to the degree to which such political beliefs could be, or were desired to be, translated into action.

Two differing interpretations emerged, each a coherent analysis which appeared to do full justice to the known facts. The first centred on Moscow. The successes of the People's Liberation Army in China coincided with mounting cold war tensions in Europe. European developments coloured and gave meaning to events in the Far East. For some Conservative MPs, the link between the two theatres of the cold war was plain. Western determination, in the Berlin airlift and in moves to establish NATO, had forced Moscow to put a halt to its plans for European expansion; therefore, 'in so far as Russia is checked in her aggression in Europe, she will turn her attention to Asia.'[18] This, the *Glasgow Herald* argued in a December editorial, would have the added benefit of 'upsetting the European rearmament programme by compelling diversion of strength to the Far East.' Soviet diversionary strategies later became an important element in British responses to the outbreak of war in Korea. It was in this context that criticism of the Yalta agreements reappeared. Bevin took up the point in May 1950, when opening his defence of the Labour government's recognition of Peking. 'We did not like doing it . . . I think that everybody regrets it now. It has made the situation more difficult.'[19] For Butler, from the Conservative opposition benches, it was pointless even to discuss China out of context: 'We have to look at Communism, whether in the East or West, as one piece, with a concerted guidance from the centre in Moscow.'[20]

The interpretation seemed to be vindicated by the events of 1949. Both Bevin and Alexander drew attention to the slogans, and abuse at British and American imperialism, coming out of China. Mao Tse-tung's essay *On the People's Democratic Dictatorship*, published in July, was widely seen as the definitive statement of China's future commitment to the cause of Moscow-directed international Communism. 'As clearly indicative of Nazi policy as was Hitler's *Mein Kampf*,' declared *The Times* in September, 'as clear on a minor scale is this article of Chairman Mao Tse-tung.' By 1949, the view that the Chinese Communist Party was composed of mere 'agrarian reformers' was already something of an embarrassment to its previous adherents. There was, one Conservative noted towards the end of 1948, 'little doubt that they are the real thing.'[21] To clinch the argument, the New China News Agency was issuing long and vituperative denunciations of Yugoslavia, which did little for those in Britain who were maintaining that the new Chinese Communist leadership was potentially 'Titoist.' Finally, the Soviet Union was quick to recognise the Central People's government in October, a move condemned by *The Times* as 'precipitate'. In the press generally, the step was seen against the background of other events: Berlin, the Soviet atomic explosion, Moscow's refusal to sign an Austrian Peace Treaty, the threats against Yugoslavia. It seemed that 'the Russians have launched the hottest offensive of the cold war.'[22]

The British government, however, was reluctant to question

publicly the propriety of Soviet actions in China. The question
was raised in the autumn of 1949 in the United Nations by the
Nationalist government, in a move that seems to have been
designed in part to delay British recognition of Peking. British
delegates approached the matter with some caution. Support
was eventually given only to a resolution which called in general
terms for States to respect the independence of China, but
which made no specific mention of the Soviet Union.[23] Soviet
activities continued to be viewed with concern in the West,
however, even by those who rejected the notion that the new
government in Peking was a puppet of Moscow. Washington's
alarm was transmitted to London in the exchanges preceding
British recognition of the regime, and seems to have been
instrumental in delaying that decision in the final weeks of
1949.

Yet at no time were British officials persuaded that the
situation in China was as simple or as ominous as this. A Soviet
role was not denied; but its importance was a matter for debate.
In the second interpretation, the causes of the Chinese
revolution lay not in Soviet manoeuvres, but deep in Chinese
conditions and history. There was widespread agreement that
the Kuomintang regime of Chiang Kai-shek had thoroughly
discredited itself. The 1946 Board of Trade mission to China
reported corruption as 'one of the most deep-rooted and
intractable of the problems of Chinese life at present.'[23] Chiang
Kai-shek brought forth invective from the left of a kind
previously reserved for Hitler and Franco. He led, Lord Darwen
stated, what was 'almost a completely Fascist government,
riddled with bribery and corruption.' The speeches of Labour
MPs on the left of the party were liberally sprinkled with
vehement attacks on Chiang for running a one-party police state
with the aid of censorship and concentration camps. On the
other hand, there was still sympathy for the problems the
Nationalist leader had to grapple with; but this sentiment
seldom prompted advocacy of his retention of power. Distaste
for the Nationalist regime was shared by the Far Eastern
specialists in the Foreign Office. Many United States officials in
China took a similar view. Two later described the Nationalist
government as 'termite-ridden', and as a 'hopelessly inefficient
and corrupt government' which had lost the support of its
people.[24]

British and United States views did not converge, however, at higher governmental levels. In Washington, the explanation of events came to be that Communists serving Moscow's, rather than China's, interests had been able to exploit conditions to their own advantage. Acheson acknowledged that the Nationalists had manifested 'the grossest incompetence ever experienced by any military command.' The 'almost inexhaustible patience of the Chinese people in their misery ended', and they 'completely withdrew their support' from the Nationalist government. Thus the Communists 'did not create this condition. They did not create this revolutionary spirit . . . But they were shrewd and cunning to mount it, to ride this thing into victory and into power.'[25] In the British view, however, the Chinese Communist Party — unlike, perhaps, other Asian Communist Parties — could lay some claim to represent the aspirations of the Chinese people.

There were frequent favourable accounts of the CCP in the liberal and left-wing press and in parliament during 1948—9, though these tended to dwindle as the year progressed. Emphasis was placed on the efficiency of Communist administrations in the liberated areas, and on their evident determination to eradicate the corruption for which Nationalist China had become notorious. This latter point, the *Guardian* commented in December 1949, had 'come to be the stock advertisement for Communist China, just as making the trains run punctually was the stock advertisement for Mussolini.'[26] Other reports observed that the People's Liberation Army, in contrast with its Nationalist opponent, was regularly paid, adequately fed, literate, trusted its officers, believed in a cause, and practised strict discipline. *The Times'* own correspondents in China and Hongkong sent similar reports home during 1949. The argument was developed that, although the basis of CCP support lay in the peasantry, the Communists had also won the admiration of the middle classes, including Chinese intellectuals. Interpretive articles such as those of Guillain in the *Guardian*, stressed that the 'New Democracy' in China meant not central totalitarian rule, but rather local and village participation in politics.

British opinion also differed from that in the United States in its attribution of nationalism to the new government as well as to the Chinese people. In the emerging American view, only the

latter was acknowledged. Thus it was argued on both sides of
the Atlantic that the Chinese people were fundamentally
conservative; that they placed family above State; that strong
provincial loyalties precluded centralized rule from Peking, as
did the basic cleavage between north and south; and that the
peasantry who constituted the bulk of the population could be
expected to put up powerful resistance to encroachments by
the State. There was also the much-quoted argument from
history. 'There have been many conquests of China,' the
Foreign Secretary stated in the United Nations, 'but no
conquerors. Each, in turn, has been absorbed by the Chinese
people.'[27] It was the British argument, in this Anglo-American
debate, that the Peking regime was Chinese. Its leaders were
Chinese Communists; but they were Chinese first and Communist second. The China Association described the Central
People's government as 'intensely more nationalistic' than any
other of China in modern times.[28] To an extent which had not
been sufficiently realised in the West, *The Economist* argued,
Communism had been able to outbid the Kuomintang as the
prospective champion of Chinese nationalism.[29] The Hongkong
correspondent of *The Times* reported that although Peking
Radio gave the impression of being a mouthpiece of the
Kremlin, in private conversations Chinese Communists often
voiced other ideas, and many appreciated that Russia's interests
did not coincide at every point with those of China. British
accounts often drew attention also to divisions evident within
the ranks of the CCP leadership. The conflict cited was usually
that which was held to exist between Liu Shao-chi as the
advocate of pro-Soviet alignment, and Chou En-lai as the
supporter of moderate economic co-operation with the West.
There were differing interpretations of Mao's stand. And the
Party itself was not a monolith. It contained a 'pre-eminence of
Marxist elements', but this concealed 'a confusion of different
and often contradictory forces beneath the surface.'[30]

The conclusion of this second interpretation was thus that
what had happened in China owed very little to Moscow. Soviet
aid to what Stalin himself had dubbed the 'margarine communists' of China had been meagre; and Soviet policy even
during 1949 was hardly compatible with the view that Moscow
was aiming at the establishment of a puppet regime. Whatever
may have been the position in the past, the Chinese Communist

Party by 1949 was thought to be independent of Soviet support for maintaining its position in China. And in the future, China and Russia would have 'as much reason to collaborate as Russia and Germany.'[31] Both *The Times* and the China Assocation argued that Moscow might itself contribute to a future Sino-Soviet split if too overt an attempt were made to mould the actions of the new regime.

On balance, then, the two levels of looking at Communist China tended towards the same conclusion as far as British policy was concerned. First, it would serve no good purpose to abandon British interests without first attempting to establish some channels of communication with the new authorities, even if this meant only trying to obtain compensation before a final withdrawal. Secondly, it seemed evident that, depsite the confusion and uncertainties of China's recent turbulent history, the leadership of the CCP was not subservient to the Soviet Union and might prove open to, though probably suspicious of, the right kinds of approaches from the West.

The British attitude to the more specific question of diplomatic recognition was not, however, a simple one. At least six different interpretations of the primary reasons for or against recognition can be discerned. There was first the officially declared position. It was often expressed as a syllogism: the regime in Peking was a fact; facts had to be recognised; therefore, the Peking regime should be recognised. Such recognition would not imply any statement as to the legitimacy of the regime, or any suggestion that Britain approved of the ideology or policies of that regime. This was, broadly speaking, the position taken by most British international lawyers, including those advising the government from inside the Foreign Office. It was articulated by Professor Lauterpacht in an article in *The Times* of 6 January 1950, the day Britain accorded diplomatic recognition to the Central People's government. Lauterpacht argued that whenever the requisite conditions of governmental capacity existed — that is, once a revolutionary government 'may fairly be held to enjoy, with a reasonable degree of permanency, the obedience of the mass of the population, and once it is in effective control of the bulk of the national territory' — then recognition was 'due as a matter of right.' A similar line of reasoning was put forward by

G.G. Fitzmaurice, then a Legal Adviser to the Foreign Office, in an article published in 1952.[32]

The notion had been applied earlier by those Labour MPs who wanted British recognition of 'North China', or the Communist-occupied areas, in the winter of 1948—9. Other ideas were mooted. The Communists, it was said, could be accorded *de facto* recognition, while *de jure* diplomatic links were kept with the Nationalists. The drawback to such schemes was that the Communist authorities themselves refused to consider anything less than full *de jure* recognition. Thus the existence of a strong, central government in China became both a necessary and a sufficient condition for British recognition in official statements. Ministers reiterated that more should not be read into the action. Malcolm MacDonald, the British Commissioner-General for South-East Asia, pointed out that Britain had granted diplomatic recognition to many foreign governments with whose politics it strongly disagreed, such as Hitler, Mussolini, Franco, and Stalin.[33] But it was Churchill, as Leader of the Opposition, who best expressed the mood: 'recognising a person is not necessarily an act of approval . . . One has to recognise lots of things and people in this world of sin and woe that one does not like.'[34] Diplomatic recognition, *The Times* commented after the step had been taken, was 'simply a recognition of fact'; it was 'not itself of great importance.'

A second view was more characteristic of United States thinking, but also found support in Britain. Here, the assumption of an identity between the common-sense and the legalistic meanings of the term 'recognition' in the syllogism noted above was questioned. Recognition was much more than an acknowledgement of facts. It implied a measure of faith in the capacity and willingness of a regime to carry out its international obligations and responsibilities. Such recognition could, and should, be withheld until such time as assurances were forthcoming on this point. During the summer and autumn of 1949, the Administration in Washington appeared to be trying to leave the alternative option open. In September, for example, Acheson said that diplomatic relations were maintained 'primarily because we are all on the same planet and must do business with each other. We do not establish an embassy or legation in a foreign country to show approval of its Government.'[35] But what later became the prevailing United States view was expressed about the same time by the State Department. There were three tests for recognition: the new regime must be in efficient control of the country; it must recognise and carry out its international obligations; and it must rule with the acquiescence of the ruled. In particular, it was to be by its treatment of American nationals and property that the Peking regime would be judged in connection with the question of recognition.[36]

This possibility was denied in London. The proper course, according to Lauterpacht, was 'to assume that the Government of a sovereign State will fulfil its obligations in good faith.' In December 1949, Mayhew refused to await Chinese assurances of respectful treatment of British staff in China. In international practice, 'the proper treatment of diplomatic and consular officials should be automatic. To ask for assurances on this point might imply that this was not the case.'[37] Ministers were more frank in some earlier statements. Thus in May, the Prime Minister said that the question of relations with the new government would 'depend on their actions, and it is premature to judge what lines they will take.' In September, the Foreign Secretary told the United Nations General Assembly that 'China has entered into certain international obligations which we feel must be honoured'; and added, in Ottawa afterwards, that 'the treatment of our nationals and the general question of behaviour towards us' would influence relations with the People's Republic. Similarly, in November, the British Ambassador in Washington confirmed that Britain's decision 'must depend on how the new government establishes itself in China and how it behaves.'[38] In a sense, these remarks were technically correct. Later, in 1951, Morrison distinguished between recognition of a government, and entering into diplomatic relations with it, maintaining that the latter step was entirely discretionary. But much use of this distinction was not made, even by specialists, until after the Chinese response to British recognition had become known. It is possible that the government was attempting to secure from Peking some broad statement which could be interpreted as a commitment to fulfil international obligations, and which would help to cushion the impact of British recognition on United States opinion.

Thirdly, diplomatic recognition could be an element in bargaining between Britain and China. *The Times'* Peking correspondent wrote in October that the regime was 'anxious to have British and American recognition', and that 'unconditional recognition without guarantee of reasonable trading facilities and fair treatment of nationals would merely mean surrendering uselessly the only bargaining counter the western Powers now have.'[39] Others pointed, in this context, to China's economic needs. Different conclusions were drawn, however, by Labour and Conservative speakers. Bevan, in his book *In Place of Fear*, wrote later that 'the outstanding need of China is for the industrial products of the urban communities of the West. These Russia is not able to supply in anything approaching the quantities required.'[40] For rank-and-file Labour supporters, this general observation prompted criticism of the British government's dilatoriness on the question of relations with Peking, and led to the conclusion that a natural economic bond could be erected between Britain and China. China's capital needs were also appreciated by the Foreign Office. Officials and traders in Hongkong made the point to Lord Strang during an Asian tour; and a similar view had been put forward by the Board of Trade mission earlier.[41] It was unfortunately apparent, though, that the Chinese did not see things the same way. It was being suggested in Peking that it was rather Britain, like other capitalist states, that desperately needed trading links with China. It followed that Mao must be persuaded of the validity of the contrary proposition. 'It is China', *The Economist* emphasised in October, 'not America, which is in need of economic favours.' Optimists suggested that this task might be easier than it sounded. Pronouncements from the new leaders in Peking seemed to indicate that there was no immediate intention of destroying private enterprise in China, whether Chinese or foreign. Further comfort was found in the conviction that all Chinese were by nature businessmen. The view was put bluntly by one Hongkong trader during the summer: 'Get one of those fellows in the back of a Packard, stick a four-inch cigar in his mouth, and give him a bank account in hard currency, and you'll find he is just the same as all the others . . . they're Chinese even if they call themselves Communists.'[42]

In a fourth perspective on diplomatic recognition, some acknowledgement was made of British needs for favourable treatment. Recognition was expedient; useful results might follow. In his defence of government policy from the Opposition benches, Churchill said that 'The reason for having diplomatic relations is not to confer a compliment, but to secure a convenience.' Establishing diplomatic relations would mean that there was some possibility, however small, of securing fair treatment of British interests in China. The Hongkong and Shanghai Banking Corporation expressed the hope that 'when diplomatic relations have been fully established . . . some information will be forthcoming as to the possibility of negotiations with the Central People's Government about China's railway debts and other financial obligations.'[43] It was not, that is, suggested that a Chinese commitment to enter into such negotiations should precede British recognition. Hongkong's dependence on supplies from the mainland set the seal on the need for official relations with Peking and Canton. In October 1949, the government announced that 'very satisfactory arrangements' had been made on this question. In general, officials and traders considered that Peking would not be averse to continuing China's traditional relationship with the colony. Hongkong's entrepot role served her interests as well as those of Britain. Some businessmen even thought that, in view of the Nationalist blockade, Canton — served by Hongkong — might become the main port of entry for goods into China. Talks were held between British and Chinese officials in October on the re-establishment of through traffic on the connecting railway. The other possibility was that British failure to recognise Peking might provoke Communist reprisals. From the Chinese point of view, the 1842 Treaty could certainly be classified as 'unequal', and British opinion was reluctant to force Peking into the position of having to demand its abrogation.

Two final considerations arose from the broader perspective of the cold war. On the one hand, recognition could be viewed as appeasement of a potential aggressor. The view was already gaining ground in the United States. In the Senate Foreign Relations Committee's hearings on the Japanese Peace Treaty in 1952, Dulles argued that American policy rested on the assumption 'that there will be a change from the present China situation . . . the alien doctrine of communism cannot permanently conquer the Chinese spirit or liquidate the innate individualism of the Chinese race . . . We should assume the impermanence, not the permanence, of the present Moscow-oriented rule of China.'[44] Diplomatic recognition, therefore, would prolong the oppression of the Chinese people, while at the same time encouraging Peking to persevere with intransigeant and aggressive policies abroad. In Britain, the Conservative Party leadership tended to support the government's China policy. Only a small minority of back-benchers expressed more vociferous demands for a more comprehensive anti-Communist programme, which would include, at the very minimum, a refusal to extend recognition to Peking. This argument was put forcibly by one Conservative in an unsigned article in *Le Soir* in December. The objective must be

> de contrarier le communisme partout . . . Aussi longtemps qu'il existera encore quelque resistance nationaliste en Chine . . . nous ne devrions accorder aucune faveur aux favoris de Moscow. Nous devons espérer que cette resistance se prolongera et nous devons faire tout ce qui est en notre pouvoir pour accentuer en Chine communiste le désappointment au point de vue économique.[45]

The counter to this case was that diplomatic recognition would encourage a 'Titoist' departure of Chinese from Soviet policies. (In the United States, by contrast, non-recognition was defended on the grounds that this would encourage 'Titoist' tendencies on the part of the Chinese people, and lead them eventually to reject the regime that had been forced upon them by Moscow.) Thus *The Round Table* argued in December that 'China's future with Moscow is by no means certain, and much will depend on the attitude of the Western Powers towards her new Government.' China, in other words, must be left with solid alternatives to an alliance with Russia. Ministers argued that diplomatic recognition 'was the only way in which we could avoid creating a complete barrier around China — a complete blackout between China and the rest of the world.'[46] A policy of recognition, trade, and contact, would strengthen the hand of moderates in Peking; non-recognition, on the other hand, would only serve to drive the new regime, perhaps irrevocably, into the Soviet orbit. Thus, in a sense, a British refusal to recognise Peking would have implied a willingness consciously to act in pursuit of what were understood to be Soviet objectives in China. The Hongkong *South China Morning*

Post referred to Western mistakes in the approach to the new Soviet authorities in the post-1917 period. Speedy recognition might help prevent Chinese foreign policy developing along similar lines. And contact with Western officials, *The Times'* Hongkong correspondent argued, might well serve to remove some of the erroneous notions about the world held by members of the Communist government. Significance was found in the fact that it was Liu Shao-chi, the most ardent of pro-Soviet advocates, who had remained in virtual isolation during the civil war, whereas Chou En-lai had established relations with Westerners.[47]

The British government's readiness to come to terms with the new Communist authorities in 1949 was the logical outcome of its response to Chinese nationalism in the late 1920s. Yet its justification for extending diplomatic recognition to Peking was neither as simple as Whitehall claimed, nor as crudely self-seeking as the government's critics in Washington believed. That the action was a recognition of facts, and no more than that, was a construction thought essential if the charge of appeasement of Communism were to be averted. It was this style, as much as substantive issues, that led the Chinese in their turn to devalue the worth of British recognition. Critics were correct in pointing to the British interests that persuaded opinion of the need for recognition. But a more decisive consideration was the growing cold war confrontation in Europe. The British government thought it vitally important that as much as possible be done by the West to prevent Moscow spreading its influence over the most populous nation on earth. And in classical balance-of-power terms, it made sense at least to try to make contact with a possible antagonist of one's enemy who happened to be conveniently placed on his other flank.

The dilemma posed in the title of this chapter is thus a false one. Some in Britain saw the Chinese Communist leaders as tyrants; others took their claim to be liberators at face value. But for most observers, the truth was thought to lie somewhere between these points. The emerging American view, that they constituted an alien entity implanted by Moscow, did not on balance find much support. Labour MPs, in line with the party's overall approach to nationalism and Communism in post-war Asia, put forward a coherent interpretation which contrasted the reformist and nationalist aspirations of Peking with the repression and expansionism of Russian imperialism under Stalin. A broader spectrum of opinion, including Conservatives as well as officials, was disenchanted with Nationalist China. Taking its cue from Churchill, the Opposition fell into line with the government on the question. The mounting threat to British interests towards the end of 1949 if recognition were delayed much longer then became crucial. Indeed, once the need to guarantee Hongkong's integrity and prosperity had been accepted, as it had been by both parties, the retention of diplomatic relations with the Nationalist authorities on Taiwan became inconsistent with the protection of British interests in the region.

3 Failure of Diplomacy

On 6 January 1950 the British government extended *de jure* diplomatic recognition to the Central People's government of the People's Republic of China. The decision represented the culmination of several months of diplomatic exchanges with the United States, Commonwealth and Western European governments. These were important influences on the character of the British action, its style and timing. The substance of the decision also reflected British interpretations of obligations under international law, and thinking more generally about the nature of diplomacy. At the same time, the government maintained contact with representatives of British interests in China. Yet recognition did not produce the desired results, even though by the turn of the decade few in Britain felt able to express optimism about the future course of relations with China. What did come as a surprise was the failure of the two governments even to agree on such an elementary step as the exchange of ambassadors.

In 1949 this obstacle was not anticipated. Domestically, the Labour government was under pressure from its own supporters in the House of Commons. This mounted towards the end of the year, when it seemed that the Foreign Office was delaying out of deference to American wishes. Yet the course of action followed by the government bore little relation, except in the most simple sense, to the kinds of policies being urged from the back benches. Socialist principles dictated two alternative China policies: either one of recognition, support and friendship, if the regime in Peking were viewed as reformist; or one of repudiation and denunciation, if instead it seemed more Stalinist than Titoist.[1] The Cabinet took neither line. The first perspective was more influential within the ranks of the party, and there is evidence that the thinking of at least some Ministers was coloured by it. But, given the higher priority of Europe, the government's deliberations were swayed by other factors. These were of a kind that would have impinged on any post-war British government, regardless of party. Thus the leadership of the Conservative Opposition, if not some of the rank and file, lent its support to the government's policy on China. Party political considerations were marginal in this alignment; but Conservatives compared the arguments being presented in favour of recognition of Peking, with those mustered by the Labour Party to deny recognition to Madrid. Younger noted later that there was no major difference between the parties on the question.[2] Even *Tribune* tended to say little during the autumn and winter that would have been out of place in *The Times*. It was only after the Chinese response to British recognition had become known that the Conservative leadership found itself unable to contain the indignation of some Tory critics; and only after the return of a Conservative administration under Churchill in 1951 that Labour MPs, freed from the injunction not to rock the boat, developed a more distinctively left-of-centre approach to China policy. Indeed, prior to British recognition, China was neither a seriously divisive nor even a much discussed topic at Westminster.

More important than party influences, then, were the grievances of Britain's China traders. The China interests waged a persistent battle during 1949 to bring home to the government the nature of the circumstances under which they were trying to operate. Shanghai, as we have seen, was particularly badly hit. In July, its Chamber of Commerce asked the China Association in London to rouse public opinion and the government with a view to devising some means of breaking the Nationalist blockade.[3] *The Times'* correspondents publicised businessmen's grievances. Its Shanghai correspondent, for example, reported that the British trading community in that city wanted government help to get ships in and out: British acquiescence in the blockade was serving only to make it effective.[4]

In Britain, contacts were kept up between officials and the China Association. The situation brought about by the Nationalist blockade was regarded as central to the whole question of China policy. The Foreign Secretary told the Commons in May

1950 that British interests in China had been 'hurt more by that than by what the Communists have done. The Communists have taxed them, charged them and done all sorts of things, but I think that in all probability their difficulties could have been got over if the blockade had not been put in operation.'[5] Various steps, all ineffective, were taken before recognition of Peking. The Nationalist authorities were informed that Britain regarded attempts to enforce the blockade by attacks on merchant shipping as illegitimate. Local British and United States officials cooperated to provide trading companies with information about hazards to shipping. The question of Royal Navy protection, however, did not seriously arise until the spring of 1950, and the increase in the number of incidents that preceded the outbreak of the Korean War. Before this, though, the British government informed the Nationalists that it was 'undoubtedly entitled to give naval protection to British merchantmen outside Chinese territorial waters.'[6] Two frigates were maintained off the mouth of the Yangtse. Mayhew stated in the Commons that the rest of the naval force on the Far East station was available if required. Towards the end of 1949, British merchant ships began a more determined drive to break the blockade, reportedly with the tacit sympathy of British officials in the region.

Diplomatic recognition of Peking was one obvious way out. The China Association reported that the blockade was arousing Chinese Communist animosity, since Peking believed that it was only through the connivance of Britain and the United States that it could be maintained. Traders were particularly indignant since it appeared that Nationalist policy was aimed specifically against British interests. Nationalist statements, for example, indicated that Hongkong was regarded as virtually a supply base for the People's Liberation Army. That diplomatic relations should be kept with the Nationalists in order to provide some mechanism for the redress of grievances was not, therefore, a proposition that enjoyed much support. Recognition also seemed the logical solution to British businessmen's difficulties inside China. It would, the *Manchester Guardian* pointed out, be the minimum price the Communists would demand for the provision of reasonable trading facilities.[7] It would, it was hoped, at least facilitate the commencement of Sino-British official talks on the subject, which would be desirable even if the only upshot were compensation for requisitioned property and the issuing of exit permits for British staff.

Yet generalisations about trading opinion are deceptive. Opinions varied considerably between different areas of China, and between different dates. In the early summer of 1949, for example, British traders tended to be more optimistic about future prospects than they were on balance later. In February, Hongkong businessmen were said to be 'strongly urging' recognition; and in June, a survey of Shanghai's foreign commercial and financial leaders found them 'almost un-animous' in the view that there should be immediate recog-nition once the Central People's government were finally established.[8] But from about July, the tone of pessimism was more in evidence. At the same time, some trading contacts were established with the local Communist authorities even in the absence of official relations. From at least as early as the beginning of 1949, British and American businessmen were trying to open up trade in the Communist areas on a semi-barter basis. Contact was established with the Communist authorities in Shanghai in September, and various arrangements, described as 'purely local in character', arrived at. This led the *South China Morning Post* to speculate in June that British traders in fact did not want their government to recognise the Com-munists, because of the profitability of unofficial transactions. But it was not the longer-term view of more responsible trading opinion. The China Association was 'on record with the Foreign Office' in October 1949, to be 'in favour of recognition of the new regime as soon as this is diplomatically practicable.'[9]

But any account of the domestic exchanges of 1949 gives only a partial picture. 'It has been our constant policy,' the Minister of Defence stated in May, 'to secure the maximum degree of harmony with other like-minded governments in meeting the exigencies of a difficult situation.'[10] The following March, the Lord Chancellor gave his 'personal assurance' that there had 'never been a matter with regard to which there has been closer or more continuous and more direct consultation between this country and the other members of the Commonwealth.'[11] The governments thus consulted, however, became increasingly divided on questions of China policy during the second half of 1949.

Differing points of view within the Commonwealth were aired at a meeting of High Commissioners at the Foreign Office in mid-November. By this time, the position of the Asian members had crystallised. Recognition was due to the Peking regime since it was in control of the bulk of China's territory, and since it in addition seemed to represent the interests of the Chinese people. Australia's thinking was more complex, and also more fluid. Canberra was said to be in favour of early recognition in the early summer of 1949. Indeed, United States sources tended to identify it with a wish to recognise a Chinese Communist government at the earliest possible moment.[12] But as time went by, greater reluctance was displayed towards falling in with Indian, or even with British, ideas about China. By the end of November, official opinion had turned. Evatt and other Ministers increasingly linked the question of recognition with the fulfilment of obligations by the Chinese. At a meeting in Canberra attended also by New Zealand officials, the British were informed of this hesitation, one reason for which was said to be the difficulty of making new departures with a General Election in the offing. Representations were accordingly made to Britain and other Commonwealth countries in November to defer recognition, at least until the question had been fully investigated at the Colombo conference due to be held in January.[13] In December, however, a coalition Liberal-Country government was returned at the polls. The possibility of an early Australian recognition of Peking now receded almost to vanishing point. New Zealand's government, reluctant to depart from Australian policy, and similarly unwilling to let China policy become a campaign issue, was also defeated in a December election.

Ottawa seems to have ended the year much closer to Britain's own position, despite its sensitivity to the movement of American opinion. In November, Pearson said that if and when recognition occurred, it would not indicate approval of communism in China. 'Of course we in Canada reject completely the Marxist-Leninist principles espoused by the Chinese Communists, but we cannot reject the fact of China and its 450 million people.' Reservations common in British remarks at the time also made their appearance. If the fact of Communist control of China were demonstrated, Pearson declared, 'and an independent — I stress the word 'independent' — Chinese government, able to discharge its international obligations' were established which was 'accepted by the Chinese people', then 'in due course and after consultation with other friendly governments we will have to recognise the facts which confront us.'[14] But being further removed from the situation than was Australia, and not facing a pre-election Opposition eager to pounce on any indication of appeasement of Communism, the Canadian government was probably prepared at the end of 1949 to follow Britain's lead after a short interval. That it did not do so is due, first, to the unexpectedly hostile Chinese response to British recognition, and, secondly, to the commencement of hostilities in Korea in June, 1950, which occurred at a time when several Western and Commonwealth governments were moving towards diplomatic recognition of Peking.

Still more crucial to Britain was the position of the United States. For much of 1949, differences between American and British approaches to China were far less prominent than they often appeared. The point of divergence can perhaps be dated at a point in January 1950, shortly after British recognition. Before this time, despite fluctuations and some degree of ambiguity, partly deliberate, in the American position, the two governments tended to move along broadly parallel lines, and, moreover, to regard such harmony as essential to the development of sound Western policy towards the People's Republic of China.

Overall policy in the region can be summarised briefly: recognition of any Chinese Communist government that might emerge later in 1949, combined with more stringent measures to combat the threat of Communism in other parts of Asia. This programme seems to have been hammered into shape early in 1949, at a time when the winter successes of the People's Liberation Army were making the advent of a Communist regime a distinct possibility. British thinking on the containment of Communism in Asia were set out in exchanges with the State Department in January. In the British view, Chiang Kai-shek's regime would be almost inevitably succeeded by a Communist one. Western governments should therefore plan to recognise such a regime, if and when it were established; but at the same time begin to implement a more active anti-Communist policy, in which economic aid would play a major role, in relation to the non-Communist states on the perimeter of China.[15] Reasoning such as this met with a sympathetic audience. The Administration was beginning to effect a retrenchment in China, one consequence of which would likely be the ultimate abandonment of the Kuomintang. In remarks which later earned some notoriety, Acheson refused demands for a re-examination of United States China policy, since he could not clearly foresee the outcome in China 'until the dust settles.' There was virtual unanimity in March in the Senate Foreign Relations Committee that 'we had best get out of China as fast as we can.'[16] The United States was, however, still heavily committed to the Nationalist government. In April, Congress approved the extension of the expiration date of $54m of unexpended funds for aid to Chiang until February 1950.

In this confused situation, it seemed unavoidable that Britain take the Western initiative in coming to terms with a future Chinese Communist government. On 6 May, the State Department communicated to Britain and other States with Far Eastern interests, American views of '(1) the disadvantages of initiating any moves toward recognition or giving the impression through statements by their officials that any approach by the Chinese Communists seeking recognition would be welcomed, and (2) the desirability of concerned western powers accepting a common front in this regard.' The result was an informal agreement that the powers would consult with and inform each other before taking action.[17] The Foreign Office let it be known that there had been informal consultations in Nanking between British, American and other Western officials on the recognition question. The United States ambassador had stayed behind in the city when People's Liberation Army forces occupied it towards the end of April.[18] In general, the summer months were marked by reports of frictions in Anglo-American relations. Even so, when Bevin and Acheson met in Paris in June, it seems to have been widely considered, at least on the British side, that both had agreed that recognition was inevitable, and that the question was one of timing.

On 5 August the State Department published its White Paper on the whole question of United States policy in China. The failure of that policy was attributed to Chiang Kai-shek's ineptitude, and the future Communist regime described as a tool of the Kremlin.[19] Acheson and Bevin met again in

Washington the following month. The meeting, stated the communique, was 'of the greatest help in developing common understanding of the situation and the development of policy along parallel lines.' After the Foreign Secretary's return to London, the 'closest consultation' between the governments would continue. According to later American versions, Acheson took the opportunity to persuade Bevin to act in concert with Washington, and expressed the view that it would be unwise to recognise a Communist regime.[20] More contemporary accounts were of the opinion that Britain had sought, not entirely unsuccessfully, a greater American commitment against the spread of Communism in the rest of Asia, and had agreed in return to proceed more cautiously in its moves towards recognition of Peking. In testimony to the Senate Foreign Relations Committee on 12 October, Acheson said that there was general agreement between the United States, Britain and France, on three 'sound' criteria of recognition. These corresponded to the criteria the Secretary of State put forward publicly in a press conference the same day: *de facto* control; recognition by the regime of its international obligations; and government with the consent of the people.[21]

By the time of the establishment of the People's Republic at the beginning of that month, however, China had become for the United States what Alastair Cooke, reporting to the *Guardian*, described as 'a raging issue of domestic politics.' Officially, the Administration continued to tie diplomatic recognition to the fulfilment of obligations by Peking. At the same time, a conference of opinion leaders held under the auspices of the State Department found overwhelmingly in favour of early United States recognition of and trade with Communist China. This uncertain atmosphere inevitably became a factor in British thinking, if only on the question of the timing of recognition. The *Daily Telegraph* reported on 19 October that Britain had given her NATO allies assurances that there would be no early British action. This was officially denied. Clearly, the Foreign Office was moving quickly towards advocacy of recognition. At the end of the month, a memorandum was sent to Acheson indicating the British government's intention to go ahead with recognition of Peking.[22] At the beginning of November, British Far Eastern officials, meeting in Singapore, recommended early recognition.

This momentum now seems to have prompted fresh representations from Washington warning against any precipitate moves.
By the middle of November, it was clear that some kind of
delay had been instituted by Britain. Various explanations were
put forward. The one most generally accepted in Hongkong was
the stiffening of the official United States attitude following the
Mukden episode.[23] It was also suggested that a pause was
necessary so that more countries could be persuaded to join in a
concerted action; or that it was connected with the continuing
Anglo-American exchanges on the banning of the export of
strategically significant goods to China; or that the Foreign
Office had become more alarmed than it had been hitherto at
the extent of Soviet involvement in China.[24] This last point was
rapidly becoming a major source of anxiety for American
officials. In addition, the British government was being sub-
jected to pressures for delay from Australia and France. There
was no official admission of the existence of a delay. Speaking
in the Commons on 16 November, however, Bevin for the first
time drew particular attention to the complexity of the
problems involved. This had been one of the main United States
objections to speedy progress towards recognition. There were
'a lot of issues involved – the United Nations . . . and the
question of the views of the United States and our own
Commonwealth. In a great changeover of this character, one has
to act with caution, reasonable speed and with an idea of
producing the best results.'[25] The weeks following saw an
increasing number of criticisms from British opinion. As early as
October, the China Association had criticised the indecisiveness
of the governments principally concerned on the recognition
question. In Hongkong, there was disappointment at the
'obvious fact' that recognition had been postponed until
January.[26]

Was there, then, any 'understanding' between London and
Washington on recognition? In this context, there are at least
three possible interpretations of the United States' position at
the end of 1949. Opinion in the two capitals on each one was
not necessarily the same. First, at the minimum, it could simply
be argued that the Administration appreciated the reasons for
the British action, but regretted it; secondly, that it saw positive
benefits for the United States in having official British
representatives in Peking; and thirdly, and more controversially,

that it was itself prepared to follow suit at an appropriate point
in 1950.

On the first, it seems clear that the State Department was
well versed in British thinking on the questions of China and of
Asian Communism. This much can be concluded from the
number and the level of the exchanges that took place between
the two governments during 1949. In Congress, however, and in
the Republican press, British policy was condemned as a
sacrifice of principle on the altar of expediency. In Congressional testimony in 1951, Acheson gave the orthodox view of
the Anglo-American exchanges. The United States

> had been in discussions with the British government . . . The
> British thought for various reasons that there were strong
> considerations motivating them toward recognition. We did
> not share that view and continued to point out reasons why
> it could not be done, why we were not going to do it, and
> why we hoped that the British would not do it, and that
> situation continued until the British let us know that, having
> given most careful thought to all that we had said to them,
> they had to take a different course.[27]

This contrasts with the view given by the Lord Chancellor
shortly after British recognition: 'So far as the USA are
concerned, they were most understanding, realising that our
position was peculiar, unique and special.'[28] British opinion, for
its part, appreciated the Americans' dilemma. Younger has
pointed out that the Administration, even if its inclination was
to implement a policy of recognition and trade, faced tremendous difficulties on account of political pressures from the
China interests and the Republicans.[29] The conclusion tended
to be drawn, therefore, that Acheson and his colleagues not
only understood the reasons why the British government was
moving towards recognition, but also that they too would take
the same step once domestic United States anger had subsided.
But Washington's anguish was not taken as a compelling reason
for postponement of British recognition beyond the short
period of delay from mid-November. Labour back-benchers
chose to interpret the pause as the result of the government's
failure to stand up to American pressures. At the time of British
recognition, *The Times* declared that friendship between the
two nations 'would not be well served by meekly deferring to

the judgement of the United States even when it seems to be mistaken.'[30]

On the second point, it was the British view that the Administration saw value in a British presence in the Chinese capital. This was one argument used by Bevin the following May in his defence of British recognition. The government was being asked to take charge of American interests. 'Suppose we had said, 'No, we will not take charge of your interests. You are going out of China, we will do nothing, we are going too,' I really think we should have thrown away our position in the Far East for ever.'[31] In a sense, then, the very fact that the United States seemed bent, at least temporarily, on non-recognition was itself seen as a justification for Britain taking the opposite course. Alternatively, it may have been that British recognition would be a useful test for the Democrats to gauge the strength of domestic American opposition to such a move on the part of the Administration. Other Western and Common-wealth governments at least saw the British action as a useful testing of the temperature in Peking. 'With regard to the other countries of the world,' the Lord Chancellor commented in March, 1950, 'they are waiting to see what happens as a result of Mr Hutchison's mission.' If it met with success (the reference is to official Sino-British exchanges following recognition), then 'I strongly suspect that the course we have already taken . . . will be followed very much more widely.'[32]

But it is the third possibility that raises more intractable problems. British observers tended to predict the date of United States recognition of Peking as, at the latest, shortly after the mid-term Congressional elections of November 1950. To do this before then, it was thought, would be too dangerous electorally for the Democrats. Acheson later denied emphatically that there had ever been any understanding, tacit or otherwise, between Britain and the United States on the question:

> Senator Johnson. Has the State Department ever advised England if it should recognise Communist China that the United States would probably follow suit later on?
> Secretary Acheson. No, sir; that is a complete mis-apprehension . . .
> Senator Smith. Then you think they had no justification — I want to get this clear — they had no justification then for

feeling that we would go along if they recognised Communist China?

Secretary Acheson. No, sir; I don't believe those who knew about the conversation had such a feeling.[33]

Yet at the time when Britain was approaching recognition, the senior British officials involved in the decision *did* expect that the United States would recognise the Central People's government within a matter of months. The discrepancy can be accounted for in several ways. First, the Foreign Office's analysis of the situation was wrong; no reasonable grounds existed for believing that the United States would take this course. In view, however, of the almost continuous exchanges between officials of the two governments on the question stretching back at least twelve months, this possibility seems remote. Acheson's remarks should be taken with the pinch of salt needed in the atmosphere of McCarthyism later prevailing in Washington. Secondly, the administration could have deliberately deceived British officials into believing that it would go ahead with recognition, simply in order to secure the benefits of a Western presence in the Chinese capital without itself having to incur any of the costs. This, too, seems unlikely. Even if it had the will, the State Department's leadership lacked the capability, including the unanimity of its own officials on the subject, necessary for carrying through such a project. A less Machiavellian possibility is, thirdly, that by the end of 1949 the United States had indeed decided to recognise Peking, that British officials were informed of this intention, but that the circumstances of the early months of 1950, and finally the outbreak of war in Korea in June, forced it to reverse its position. The problem with this interpretation is that studies of United States China policy in this period have been unable to unearth anything resembling a firm American decision to recognise. On the one hand, Kubek argues that the State Department 'would have openly advocated recognition' but for Chinese seizures of American consular property in mid-January 1950. On the other hand, Tang Tsou, concludes that 'contrary to the widespread impression in the autumn and winter of 1949, the top officials of the administration had not decided on an early recognition of Communist China.'[34]

The conclusion would therefore seem to be this. In the

turbulence of late 1949, both in China and the United States, Washington's only option was to postpone making the decision whether or not to extend recognition to Peking. But it also seems evident that the option of recognition was kept alive by Acheson and his senior colleagues into the spring of 1950, and possibly even until after the beginning of the Korean War.[35] In this situation, it would have been a reasonable inference – in Washington as well as in London – that American recognition, though not formally then a commitment, involved little more than a rather delicate question of timing, manner, and careful preparation. Officials in both capitals not surprisingly underestimated the capacity of events in the Far East and of Congressional opinion to impose serious constraints on the Administration's freedom of manoeuvre. In the British view, American recognition had an air of inevitability about it: it was the logical conclusion of United States policy during 1948–49; and Chiang Kai-shek's final stronghold on Formosa would in any case fall to the Communists later in 1950. In addition, British officials may have been influenced by an exaggerated assessment of the influence of those State Department officials either apparently or genuinely sympathetic to British thinking on China. The evidence from the American side on this is anecdotal. Philip Jessup's comment on the day of British recognition was said to be that the United States would follow within two or three weeks.[36] In the period between October and January, he and others gave the same impression to a number of American officials and Senators.[37]

Of the other NATO allies, France was more prepared to take the plunge. Close contact was maintained between London and Paris in the deliberations preceding British recognition. The coincidence in the timing of British recognition of Peking with that of the Bao Dai regime in Indo-China is itself indicative of this. In November 1949, it seems that the French were happy to see a delay in the establishment of Sino-British diplomatic relations at least until after this regime were more firmly entrenched. It was generally felt in Britain at the end of the year that France would follow Britain's lead in the near future, though *Le Monde* denied this. Postponement of French recognition of Peking was due to the Soviet and Chinese recognitions of Ho Chi Minh's regime.

We have so far only touched briefly on the views of British officials themselves. The Foreign Office position was the decisive one. A few weeks after the setting up of the Communist regime in China, British officials in the Far East and South-East Asia met in Singapore to discuss, *inter alia*, the implications of this development. Though the Foreign Secretary refused to comment on the meeting in parliament, it soon became known that the officials had unanimously approved a recommendation that the new regime be accorded diplomatic recognition.[38] This view was also put in despatches to the Foreign Office from British officials in China during 1949. In June 1949, the Consul-General in Shanghai stated publicly that 'if there are outstanding features of the new military authorities, they are restraint, moderation and realism.'[39] In particular, M.E. Dening, who was later chosen to be the first British ambassador to the People's Republic, was closely associated with the moves towards recognition from the winter of 1948-9, and was present at all the major Anglo-American and other intergovernmental exchanges on the question during 1949. The view of the Foreign Office's legal advisers also fitted in with this evolving policy. However, that the decision to recognise Peking was heavily couched in legalisms was due more to political than to strictly legal considerations. In sum, there appears to have been no fundamental objection to the principle or the timing of recognition either within the Foreign Office, or on the part of other interested departments. The step was a commonplace one the magnitude of which could easily be exaggerated: the real problems would arise in negotiations after an exchange of ambassadors.

British actions did not come in one fell swoop. Between the civil war period proper and that following British recognition of the Communist government, the Foreign Office implemented an interim course of tentative probing. In April 1949, the Prime Minister confirmed that British consular officers in Mukden, Peking and Tientsin had tried to reach day-to-day working arrangements with the local Communist authorities. Their approaches had, however, been 'rejected on every occasion without any reason being given for such a rejection.'[40] These approaches none the less continued. The Foreign Office emphasised that the question of formal recognition must not be implied to be under consideration. Close contact was kept, where possible, with United States officials. The United States ambassador was contacted by Communist officials on the question of American recognition and possible economic assistance; Nanking officials approached the British and American embassies in May 1949, to clarify Chinese Communist conditions for the establishment of diplomatic relations. A number of local trading arrangements were also set up between Communist authorities and British businessmen. Opinion in Britain was divided on the significance of these preliminary contacts. In September, *The Times* said that British consuls had been 'cold-shouldered in every way and treated with a disregard that indicates not the slightest desire for friendly relations'; while the *Manchester Guardian*'s Shanghai correspondent argued at the same time that there were 'many signs that the new regime is anxious to renew Chinese relations abroad, and not to cut itself off from the West.'[41] British officials were at least not mistreated, so the problem that later dominated American thinking on the question of relations with Communist China did not arise. Non-essential British personnel were, however, evacuated from China, and the British government joined in the international protest at the end of November over the treatment of United States officials in China.

Such *ad hoc* relations as were possible were no surrogate for an exchange of ambassadors. And the Chinese made it clear that nothing short of full *de jure* diplomatic recognition, and the abandonment of all links with the Nationalists, would be acceptable. By the autumn of 1949, this had become the only workable British option. It had been agreed on in principle earlier, but delayed towards the end of the year in the hope of soothing American anxieties. But the prospect of joint Anglo-American action had greatly diminished; while postponement far into 1950 carried with it the danger of an open breach within the Commonwealth. Younger said in a 1958 interview that 'since the Commonwealth was going to be divided for some time on the issue of recognition, the government was determined that it would not countenance the division being along racial lines.'[42] Further delay was also ruled out by developments in Sino-Soviet relations. The earlier optimism about Mao Tse-Tung's 'Titoist' tendencies had begun to evaporate, but it was still thought that in the long term the Russians and the Chinese would not be able to work harmoniously together. Mao arrived in Moscow for negotiations on the treaty (which was eventually signed the following February) on 16 December. Britain informed the United States the same day of its intention to recognise his regime on 6 January.[43]

Neither British officials nor the trading community expected great things of recognition. Few, however, anticipated any serious Chinese objection to the establishment of diplomatic relations. Statements from Peking were full of anti-Western propaganda, but these were taken as items for internal consumption put out by revolutionaries flushed with success, rather than as guides to future Chinese government policy. In May 1949, the People's Liberation Army strongly criticised British military aid to Chiang Kai-shek. 'During the past year, the governments of the USA, Great Britain and Canada have been helping the Kuomintang against us. Has Mr Attlee forgotten this? Which country presented the heavy cruiser *Chungking* which was sunk recently?'[44] Chinese commentary was for a long time dominated by the *Amethyst* incident, which was held out as indicative of the true face of British imperialism. The Chinese interpretation was that 'British naval vessels illegally sailed into the Yangtse River . . . and helped the reactionary Kuomintang to bombard the troops of the Chinese people.'[45] The New China News Agency waged a sustained campaign against British policy in Hongkong, with particular reference to regulations which called for the registration of certain organisations with the authorities.

This line grew, rather than subsided, after British recognition. Indeed, that action itself provided ammunition. Britain had 'crudely misrepresented the Central People's government as "the Chinese Communist government" ', and had insisted that the step did not imply approval of it. The official British statement to this effect was given wide circulation inside China. Britain, it was argued, had even gone out of its way to identify Mao Tse-tung with Hitler and Franco — MacDonald's speech, to which this alludes, was also heavily publicised — and British statements continued to 'defame the Soviet Union, China's friend.'[46] As before, British actions in China in the nineteenth century received prominent coverage in commentary on British recognition. The move was attributed simply to Britain's supposed need for trade with China, a traditional response to

British overtures as well as one suggested by Marxist-Leninist tenets.

It was several months before a more substantive response was issued by the Ministry of Foreign Affairs, although the Chinese position had been put earlier in exchanges with British officials in Peking. This statement was issued on 22 May 1950, two days before the Foreign Secretary was due to address the Commons and defend his government's China policy, which then seemed in ruins. The Chinese had informed Britain 'that the question which was most important and which must first be settled. . . was the relationship between the British Government and the remnant reactionary clique of the Chinese Kuomintang.'[47] The most obvious symbol of this relationship, the retention by the British government of a consul at Tamsui on Formosa, does not seem to have troubled Peking. The consulate was mentioned in the first public reactions to British recognition, but did not become an issue in the later exchanges. It is possible that the Chinese accepted the British view, that the consul was accredited to the provincial Taiwan authorities and not to the Nationalist regime. It is more likely that they viewed it as a minor matter; Formosa was expected to be liberated during the coming summer.

Two other questions were specifically raised as bearing on Britain's relationship with the Kuomintang: the question of Chinese representation in the United Nations, which will be discussed shortly; and the question of certain property formerly owned by the Nationalists. This chiefly concerned aircraft sold by Nationalist officials to an American company; Peking, disputing the validity of the sale, claimed that in international law it inherited the property of the state of China. The aircraft in question were grounded at the time on an airfield in Hongkong. The matter had arisen before British recognition. In December, Chou En-lai had stated that only the Central People's government and those entrused by it had a right to deal with the properties concerned, adding that 'such a sacred property right of the Central People's government should be respected by the Hongkong government.'[48] After British recognition, China claimed that British officials had 'obstructed in many ways' the flight of the aircraft to China, and had failed to protect them from damage. Britain was also accused of 'ordering' the court in Hongkong, which ruled that the aircraft were in law the property of the People's Republic, to detain them regardless of the legal position.

The reaction in Britain to the Chinese response was sharp and indignant. Other events in the new year seemed to vindicate opposition to a conciliatory Western approach to Peking. On 14 January, within a few days of British recognition, United States consular property in Peking was seized. The proclamation was issued by the authorities on the day the British Note was delivered. Both British and American officials made representations in an attempt to avert the occupation. The event significantly hardened American opinion against recognition of Peking. Acheson promptly issued instructions for preparations to be made for the recall of all American officials in China. In the following weeks, the American China policy debate intensified. It was in February that Senator McCarthy's radio broadcast, in which he claimed that Communists were working inside the State Department, received national coverage. Officials became increasingly preoccupied with countering Republican condemnation of the Truman Administration's China policy. The expiration date on funds appropriated for assistance to China was extended to 30 June. Referring to Chinese treatment of American property and citizens, the Secretary of State said that the United States 'would certainly not recognise Peking in such circumstances.'[49] The now open divergence between United States and British official attitudes showed up in April, when the Communist authorities seized the military compound adjoining the British embassy. British officials pointed out that their government did not object to this action in principle, and had been ready to enter into negotiations with a view to relinquishing Britain's rights; all that was questioned was China's right to take over the compound simply by unilateral administrative action. Far from publicising the incident as an attack on British interests, the Foreign Office emphasised that the Chinese had indicated their readiness to pay compensation, and had given advance notice of their intention.[50]

The Chinese insistence on negotiations prior to an exchange of ambassadors did, however, surprise London. Chou's Note of 9 January accepted Mr. Hutchison as the British representative 'sent to Peking for the purpose of carrying on negotiations on the question of establishing diplomatic relations.' It was thought that the proposed talks would be of a technical nature, covering such matters as immunities, communications, and where consuls might be stationed. In earlier statements, the Chinese government had indeed stated its position as being that, if the conditions on the part of the recognising government were met, it might 'negotiate' the establishment of diplomatic relations. However, this term was either absent from British accounts, or else ignored as a formal mode of expression. Discussions began in March 1950. In May, the Foreign Secretary, embarrassed by the turn of events, took a tough line in the Commons: 'What is happening at the moment is that the Chinese are attempting to raise side issues . . . To that we have no intention of submitting.'[51]

The British explanation of the status of the Tamsui consulate was given at the time that recognition of Peking was announced. It was not an issue for the Chinese. The government also denied emphatically that the question of Chinese aircraft in Hongkong could in any way be linked to the question of establishing diplomatic relations. When the question was raised in an adjournment debate at the end of March, it was pronounced *sub judice*. It was 'our principal duty' to preserve the rule of law; it would be 'improper to do anything other than leave the situation as it is now.'[52] The problem eventually disappeared in seemingly endless litigation. The court in Hongkong declared the aircraft to be the property of the Central People's government; one factor influencing this judgement was that they were being physically held by pro-Communist workers on the airfield, and these had claimed that they were the representatives of Peking. However, the planes were retained until such time as a final decision in law could be reached, pending, that is, the hearing of an appeal by Nationalist and American interests. The British government's legalistic reasoning owed something to political considerations. The United States ambassador in London was active throughout the spring of 1950 making representations in which the potential military value of the Hongkong aircraft was stressed. This was the decisive criterion for Conservative MPs, several of whom expressed strong opposition to handing the plans over to Peking. In turn, Ministers pointed out that the aircraft in question were in fact civil, not military.

Yet public opinion, though generally critical of the Chinese attitude, was not unanimously so. Those who had been opposed to British recognition, or who had reluctantly acquiesced, found their convictions strengthened. That Peking had behaved contrary to expectations by seeming to reject British overtures was not seen as invalidating their case. Peking was simply achieving its aims by other means. Britain had been 'humbugged and humiliated'; Peking's response was 'a virtual snub for Britain.'[53] For its part, the government denied that delay in the setting up of formal relations was harmful to British prestige. Conservative critics also seized upon the consequences of British recognition on the situation in Malaya, and the lack of any compensating benefit for British businessmen in China. 'The truth is,' as Eden summed up Opposition feeling, 'that recognition has in fact brought out no advantage at all today.'[54] Two further drawbacks were noted. First, Britain had by her action gravely offended the Nationalist authorities on Taiwan. The consequence was that neither side in the Chinese civil war was friendly; Britain was getting the worst of both worlds. The British government had, secondly, given the appearance of having stepped out of line with the United States and other Commonwealth nations. This was argued to be dangerous, as China could now try to play off one ally against the other. Each of these factors made still more menacing the situation brought about by China's formal alignment with the Soviet Union in the treaty announced in February 1950. During the spring, British commentary tended increasingly to highlight evidence of unrest in China, support for the Kuomintang resistance, the inability of the new authorities to cope with famine or economic and administrative problems, and indoctrination and the enforced mobilisation of the Chinese people.

Yet there was also some attempt to understand, if not always to sympathise with, the Chinese point of view. Purcell wrote that 'we are, it seems, to make it clear that we are entering into the most reluctant relations with criminals with whom no honest dealings are possible . . . In fact we are to make the recognition so humiliating, so insulting, and so absurd that no government, not even a Communist one, will accept it.'[55] Later, in June, *The Times'* Hongkong correspondent tried to summarise how British actions seemed through Chinese eyes. Britain had delayed three months before recognising; secondly, the most vociferous group in favour of recognition were the traders, 'so that the Communists not unnaturally concluded that our action was based primarily on commercial considerations, not on genuine good will'; thirdly, it had been made abundantly clear that no approval was implied, that the regime in Peking was comparable with that of Franco, and that there would be no let-up in the persecution of the Malayan insurgents or in support for the French and the Bao Dai regime in Indo-china. All this, he continued, came on top of an ingrained suspicion of the West bred by ideology, American support for the Kuomintang, and the *Amethyst* incident; and contrasted sharply with the immediate Soviet recognition. Britain had not paid due regard to the justifiable feelings of pride at their achievement of the new Chinese leaders.[56] The theme was taken up by Labour MPs, who criticised the government's continuing links with Chiang Kai-shek on Formosa, and its refusal to support Peking's claim to China's United Nations seat. But as time went on, the intransigeance of the Chinese tempered this argument. 'If the British government might have done more when first they offered to recognise Peking,' *The Times* argued in May, 'the fault for the delay in exchanging Ambassadors now lies chiefly with Peking.'[57] Even so, the Sino-Soviet treaty was not in general taken as conclusive proof that Mao and Chou had sold their Titoist souls for roubles. Observers pointed to the length of the negotiations in Moscow, which indicated that there had been difficulties in the way of an agreement. Moreover, Peking had failed to jump at the opportunity provided by British recognition to split the Western allies, and fill vacant consulates in Malaya. There still lingered the suspicion that Western actions were forcing the Chinese to turn to Moscow. If the Chinese wanted protection from the American-supported Nationalist air raids on the mainland, a writer in the *Guardian* argued, 'then, whether moderates or extremists, they have no option but to accept Stalin's terms.'[58] The Chinese response was duly noted in Australia, Canada and the United States, and lent weight to the case against recognition. Pearson said that Peking's cold reception of British recognition would definitely be taken into consideration by his government before Canada decided on the matter.

The crux of the issue was the question of Chinese represen-

tation in the United Nations. In 1949, some difficulties in the
UN were expected; but these were not held to justify
non-recognition of Peking or substantial delay. The Foreign
Office view was that wider Western and Commonwealth
recognition would be followed by the Communists' taking the
UN seat. This was not seen as raising intractable problems.
Indeed it appears that the Foreign Office officials handling UN
affairs were not even consulted on the recognition question.
However, it was also felt that, particularly in the light of United
States sensitivities, a solution should not be hurried. On 10
January 1950, the Soviet delegate to the Security Council raised
the matter for the second time (the first had been at the end of
December). The British view was that the proposal had been
raised prematurely. 'At this moment, not many governments
have recognised the new government in China, and, therefore, it
might be premature and precipitate on the part of this organ . . .
to take, or attempt to take, a definite decision in the near
future.' The Nationalist delegate, Bevin said later, was still the
representative of China; 'we could not in the transition period
come to a conclusion to throw out one representative and to
take on another.'[59] After the Council had voted not to consider
the question, the Soviet Union began a spreading boycott of UN
organs.

Britain's position at this time is an interesting one, for it was
one that, in the government's view, served Soviet rather than
Western interests. The stand was not taken with this consideration in view. But in May, the Foreign Secretary expressed
his belief that the Soviet Union 'was not really interested in
seeing Peking seated as a Member because an isolated China
would be more susceptible to Soviet control.' A *Times*
correspondent thought Soviet actions seemed 'precisely cal-
culated to impede further recognition and in the upshot to
reduce the Peking prospects of admission.'[60] This was also a
common American view. The suspicion of underlying Soviet
motives was seen to be supported by Soviet propaganda, which
blamed the paralysis of the UN on Britain and the United
States, and which claimed the West was opposed to Peking's
admission since it preferred 'the Chiang Kai-shek criminal
clique.' Apart from a wish to avoid undue haste, British
reluctance to have the Security Council consider the question
grew from a refusal in principle to give way to what were seen

as Soviet blackmailing tactics.

During February and March, London instituted a cautious policy aimed at eventually securing China's seat for Peking. Two developments eased its path. First, the United States delegate to the Council had already made it clear that Washington regarded Chinese representation as 'a procedural question involving the credentials of a representative of a member.' The United States would, therefore, accept the decision of the Security Council 'when made by an affirmative vote of seven members.'[61] American officials stuck to this position. In June, Acheson confirmed that the United States would accept the decision of any organ of the UN made by the necessary majority; that the veto did not apply; and that the United States would not influence nations in the decision of how they were to vote on the question. This position was welcomed in London. It was closely related to a second factor. A consensus gradually emerged that the UN question was quite separate from the question of diplomatic recognition. The American view was that acceptance of a Chinese Communist delegate in the UN would not imply American recognition of that regime. The Soviet delegate had based his case at least partly on this argument in January. Early in February, the Secretary General drew up a key memorandum on the general question. Lie argued that 'it would appear to be legally inadmissable' to condition decisions on representation of a State in the UN by a requirement that they be preceded by individual recognition. He also gave powerful implicit support for the seating of Peking by suggesting the need for an inquiry 'as to whether the new government exercises effective authority within the territory of the State and is habitually obeyed by the bulk of the population.'[62] This statement of the position was noted approvingly by the British government.

At this time five members of the Security Council — the USSR, Britain, India, Norway and Yugoslavia — recognised Peking. Approaches were accordingly made by Britain to France, and also to Egypt, which in February was thought to be on the verge of recognition. 'We have tried, quite frankly,' Bevin told the Commons, 'to see if we could get this cleared up by seeing whether seven votes could be collected, our main object being that we think it is better for the New China to be inside the UN. We do not want to ostracise anyone on political grounds.'[63] That little progress was made was due partly to American pressures. Despite the official stand of aloofness, Acheson stated bluntly in January that the United States was 'opposed to seating the Communist regime.' According to the Secretary-General, delegates brought influence to bear on a Latin American state (possibly Ecuador, which had also been approached by the British) that had planned to support the seating of the People's Republic. Everything seemed to depend on the attitude of the United States, Sir Gladwyn Jebb commented, and she was 'unwilling to give even informal encouragement to Member states considering supporting the admission of the new Chinese Government's representative.'[64]

By April, it was apparent that an impasse had been reached. Only two things seemed capable of breaking it: a change in the American position, or the fall of Formosa. Britain's talks in Peking on the establishment of diplomatic relations also appeared deadlocked. In May, the Foreign Ministers of the United States, Britain and France discussed China policy. Officials in Washington interpreted the result of the meeting as a decision by the three allies not to make any move for the present on the admission of Communist China. This was explicitly denied by Britain. 'In fact,' said Younger, 'we have been anxious to see this matter solved; we have been trying to get support in the relevant bodies of the UN for a course that would bring the People's government into the UN, and there is no restriction upon our activities in that regard during the coming period.'[65]

The link between the talks in Peking and the events in New York was stressed by the Chinese. Britain had 'submissively followed the lead of American imperialism' in the Security Council, and was thus not meeting the criteria established earlier for the exchange of ambassadors. From the end of May, indications began to emerge that both the Peking exchanges and the UN situation could be satisfactorily resolved. The Chinese first offered a package of concessions to Britain in return for acceptance by London of Peking's criteria. Five were mentioned: a guarantee that no discriminatory action would be taken against British business in China; British-registered ships would be permitted to ply freely along the China coast; through traffic on the Kowloon-Canton railway would be resumed; a promise would be given not to effect any blockade, 'material or moral', of Hongkong; and trade agreements would be concluded with Britain on the basis of equality.[66] Peking kept up its demands on the UN and Hongkong aircraft questions, and continued to press for changes in the regulations introduced with respect to the movement of Chinese nationals into and within Hongkong, and to the Chinese communities in Malaya. Hongkong observers saw no wish on the part of Peking to break off the talks with British officials. Some minor diplomatic concessions were made. British officials in Nanking were permitted to move to the capital; and the British diplomatic courier was still being allowed to travel regularly between Hongkong and Peking. The tone of anti-British commentary mellowed.

But the key obstacle remained. Asked a few weeks later, in July, why Sino-British negotiations had not been successful, the former British Consul-General in Shanghai replied: 'The answer is quite simple. I am convinced that Peking did not intend to establish diplomatic relations with Britain until her government is recognised in the United Nations.'[67] British concessions by way of the Hongkong aircraft issue were not possible because of strategic considerations, American pressures, and judicial questions. A renewed attempt to change the situation in the UN was therefore sought. Criticism mounted in Britain of the government's position in New York. It was argued to be unrealistic, incompatible with diplomatic recognition, and doubly dangerous: it drove the Chinese still further into the arms of the Russians, while the Soviet boycott damaged the prestige of the UN and threatened to render it incapable of functioning at all.

Thus on 19 June, it was announced in New York that Britain had decided that the time had come to break the deadlock. Several delegations, including those of Commonwealth countries, were informed that when further votes were taken on the question, Britain would probably pass from its present policy of abstention to an unqualified affirmative. Of equal significance was the British disposition now to approach the problem through organs of the UN other than the Security Council itself. Until then, British officials had maintained that the decision on Chinese representation belonged properly to the Council. The next opportunity to implement the new policy was 3 July, when the Economic and Social Council would meet in Geneva. Commenting on the British move, *The Times* stated that 'the admission of Communist China would be no more than the recognition of fact, however distasteful; and the chance would remain, no matter how slender or limited in value, of averting a final rupture' of the United Nations.[68] Commentators drew attention over the next few days to the importance of the forthcoming ECOSOC meeting. On 21 June, its chairman visited London for two days of talks with British ministers and officials.

British optimism that the end might be in sight, both for the negotiations in Peking and for the representation issue in the UN, now also rested on expectations of a shift in the French position. In May, Bidault, stating the reasons why France had not recognised Peking, added that nevertheless 'on pourrait s'arranger', provided China took no active steps to imperil French interests in South-East Asia. The French ambassador in London explicitly separated the two issues. French recognition of Peking was 'another question to be settled on another plane', rather than, as it had been hitherto, one intimately connected with Peking's recognition of Ho Chi Minh. Officials in New York put forward arguments about the need to recognise facts. At the same time, the French trading community was putting increased pressure on Paris to reach accommodation with the Chinese; and dealings between Shanghai and the leading French bank in the Far East were reopened.[69] The French view seems to have been that a decision would have to be taken with some urgency, as the Security Council could not normally operate later than July.

This coincided with the opinion of the UN Secretary-General. On 20 June, the day after the announcement of the new British policy, it was confirmed that Lie would visit London on 3 July, the opening day of the ECOSOC meeting in Geneva. It was later stated that his speech in London would be 'of major political importance', and that after it he would fly to Geneva. While in London, Lie said, he would have 'further important talks' with members of the British and French governments.[70] It seems evident that the gound was being prepared for a successful vote on Communist Chinese entry to the United Nations through one of its subsidiary organs. Events in Korea, however, intervened. The last of these reports on the forthcoming British initiative appeared on the Saturday after it had been anounced. On the next day, news came of the North Korean attack.

This final British initiative before Korea gives some indication both of the persistence of the British government in clinging to its earlier stand on China despite American criticism and Chinese hostility, and of the magnitude of the impact of that war on the evolution of Sino-Western relations. After 1950, Western China policy was tilted in an American rather than, as previously, in a British direction. The consequent tightening of Western trade controls, amounting in the United States' case to a complete embargo, and the formal denunciation by the United Nations of China as an aggressor in Korea early in 1951, had implications far outlasting the duration of the war itself. More immediately, the neutralisation of the Taiwan Straits barred Communist occupation of Taiwan, expected in a matter of weeks; the wider Western and Commonwealth recognition of Peking that would have followed, and in some significant cases preceded, Chiang's fall did not therefore materialise; Peking's first admission to a body of the United Nations, expected in a matter of days, was postponed. All of this does not, however, support the argument that a beleagured administration in Washington deliberately overreacted to events in Korea in order to salvage the Democrats' crumbling position before the 1950 mid-term elections. That would imply an American official perception of the separability of Far Eastern developments that did not exist. And there is some evidence that Acheson was still at this late stage trying to keep open the option of recognition of Peking by the United States.

The British government went as far as it considered it reasonably could at the end of 1949, and again in the spring of 1950, to meet with United States reservations. All other considerations pointed towards recognition: the facts of Communist power in China, the presence of British interests, and British interpretations of the international law of recognition; the views of British officials; the support of the Conservative Opposition for the government's move; the opinions expressed by the governments of the Asian Commonwealth. It is in this context that the Chinese response, and the British reaction to it, can best be understood. For Britain, the act of recognition was — despite the official camouflage — a step of major importance. Because of her leading position in both NATO and the Commonwealth, she would be giving Peking an immense accretion of prestige and international legitimacy. And the government was conscious too of the potential costs of recognition in terms of British interests in Malaya and of the Anglo-American alliance. For China, British recognition was a test case for future Sino-Western relations. The price that Britain had paid seemed negligible when compared with the trading benefits she hoped to obtain in return. Yet from May 1950, both sides seem to have developed an impetus to break through the obstacles impeding an exchange of ambassadors. That they failed was due to factors beyond the control of either.

4 The Containment Debate

China did not exist in a vacuum. She was very much a part of international relations in Asia. Further, what happened in China had repercussions for world politics generally. Such considerations forced British observers to ask fundamental questions about Asian Communism in the context of forming judgements about the People's Republic of China. It was taken as an article of faith by all but the fringe elements of British politics that the Soviet Union was beyond the pail of respectability: internally repressive, externally expansionist. No such certainty touched thinking about China. The dilemma of 1949 was to decide whether Asian nationalism or Moscow-inspired Communism best characterised the leadership in Peking. It was resolved for many by the events of 1950 and afterwards: the Sino-Soviet Treaty, the Korean War and Chinese military intervention in it, the occupation of Tibet, and the later support to the Vietminh forces. But traces of the earlier conflict remained. In 1954, Britain approached the question of the establishment of a South-East Asia Treaty Organisation (SEATO) in a manner that highlights the divergence of opinion on these questions that existed between London and Washington.

In 1949, the view that Asian Communism was a tool of the Kremlin was not confined to any one political party. The attacks of the left on Soviet imperialism in Asia frequently surpassed in vigour those emanating from Tories. Asian Communist Parties, Wyatt argued, were 'run by somewhat half-baked lunatics who hardly know what they mean by Communism anyway, who specialise in terrorist methods, and whose only aim is to throw all foreigners out of their country straight away . . . as well as blindly following every manifesto and edict that comes from Moscow and believing implicitly in the great god Stalin.'[1] The Czech coup of 1948 became a model, readily applied to the Asian context, of how a country could be brought under the thumb of Moscow through internal subversion. Nationalism and Communism were thus opposed. Communism, Macmillan said in May 1949, 'with all its reinforcements of malignant propaganda', was 'exploiting and fomenting these national, and not unnatural, sentiments.'[2]

Yet the consensus, such as it was, was that this analysis was too simple. The alternative proposition was articulated most fully to the left of centre of British politics. In March 1950, Crossman maintained that it was a 'very dangerous conclusion for us to draw that, because in Europe Communism is virtually identical with the expansion of Russian imperialism, the same is also true of the Far East.' Europe, which used to dominate the world, was 'now merely just one part of the world, and the peoples in Africa and Asia are asserting the right of nationhood, and they have grasped Communism as the means of asserting it.' Primarily, Communism there meant 'something to fill empty bellies and something to achieve self-determination.' It was 'against white imperialism which has lasted one hundred years, that they are now rising.'[3] Though attitudes varied – and the Korean War introduced a new dimension to the problem – it was Ho Chi-minh and Mao Tse-tung that tended to be singled out as men who exemplified this combination of a reforming, socialist programme at home, with a nationalist and independent foreign policy abroad. China, then, was both nationalist *and* Communist. This dual characterisation was not thought to contain an inner inconsistency. In the jargon of the period, China's leaders had significant 'Titoist' traits.

On balance, however, China was seen as an exceptional case. Quite different lines of argument were developed in relation to local Communist Parties in India, Hongkong or Malaya. These, it was argued, unlike the CCP, could lay no such claim to be representative of the population. The point is worth making since Malayan and China policy often made contact. During the summer and autumn of 1949, for example, it was reported that the British government was trying to secure a greater measure of United States support for British policies in the Malayan territories, and that it was prepared to slow down the momentum towards diplomatic recognition of Peking in return. Similarly, after recognition, Tory critics claimed that this action had been responsible for a stepping up of guerrilla activities in Malaya. This the government denied. Younger admitted, however, that the successes of the Chinese Communists had aggravated the situation in Malaya and in other parts of South-East Asia.[4] Before Korea, British opinion tended to point to Indo-China, Burma, and Thailand, as countries most likely to be affected by the victories of the Chinese People's Liberation Army. There was also intermittent discussion of Tibet during 1949, but the situation there was complicated by the British government's interpretation of Tibet's status in international law.[5]

Thus a cautiously sympathetic appraisal of Chinese Communism was not held to be incompatible with harsher judgements on Communism in other parts of Asia. This balance was nurtured by the interpretations prevalent in India and other Asian Commonwealth nations. Defending his government's recognition of Peking, Nehru in 1950 gave a matter-of-fact justification that took its cue from British rationales. The Indian government had recognised the new regime when it was quite clear that it was 'in possession of practically the entire mainland of China . . . that this Government was a stable Government and that there was no force which was likely to supplant it or to push it away . . .'[6] The statement does not do justice to Indian thinking at that time about China. The central People's government was seen to be dedicated to achieving the aims of modernisation, reform, the ending of the corruption of the Kuomintang period, and national unity. It was seen as having its natural roots in the peasant masses, while at the same time enjoying support from other groups in Chinese society. In its foreign policy, it would be suspicious of the West for obvious historical reasons, and because of that disposed to look favourably upon overtures from Moscow. It would, however, be an intensely nationalist regime, having as its objective a China 'standing up' and taking part in the affairs of Asia and, through membership of the United Nations, of the world.[7] Recognition would thus help to prevent the emergence of the hostile attitudes and actions that could arise out of strongly felt grievances.

The idea of some kind of alliance grouping for Asia, possibly similar to NATO in Europe, was discussed as early as 1949. A number of Conservatives, including Macmillan and Butler, thought such a scheme desirable. Macmillan argued that

> the Great Alliance has brought a temporary stability to the
> West. It must be extended to the East, for it may well be that
> the supreme Communist High Command in the Kremlin will
> for the moment accept a pause . . . in its expansion in the
> West in order to seek out more profitable and spectacular
> successes in the East. A Pacific Pact, therefore, must buttress
> and complete the Atlantic Pact.'[8]

In 1949, however, too many obstacles stood in the way. The
State Department was firmly opposed to an American commitment with respect to territories on the mainland of Asia. It was
in any case reluctant to involve the United States in ventures
which might be interpreted in Asia as attempts to bolster British
and French imperialism. NATO, Acheson pointed out in May,
was the product of particular circumstances and the culmination of previous actions. It was based on a solid foun-
dation. By contrast, internal conflicts in Asia meant that a
Pacific defence pact could not take shape.[9] The objection in
Britain tended to be somewhat different. The answer to the
problem of Asian Communism was not seen to be primarily a
military one. The Colombo Plan better embodied this notion. It
also reflected the principle that Asian governments themselves
ought to have a say in determining policies in the region. And
for many in the Labour Party, there was the further danger of
the West, by such methods, extending its support to Asian
regimes that were helping to perpetuate social injustices, and
which themselves, therefore, served indirectly the cause of
Communism. Crossman, for example, contended that 'the only
chance we have of defeating the Russians is to split Communism
— to split the Communists who believe in their nationhood
from the Communists who are merely satellites and serfs of the
Russians.'[10]

This principle already underlay the British approach to the
problems posed by Communist China. The Chinese were
Communists who, with luck and the right policies, could be
persuaded to detach themselves from entanglements with
Moscow. Thus Britain's China policy from late 1948 to early
1950 can be seen as part of a broader framework of thinking
about post-war Asia. The Communist victory in China had to be
recognised as a fact, while the spread of Sino-Western contacts

would alert Mao and Chou to options other than a close alliance with the USSR. But at the same time, Communism had to be contained within its present limits. This was to be achieved not only through the strengthening of the internal and external defences of threatened areas. It could not succeed without emphasis on the elimination of those economic and social conditions which could with ease be exploited by local Communists, to the ultimate benefit of Moscow and the hard-liners in Peking.

This background is essential to understanding the British response when the alliance idea was raised again in greater earnest some five years later. New factors had emerged by 1954. China had, in Korea and Indo-China, proved herself able and willing to intervene, directly or indirectly, on behalf of Communist movements in neighbouring Asian states. It was in this context that the SEATO concept came to fruition. Another factor in the intervening period had been the signing of the ANZUS Treaty in San Francisco in September 1951, between the United States, Australia, and New Zealand. Britain's exclusion from the pact rankled, especially since two senior members of the Commonwealth had participated without her. It had been argued in Washington that British membership of such a grouping would involve its members in additional and unacceptable burdens of defence commitments.[11]

As previously, the British position fell somewhere between those taken by the United States on the one hand, and the members of the Asian Commonwealth on the other. In 1954, Washington saw the primary Western defence need as being to save Indo-China from a Chinese assault. After the Geneva accords, Bedell Smith stated that the main object of any defence organisation in the area would be to 'draw the line' against further Chinese advance in that part of the world. The three Indo-China States, he added, had been left 'almost defenceless' by the agreements signed in Geneva.[12] The *New York Herald Tribune* expressed the issue succinctly in an editorial on August 8, in which it declared that plans for an alliance organisation were 'aimed at deterring open aggression by Communist China and preventing indirect aggression by means of Communist-inspired subversion or civil war.' Comparisons between NATO and an equivalent body for Asia were drawn with increasing freqency and confidence. The precise form it might take was not clear. Indeed there was a persistent background debate of the virtues of a grouping encompassing Nationalist China, Japan and South Korea, possibly alongside a South-East Asian organisation.

Australia, too, was coming round to a similar verdict. During the first half of the year, government statements grew steadily more anxious. Stating the case for a defensive grouping in the region, Casey referred to 'the black clouds of Communist China' hanging to the north of Australia. In March, he said that 'the menace of the southward march of international communism from Russia and China' was keeping him awake at nights. It was doubtful, he said in May, that, bearing in mind the manpower, resources and territorial ambitions of Communist China, an individual South-East Asian country could resist Communist infiltration solely on its own resources.[13] The *Sydney Morning Herald*, and the Australian press generally, similarly made much of the supposed analogy between the Asian and European contexts in this regard.[14] Australian indignation over what was seen as a failure by Britain to take this threat seriously grew during the summer.

British official opinion was sensitive to United States and Australian fears. But the government was also closely in touch with Asian Commonwealth governments. Very different re-actions to SEATO came from New Delhi. Speaking in London in September 1954, Menon summarised his government's views on the question. 'If we want peace, we must avoid many things that create an atmosphere for war. No country wants aggression against itself or its friends. And yet the steps they take in the name of preventing aggression itself encourages aggression.'[15] The creation of military alliances, he maintained in a series of public statements in the summer, caused international tension. Nehru, too, contrasted the alliance concept with the kinds of understandings reached at Geneva. SEATO, he declared in August, would serve to lead the world 'away from the new atmosphere of peace created since the Geneva Conference.'[16] The Indian press considered the pact to be aimed solely against China. The *Hindu* expressed the opinion that, particularly when the types of regimes which had associated themselves with the idea were considered, the alliance could be seen as 'a sort of colonial wing of the NATO itself.'[17]

The debate inside Britain was symptomatic of this bi-furcation of external opinion. Conservatives tended to be more prepared to give United States and Australian views a fair hearing; Labour supporters to be more sympathetic (though not uniformly so) to Indian opinion. Assessments of Chinese objectives were dominated by the incontrovertible facts of Chinese military intervention in Korea, and aid to the Vietminh. Opinions were divided on the significance of the latter point. In April 1954, *The Times* voiced the opinion that the Chinese part in prolonging the Indo-China war had been exaggerated. The same month, Nutting stated that it was the British government's view that the Vietminh were 'entirely dependent on aid from China' for the conduct of regular military operations against French Union forces.[18] It was widely believed that China, as a result of its involvement there and the subsequent Geneva settlement, had gained prestige, sowed divisions between West-ern governments, strengthened itself domestically, and, more-over, achieved a large part of its immediate objectives.

Concern about what *The Times* referred to as the 'long-term ambitions' of Peking were thus crucial to British thinking about SEATO. The fear was not so much of direct aggression. The danger from 'the Chinese advance in Asia', as the *Manchester Guardian* termed it, was more one of subversion and infil-tration. Commentary in the national press was split on the question of where the weak spots in Asian defences were located. Thailand, Burma, Indonesia and the Philippines were generally placed in the front line, as were Malaya and North Borneo. British interests were hence affected more directly. The Foreign Secretary's own first expression of support for the SEATO idea in April 1954, dwelt on British interests in Malaya. Eden wrote later that he had welcomed the United States proposal 'since this would contribute to the security of Malaya and Hongkong.'[19] The two front benches in the Commons were not in fundamental conflict. In November, Brown related the Opposition's view: 'again and again aggressive Powers get into a war because they find it impossible to ascertain the point beyond which they cannot go without a war resulting.' It was 'well to say to potential aggressors in Europe and in Asia that a line is being drawn, and to tell them, in the good old trade union parlance, "Thus far, brother, and no farther." '[20] Such comparisons with the Soviet threat in Europe were frequent. In turn, the Sino-Soviet Treaty of 1950 became a major justification for the British government's signing the Manila Treaty.

More telling, however, were the arguments undermining the comparability of the two regions. First, and most obviously, the non-Communist Asian nations — such as India and Pakistan — were clearly more deeply divided than were those of Western Europe in 1948—9. Secondly, there was the sheer military problem. A nucleus of land powers with forces on the spot simply did not exist. The *Guardian* spelt out the implications of this fact in a sequence of editorials during the summer months. It meant that such forces would have to be supplied by the West. But this raised the alternatives of a commitment to fighting a land war in Asia, which the United States was not willing to accept; or Western bases on the continent, which was undesirable in view of Asian sensitivities, would feed Communist propaganda, and might contribute to the spread of Communism; or else, thirdly, a willingness to use nuclear weapons in the last resort. This last possibility raised the unattractive prospect of the Western powers becoming embroiled in a nuclear war with the USSR as a consequence of an increase in guerrilla activity in, say, Thailand; or, alternately, of the Communists advancing with impunity armed with the knowledge that the West would not use the nuclear option.[21] Other factors, such as geography, made it difficult to 'draw a line' as NATO had in Europe. And the wisdom even of making explicit those areas that were to be defended was questioned, on the grounds that this might imply that territories not so mentioned would be readily sacrificed by the West. It had become a common argument in the United States that one source of the Korean War lay in Western failures earlier in 1950 specifically to mention South Korea as part of the Western defence perimeter.

Thirdly, China in 1954 was different from the Soviet Union in 1949. It could be argued, as on balance *The Times* tended to do, that after Korea and Indo-China the Chinese government would want to wind up its international commitments and concentrate on domestic issues, and that in foreign policy its immediate preoccupation would probably be the creation of spheres of influence to act as buffers against the outside world, rather than outright mastery of South-East Asia. As Attlee put it in June, 'They have 603 million people to look after. Surely that is enough for any government.'[22] China, however, might be forced into a position of becoming like the Soviet Union of 1949. Bevan, for example, expressed his opposition to any move designed to encircle China by military entanglements. The criterion of whether or not Western actions were provocative, Wyatt maintained, would be 'a subjective test applied by the Chinese.'[23] And even those sympathetic to the pact idea proclaimed the need to allay the reasonable fears of China about its intent.

Asian sensitivities constituted a fourth basis for British reservations. Suspicions of the West, and memories of colonial rule, were still deep, *The Times* noted; they could easily be fanned into resentment. British interpretations of the evident Asian mistrust of the scheme varied. Some, particularly Conservative back-benchers, put it down to lack of understanding, arising out of lack of experience, of the reality of Communist imperialism. This would change, presumably, as the nature of the threat became more vivid. Asian misgivings were often attributed on the Labour side to United States dogmatic anti-Communism, and to Washington's failure to distinguish between nationalism and Communism, or between different types of Communism, and its consequent espousal of feudal and military regimes in the region. SEATO would give the impression, Bevan suggested, that an alliance was being established in Asia 'for the purpose of imposing European colonial rule.' It would, therefore, be self-defeating. Donnelly went so far as to claim that 'the surest way of spreading Communism in Asia would be to adopt the policy of a Western-planned, Western-dominated, and Western-instigated military alliance in Southeast Asia.' This was 'the surest way of bringing people in the political no-man's-land into the Communist camp, because it makes the Communists the champions of Asiatic nationalism.'[24] Something like the same point was made by Eden in a memorandum to Dulles at the beginning of the Geneva Conference. Communism in Asia, he wrote, could not be checked by military means alone. The problem was 'as much political as military; if any military combination is to be effective, it must enjoy the widest possible measure of Asian support.'[25]

One way of guaranteeing that an Asian grouping did not antagonise China was to have her as a member of it. For United

States opinion, such an idea was anathema, even incomprehensible. Different kinds of Asian collective security options were investigated by Labour MPs. From the government's own perspective, however, the reasoning behind such schemes was defective, since they implied the granting of a veto power to the Communist side in any moves to shore up the Indo-China settlement. Yet Eden did table a combined proposal, much to the irritation of the State Department. This called for 'a reciprocal agreement in which both sides take part, such as Locarno', together with a defensive alliance along the lines being discussed. In the first, the Geneva settlement might thus be guaranteed by 'an Asian circle, consisting on the one hand of China and Soviet Russia, and, on the other, of France, America and ourselves — and perhaps India and other countries too. . . '[26] But even this failed to satisfy Labour back-benchers, a group of whom continued to urge a more comprehensive settlement which would hinge on the wider diplomatic recognition of Peking, and on the Communists taking China's seat in the United Nations.

Fifthly, the economic roots of Asian Communism were emphasised. Communism in Asia, stated *The Times* in May, fed on poverty and on the twin appeals of anti-Westernism and anti-landlordism.[27] For much of British opinion, economic policies of the type inaugurated in the Colombo Plan were of central importance. This converged with a marked British reluctance to be associated with the regimes in Thailand, South Korea, Vietnam, or Nationalist China, in the course of tackling Asian Communism. Dealing with aggression and subversion was a primary aim, the *Guardian* insisted, but 'the Western Powers cannot afford to find themselves at the beck and call of a local government which finds it convenient to dub its legitimate opposition as Communist.'[28]

The genesis of SEATO Eden later regarded as a proposal put to him in June 1952, by Schuman. But prior to March 1954, there was little discussion of the subject. To the degree that some kind of Asian pact was considered, it tended to be dismissed in Britain as impractical, old-fashioned, as only a partial solution, or as only a very long-term possibility. Until the spring of 1954, the objections seemed overwhelmingly to indicate its unrealism in the world of the mid-1950s.

The initiative came from Washington in March. Dulles, addressing the Overseas Press Club in New York, said that 'the imposition on South-East Asia of the political system of Communist Russia and its Chinese Communist ally, by whatever means', would be 'a grave threat to the whole free community', and one which 'should not be passively accepted but should be met by united action.'[29] The first British reaction did not give to the speech the significance which later events seemed to justify. However, the trend of United States thinking was then put more explicitly by Eisenhower in a letter to Churchill on 4 April. Geneva, he pointed out, was less than four weeks away. He had in mind the establishment of 'a new, *ad hoc* grouping or coalition composed of nations which have a vital concern in the checking of Communist expansion in the area." The President mentioned in particular the ANZUS powers, together with Britain and France, and also Thailand, the Philippines, and the Associated States.[30] Eden gave the proposal a reserved welcome. Though it did not correspond with British thinking at that time, it at least represented an improvement on American public airing of the possibility of armed Western intervention on the mainland of Asia. At first, the Foreign Secretary's grounds for qualified support were twofold: a grouping would enhance the security of Malaya and Hongkong, and it would go some way towards rectifying the situation brought about by Britain's exclusion from the ANZUS pact. Eden did, however, object strongly to the forming and proclaiming of such a defensive coalition *before* Geneva. This 'would be unlikely to help us militarily and would harm us politically, by frightening off important potential allies.'[31]

It was this question of timing that more than anything else exacerbated Anglo-American relations in the weeks following. For Washington, well publicised progress towards the forming of an alliance was an essential preliminary to Geneva if the West was not to bargain there from a position of weakness. In a visit which produced in its wake a host of misunderstandings, Dulles argued the case for speedy action in talks held in Paris and London in the second week of April. The Secretary of State no longer had in mind a warning declaration specifically directed against China, which removed one headache for British officials; rather, the planned coalition would itself deter China from further interference in the affairs of South-East Asia, and would in addition strengthen the Western position at Geneva. Eden raised the British concern that Asian Commonwealth countries not be excluded. Dulles replied that United States opinion would tolerate this only if the pact were extended eastwards also, to include Nationalist China and Japan. Such a membership was clearly unacceptable to London. The Anglo-American talks ended with a joint condemnation of Communist activities in Indo-China, together with the crucial declaration that 'we are ready to take part, with the other countries principally concerned, in an examination of the possibility of establishing a collective defence, within the framework of the Charter of the United Nations, to assure the peace, security and freedom of South-East Asia and the Western Pacific.'[32]

Churchill and Eden both took care later to stress the tentative nature of the agreement reached. This did little to soothe the Opposition. Labour critics hinted that the United States proposal had been made for political purposes as part of a deliberate attempt to sabotage the Geneva conference. The government did, however, cling firmly to the principle involved in the timing of moves towards an alliance. Churchill confirmed that no final decision could be taken until the outcome of Geneva was known. Hence Eden's objection to the momentum being spurred along by the State Department. In particular, he resisted Dulles' call, on his return to Washington, for a conference of ambassadors from countries previously suggested as members of the pact: the countries invited would be regarded as already constituting the proposed organisation, and 'I could not possibly accept this.'[33] The meeting nevertheless took place, though Dulles converted it into a general briefing session prior to Geneva.

The Foreign Secretary's approach was endorsed by the Cabinet on 25 April. If, that is, a settlement were reached at Geneva, Britain would join in guaranteeing it and in setting up a collective defence in South-East Asia. If no settlement were reached, then 'we shall be prepared at that time to consider with our allies the action to be taken jointly in the situation then existing.' But, crucially, 'we cannot give any assurance now about possible action on the part of the United Kingdom in the event of failure to reach agreement at Geneva.'[34] British views were communicated to Dulles by Eden at the NATO Council meeting in Paris in April, and at the end of the month in

Geneva. By this later date, however, Britain's stand had been overtaken by events. Faced with the imminent danger of a French military collapse in Indo-China, Eden, in meetings with Bedell Smith in Geneva at the beginning of May, proposed an immediate and secret Anglo-American examination of the political and military problems involved in the setting up of SEATO. A marked improvement in relations between the two governments had now become visible.

Eden's idea was that Britain, France and the ANZUS States should take part in this study through the five-power Staff Agency in Singapore. This body had grown out of an earlier arrangement which Britain had developed with France for the exchange of military information and opinions, and which had been extended in 1953 to include the ANZUS governments. Eisenhower regarded the British decision as critical. It represented 'a considerable advance in the British position: it visualised including Indo-China in British planning and for the first time showed their willingness to try to do something before the end of the Geneva Conference.'[35]

As in April, differences between the British and the American positions persisted, though these had now narrowed. On 5 May, Eisenhower stated publicly that plans were proceeding for the realisation of a South-East Asian security organisation. Such publicity was an important ingredient in American policy. But it was in stark contrast to the British approach. Lloyd, finding himself in the disquieting position of having to square the President's remarks with his own statement earlier — to the effect that no such steps were being taken — explained that Eisenhower had been referring to 'informal and exploratory conversations,' whereas he himself had meant 'more formal discussion attended by representatives of a number of states.' Any examination that might be undertaken, he concluded, was without commitment.[36]

From the decision of the first week of May, the ball remained firmly in the American court. Dulles now more openly discussed analogies between the planned organisation and NATO. Successful representations were made to switch the location of the talks from Singapore to Washington, and the Australian and New Zealand governments came out strongly and publicly in favour of five-power talks as a matter of some urgency. Further, United States newspapers were full of ambitious schemes to include Nationalist China, South Korea and Japan in a North-East Asian pact which might be closely tied in with SEATO. Finally, the possibility of an alliance organisation being formed without British membership was discussed. Australia, for example, was said to be in favour of a pact with or without Britain.[37] Eisenhower himself was ambiguous on the point in remarks on 19 May. Australia and New Zealand, he said, were the Commonwealth countries most directly concerned, while the participation of 'the proper Asian nations' was *sine qua non*; on this basis, it would be possible to arrive at 'something which could be workable.'

Thus a combination of British fears of a repeat performance of her exclusion from ANZUS, together with anxieties lest Washington go ahead with plans for more provocatively anti-Chinese measures in Asia, gradually edged London into a firmer commitment to SEATO. The Foreign Office reiterated that the Washington talks in June were without commitment. They were, Churchill told the Commons, directed to 'immediate practical issues' and were 'quite distinct from the question of collective defence organisation for South-East Asia, which would in any case take a considerable time to bring into effective working order.'[38] As far as possible, the government distracted attention away from the talks, lest they affect adversely the Geneva negotiations. No statement was issued upon their conclusion on 11 June, though a technical report was evidently drawn up by officials and presented to the five governments on the steps that would have to be taken to improve the military defensibility of South-East Asia. British officials playd down, while American officials emphasised, the importance of the talks. As *The Times* put it, the government had merely recognised that the contingency of failure in Geneva had to be planned for. Eisenhower's view was that the discussions 'helped to make the world aware that the Geneva Conference could not be used as a vehicle for handcuffing the Western world into inaction in Indo-China.'[39]

Towards the end of the month, the Prime Minister and the Foreign Secretary themselves visited Washington. The day before their departure Eden elaborated his concept of an Asian collective security system based on the Locarno model. Anglo-American discussions thus took place against the background of public uproar which greeted this suggestion in the United

States. The reaction seems to have surprised British officials; Eden himself later attributed it to the erroneous assocation in many American minds of Locarno with Munich. He repeated the British view that 'there must not be, before the [Geneva] Conference was over, any publicised meeting to plan and proclaim an anti-communist alliance in South-East Asia.[40] The final communique nonetheless stated that the consequences of failure and success at Geneva had been discussed, and that the two governments would 'press forward with plans for collective defence to meet either eventuality.' An Anglo-American de-claration of principles issued on 29 June included the phrase: 'As regards formerly sovereign states now in bondage, we will not be a party to any arrangement or treaty which could confirm or prolong their unwilling subordination.' Eden's Locarno proposal had thus been shelved, at least as far as Washington was concerned; the phraseology was among standard United States usage for describing Communist China.

A working group on South-East Asia, composed of British and American officials, was set up in Washington after the talks. A few days later, Dulles said that the talks in the study group were proceeding under a note of urgency, and expressed the hope that they would be concluded quickly. An ANZUS meeting at the end of June in Washington had already called for 'immediate action to bring about the early establishment of collective defence in South-East Asia.' In Britain on the other hand, Ministers stressed that the nature of the defence arrangements being discussed would depend on the results of Geneva. It was now also argued, however, that the notion of a collective defence system was not incompatible with the settlement which was hoped for at Geneva. The recommen-dations of the study group were submitted to the two governments on 17 July.

The British government had throughout this period of intense activity kept in close touch with Asian Commonwealth govern-ments, on the Geneva as on the collective defence questions. Churchill repeated in July that there was 'no intention of presenting cut-and-dried formulas on a "take it or leave it" basis to potential Asian members.'[41] For a long time, the hope was kept alive that somehow the future alliance organisation would comprise independent Asian membership as well as governments like those in Thailand and the Philippines. Soon after Dulles'

March speech, the British High Commissioner in India reported to the Foreign Secretary the 'widespread suspicion' in that country that the United States was determined that nothing should come out of the Geneva Conference. These exchanges stimulated United States fears. Dulles, for example, thought that Eden's objecting to his proposed April ambassadorial conference was 'possibly due to pressure from Nehru.'[42] But if so, such influence was mutual. Eden informed the Secretary of State later that month of his belief that British representations had been successful in persuading the Colombo governments to refrain from coming out publicly against the Anglo-American proposals. Nehru had been diverted 'from his original intention of condemning it root and branch.' But it was clear that Asian capitals had 'not hesitated to react unfavourably to informal soundings as to their attitude towards SEATO.'[43] Eden at several points sought their participation in the proposed organisation. Asian Commonwealth objections were summarised by Nehru in a letter to Eden. It was recognised that in certain circumstances united action was necessary. That was why India was a member of the United Nations. There was understanding of the need for NATO, and of Britain's special interests in Asia. But India felt that the Asian Communist countries must be given a chance to prove their sincerity in Indo-China. Nehru, finally, expressed support for the five principles of the Sino-Indian treaty, and his preference for an arrangement similar to Locarno rather than the alliance envisaged.[44]

By August, then, both the principle and the main outlines of SEATO had been accepted by London. The Manila Treaty was signed on 8 September by the Foreign Ministers of the participating States (except for Britain, whose delegation was headed by Lord Reading, Eden pleading pressure of EDC business as a reason for non-attendance). It received parliamentary ratification in Britain in November without a division, though not without Labour criticisms.

Not all the issues had been resolved before Manila. The objectives of SEATO, its membership, and the proper balance between military and economic policies in the struggle against Asian Communism, all continued to be the subject of Anglo-American disagreement. On the first, United States opinion remained undeflected from the notion that SEATO was aimed against the Chinese threat. Hence British objections to specific mention of 'Communist' aggression in United States drafts. In that leaked in the *Manila Bulletin* of 31 August, Article 4 stated that 'Each party recognises that Communist aggression by armed attack in the treaty area . . . would endanger its own peace and safety.' The aim of the parties was stated as being to co-ordinate collective defence efforts 'so that a potential Communist aggressor will appreciate that the parties stand together in the area.' British reservations were put during the meetings of the committee of experts which sat at the beginning of September. The alliance, it was argued, should not appear to be overtly anti-Chinese. As a result, the specific references were removed from the body of the Treaty, though they figured in separate American reservations. Dulles managed to accommodate both the British and the United States positions in a speech on 6 September: 'What we do is directed against no nation and no peoples . . . We are united by a common danger, the danger that stems from international communism and its insatiable ambition.'[45] Though in Britain there was reluctance to adopt a phrasing that would exacerbate other disputes, notably that between India and Pakistan, it is also true that other sources of potential aggression – from Japan particularly – were at the back of some British, and Australian, minds. Canberra opposed the specificity of United States references on similar grounds to London's. Sir Alan Watt, the head of the Australian delegation, described them as unprecedented among similar treaties. Yet, quite clearly, Chinese Communism did lie at the root of Western anxieties. If there was to be aggression, Younger stated for the Opposition in the November debate, 'let us be frank: it could really only be Chinese aggression.'[46] And this underscored Indian condemnation of the alliance. 'Do you think they can fool us by dropping 'Communist' from the wording of the Treaty?' was one response; 'If eight anti-Communist nations meet to sign a treaty, we are able to understand whom that treaty is against.'[47]

Of the Colombo powers, only Pakistan attended the Conference. Asian Commonwealth participation, as noted earlier, was unacceptable to Washington. The threat of bringing Nationalist China, South Korea and Japan into a related grouping had been quite explicit in earlier exchanges between Eden and Dulles. For his part, Dulles said he was not surprised at the disinclination of some powers to take part. Those attending the Conference were precisely those countries which the State Department had expected to take part as early as April. Asian absences were, however, of concern to British opinion. Even after the signing of the Manila Treaty, newspaper editorials continued to express the hope that the Colombo governments might eventually join. It was also argued that they were privately relieved that the alliance organisation had been established. In November, Eden stated that 'We should, of course, have liked to see more Asian States join us at the outset in this essential and pacific task.' Provision had been made in the treaty for them to come in; and 'we hope that once they get a chance to study the terms of the Treaty and to see how it works in practice, some of our Asian friends may change their minds.'[48]

The Foreign Secretary added, 'We are absolutely convinced that for the Manila Treaty to be successful it has to do two things: it has to give the assurance of military security and the positive encouragement of economic help.' It was apparent, however, that military forces were not available in SEATO for the kind of task that NATO had attempted in Europe. There were further difficulties involved in the creation of a command structure, not to mention problems of liaison and overlap with ANZUS machinery. During the summer, Washington gradually shifted from its original view that the organisation should be one with teeth, despite expresssions of alarm from the Philippines, Australia and New Zealand. Such was the extent of the American shift that there were complaints from the *Manchester Guardian* and elsewhere in September that the organisation was weaker than was desirable.[49] By then, it was Britain rather than the United States that was tending to argue the need for more effective machinery and facilities; Dulles was developing the theme that it would be self-destructive for the signatories to attempt to support formidable land-based forces at every danger-point throughout the world. Ironically, critics of the watering-down of the Treaty's provisions more usually attributed the blame to the British government.

SEATO differed from NATO in that subversion rather than direct aggression was seen as the threat. In his criticisms of the treaty's provisions, Younger cited Walter Lippmann's view that it was the first international instrument of modern times to justify intervention in the domestic affairs of other nations. Nutting replied that Paragraph 2 of Article IV, which covered dangers from subversion, did 'not, of course, authorise intervention in the day-to-day internal affairs of the country.' Rather the third paragraph, which concerned the necessity for invitation by the particular government as a prerequisite of intervention by troops of other signatories, was, the Foreign Secretary added, 'one to which Her Majesty's Government attach particular importance.' It had been inserted at the suggestion of Britain, since 'it was, in our view, essential that any country designated under paragraph one should be assured that its territory shall not be turned into a battlefield against its will.'[50]

SEATO's apparent lack of interest in economic policy was a more important target of Labour's attacks. 'We do not cure gangrene by pouring lavender water on it,' Davies commented. 'While the SEATO may smell sweet, it does not cover the hunger, the wretchedness and the poverty which underlies the struggle of the Asiatic people for their liberation.'[51] Towards the end of August, economic provisions became a British preoccupation in dealings with other governments. At the end of the month, Dulles declared that the absence of Asian members did not mean that some of those who were not at the conference might not take part in the economic and social programme. Yet on the other hand, Younger and his Opposition colleagues also made the point that fresh SEATO machinery for economic assistance might be superfluous in view of Colombo, ECAFE and Point Four. A few weeks after the signing of the Manila Treaty, Thailand, the Philippines and Japan joined the membership of the Colombo Plan, a move that was welcomed by the Foreign Secretary.

Chinese opposition to SEATO was not, obviously, in itself a decisive argument against the Manila Treaty. It could be argued, indeed, that condemnation by Peking was sure proof that the organisation was of value. Yet a number of Labour MPs, and to some extent Eden himself, were conscious of the danger of unnecessarily arousing Chinese hostility. Chou En-lai told Eden at Geneva that the main grounds for Chinese unease were a belief that the West was planning to 'split South-east Asia in two with an anti-communist alliance'; that consideration had been given to having the Associated States as members; and that the Western preparations were damaging to the chances of success of the Geneva Conference.[52] The Chinese press and radio maintained a steady barrage of attacks on the alliance, and on British participation in the moves leading up to its establishment. SEATO, the *People's Daily* stated in August, was 'an aggressive organisation directed against the Chinese people.'[53] Plans for it were held to conflict with the Geneva agreements, and were interpreted as a direct result of the serious diplomatic defeat of Dulles' 'aggressive policies' at Geneva. The aggressive and colonial nature of the pact was indicated clearly by its membership; by its recognition of the right of intervention in the domestic affairs of Asian States; by the Western attempt to ensure domination through the bribe of aid after earlier attempts to secure Asian approval had failed; and by the designation of the status of the Associated States so as to clear the way for American aggression in Asia.[54] Britain's earlier attitude was contrasted favourably with that of the United States. During and immediately after Geneva, Britain had voiced a desire for peaceful coexistence. However, 'active British support of the US South-East Asian aggressive bloc' was contrary to this. Its former policy had been correct, but the British government was 'succumbing to US pressure' by supporting plans for SEATO. This 'conflicting attitude of the British government' was 'hard to understand.' And, taken together with Britain's following the American lead in preventing China from attaining her proper status in the United Nations, this action was yet another obstacle in the way of improvement of Sino-British relations.[55]

The combined events of 1954 of the SEATO and Geneva negotiations brought to a head the latent clash of China policies of Britain and America. While London went along with the proposed pact, it did not do so out of a firm conviction that the thinking behind it was sound. British objections to such an arrangement had been enumerated in the debates of 1949-50, and seemed as valid at the later date. New factors had emerged by then – in particular, China had intervened directly or indirectly in the conflicts in Korea and Indochina, and Britain, for her part, had been left outside the 1952 ANZUS grouping – but these did not quash British reservations.

Washington's stated aim was simple: to contain Chinese Communism. The goal was further promoted, in the American view, by the signing, in December 1954, of a Mutual Defence Treaty between the United States and the Republic of China. This was interpreted by American opinion as a simple extension of the Manila Treaty, involving no new departure from it; a gap had been plugged. The thinking underlying such schemes ran directly counter to that in Britain. The British approach surfaced in Eden's ill-received Locarno proposal, in which all the major interested powers — including the People's Republic of China — would have a say in an Asian collective security organisation. This was clearly incompatible with the American conception, as were British proposals to expand the membership of the alliance to include if possible India and other independent Asian powers, or to delay work on it until the Geneva Conference had been given a chance to succeed. That the essentials of the American view prevailed was due both to developments in Indochina and to the unwritten rules of the Anglo-American partnership. From day to day, it also owed something to American bargaining tactics: in the publicity given to exchanges which the British would have preferred to remain secret; in the interpretations placed on Anglo-American exchanges by officials in public statements; and in the use of implied or explicit threats, such as the possibility that Washington might go ahead and establish a pact without British participation, or broaden the membership to include Japan, South Korea and Taiwan, or unilaterally adopt a much tougher line, perhaps by some form of military strike, against China.

5 Lure of the Market

By the time of the establishment of the People's Republic in 1949, China had experienced a long history of encounters with Britain. The period from 1949 until 1954-5 was one of major revision of the trading relationship between the two countries. It is the purpose of this chapter to probe more deeply the nature of the changes that took place in these years. History is important here, not least for shaping the attitudes on either side that persisted into the 1950s. British enterprise in China has been viewed as an expression of the dynamic spirit of the West, and as a valuable contribution to China's own economic development, carried out in the face of opposition from an aloof and hostile Chinese bureaucracy. The historical record continues to be viewed by Chinese as one of exploitation of China's resources and of humiliation of the Chinese people at a time of weakness, perpetrated with the aid of 'unequal' treaties signed under duress. There is some truth in each position. Fortunately, in view of the complexity of nineteenth-century Sino-British relations, it is not the task of the present study to offer a judgement on the question.

However, the magnitude of the changes that have taken place deserves emphasis. It used to be common to distinguish between trade *with* China and trade *in* China. The distinction is a useful one. Far more was involved than commerce between traders in two countries. British entrepreneurs were actively engaged in trade and industry inside China. The history of these contacts has been discussed already. They proceeded slowly after the exchanges of the late eighteenth century, but gathered pace rapidly from the 1840s. During the rest of the century, virtually every restriction upon the foreign trade of China was removed. The process was virtually complete by 1895. As a result, the great bulk of China's foreign trade fell into Western, and also Japanese, hands. The British role was pre-eminent. In the earlier nineteenth century, trade took the form of the export of silk and tea by British merchants against the import of silver. There later developed a three-way trade: exports of manufactured goods and services from Europe to India; of cotton and opium from India to China; and of silk and tea from China to Europe. By the turn of the century, however, the pattern of exports and imports had become much more diversified. London, moreover, had become the centre for trade between China and third countries.[1]

But for a number of reasons, such as early deficiencies of supplies, British merchants dealing in the China trade had entered manufacturing industry inside the country. They were also involved in the processing of the various goods which China supplied for export: bristles, egg products, vegetable oil, brick tea, braid, and other items. Under the 1895 Treaty, it became legally possible for foreigners to set up large-scale manufacturing undertakings in the concessions. In the next few years, the British in particular had turned to textiles, especially cotton textiles. Of British-owned enterprises, perhaps the most famous was the large Kailan Mining Administration. Others included the British textile factories in Shanghai, and the cigarette factories of the British-American Tobacco Company in Manchuria. British entrepreneurs also developed and utilised a network of specialised banking and insurance facilities. The banks, the most well known and prosperous being the Chartered Bank of India, Australia and China, and the Hongkong and Shanghai Banking Corporation, also discharged functions similar to those carried out by central banks. They even became responsible for furnishing a considerable part of the Chinese currency.[2] Britons also founded municipal administrations, set up port installations, and provided ships both for the ocean-going trade and for the efficient distribution of goods within China by river and coastal services.

Even before 1949, though, British enterprise had passed its peak. The emergence of Communist China simply accentuated the difficulties already encountered in Nationalist China. Thus general economic conditions in the country had been deteriorating long before the establishment of the People's Republic. Apart from the transportation and other problems posed by the civil war, and later by the Nationalist blockade, British businessmen were hard hit by the Chinese inflation of the 1940s. And at the beginning of the Communist period, the People's Bank Dollar declined in value from US$1 = PB$1,800 in June 1949, to US$1 = PB$38,000 in March 1950.[3] Pressures from the Communist authorities constituted a second source of frustration. This did not represent a radical break with the past. The report of the 1946 Board of Trade mission noted that 'foreigners in China will have to adapt themselves to the ebb and flow of conditions . . . the accusation of "co-operation with foreign capitalists" can be made a political weapon.'[4] For example, British merchant ships had lost the right to participate in Chinese coastal and inland water trade in 1943. After 1945, the Labour government made several representations to the Nationalist authorities with a view to obtaining a relaxation of these restrictions.

Controls on private capital, both foreign and Chinese, were instituted by the new regime. For example, a system was introduced whereby wages paid to workers had to be directly related to the cost of essential commodities. With high rates of inflation, the wage costs of British enterprises rose steeply in 1949-50. Further, Chinese trade unions demanded six months' wages for their members as severance pay from British firms. Taxation by the Communist authorities was high and growing on businesses, income, land, cars, and other items. From December 1949, regulations in Shanghai, the main centre of British enterprise, began to provide for eventual Chinese government control of all non-registered land and property. Various administrative difficulties, such as problems in obtaining credit facilities, impeded the flow of trade. Raw materials were often in tight supply, and many British firms were made idle as a result. This, together with the effects of the trade union and taxation demands, meant that sterling had to be pumped into Shanghai and other cities simply to enable British companies to meet overheads. The sums involved were estimated at between £375,000 and £500,000 a month.[5] Moreover, there was a general feeling on the part of many traders that the sterling-dollar rate was unrealistic, and was itself hampering the resumption of normal trading activity. Not surprisingly, many British firms simply left China altogether in a general exodus to Hongkong, leaving behind skeleton staffs or else handing over responsibility to Chinese managers. But even this step was not a straightforward one. Great delays were frequently experienced before exit permits could be obtained. Businessmen complained that the Chinese authorities were in some cases making the granting of these dependent upon the fulfilment of financial obligations to Chinese employees. All of this, however, was not necessarily the result of a concerted and systematic drive by the Communists to rid China of foreign traders. Both British and American businessmen publicly acknowledged a helpful attitude on the part of many Chinese officials during 1949. In Shanghai, Chinese officials held discussions with British traders, and put a stop to the more extreme demands of local trade unions.

Outside China, however, there seemed little that could be done about the Nationalist blockade. Incidents between British merchant ships and units of the Nationalist armed forces mounted to almost a crisis level by early June 1950. Later that month, indeed, one such incident led to retaliation by the Royal Navy, the first time that British forces had taken such action since the start of the blockade.[6] The other side of Nationalist tactics, the bombing of mainland installations, similarly went on unabated. It was thought in some quarters that British property was being deliberately singled out by the Nationalists, and that through his air attacks Chiang Kai-shek was planning 'the ruthless destruction of British holdings in retaliation for the withdrawal of recognition.'[7] British officials made a series of unsuccessful representations to the Nationalist authorities through the consulate in Tamsui. Incidents involving British shipping continued for some years afterwards, although Nationalist raids on the mainland came to a halt with the neutralisation of the Taiwan Straits at the outbreak of the Korean War.

It was a source of bitter complaint by traders that diplomatic recognition of Peking did not bring about any noticeable improvement in conditions. Some felt that, by provoking the Nationalists while at the same time cutting off channels of communication with them, recognition had in fact worsened their plight. British businessmen's grievances with respect to the Communist authorities can best be summarised by quoting from the list forwarded by Britain to the Chinese government in a note of April 1952:

(i) The making of each individual manager *personally* responsible for the policy and acts of his company, in some cases for acts before he became manager. (ii) The increasing restrictions on the entry and exit of foreign staff. (iii) The cancellation by the Chinese government's trading organisations of former contracts, even though raw materials have been paid for and processed. (iv) Taxation and legal judgements which both appear to be discriminatory against foreigners. (v) Uncertainty caused to British subjects by the fear of arrest and detention *incommunicado* and without charges being preferred. (vi) Pressure by the labour unions and reluctance by the local authorities to give any protection to firms who are being accused by the unions of malpractice.[8]

The China Association acted as a channel of communication between the traders and British government officials. It did 'everything possible to impress upon the British government the seriousness of the situation' in the months following diplomatic recognition.[9] By 1952, the government was also making representations in Peking about fifty-five British, Commonwealth, and United States citizens held in gaol, and about a further twenty Americans held under house arrest. A few British enterprises did continue in these circumstances to make a profit. However, the China Association pointed out that this was mostly in terms of local currency not remittable to Britain, and that many firms had in fact been operating at a loss for a considerable time. Others had been requisitioned. The value of capital seized was estimated officially in October 1952, at £9m.[10] Finally, as a last straw, there was a sharp deterioration in the quality of social and cultural amenities for members of the British communities in China. By 1953, movement had become restricted to the town of domicile, and virtually no recreational facilities were available.

Despite the severe constraints under which they were operating, businessmen were reluctant to leave China. Optimism about future prospects, even within a Communist China, died hard. The danger of making a break, many felt, was that relationships might not so easily be restored later. A return to something like normality in Sino-British commerce was bound to come eventually, and it was argued that traders who left the scene under pressure of immediate circumstances would suffer over the long term. And losing the competitive edge to the French, the Germans, the Japanese, or even the Americans, was a powerful inducement to stay on and keep whatever toehold was possible under the new regime. Two comments from China Engineers Ltd., are typical of this frame of mind: connections, once broken, were not easily repaired, and "we might have to wait a decade or two before we could patch up our friendship'; and 'we stay in China on principle, and not for profit.'[11]

This view quickly became exceptional. For most firms, withdrawal was the only realistic option. Serious consideration of withdrawal began soon after it was demonstrated that British diplomatic recognition of Peking had done little to alleviate the situation. At the end of 1950, the China Association reported that the majority of British businessmen in China had concluded that their investments in the country were unlikely to return any dividend in the foreseeable future, and were not worth the hazards to person and property which they entailed.[12] Between 1950 and 1952, many firms with long-standing ties with China took the road out. Others remained behind for only as long as it took the authorities to grant exit permits for managers. The turning-point seems to have been reached in the spring of 1952. The Hongkong and Shanghai Banking Corporation concluded during 1951—2 that with the spread of State control, there would be little room for foreign banks to operate in China; its interest in China was soon confined to liquidating its position and withdrawing staff.[13]

An indication of the extent of this movement can be gained by comparing the size of the various British communities in China during these years. From a pre-war figure of 8—10,000 in Shanghai alone — there were sizeable communities also in Tientsin, Hankow, Canton, and other centres — the total fell to 4,000 at the time of the Communist occupation of Shanghai in the spring of 1949. It was down to 3,000 at the time of British recognition the following January; to 1,000 or less at the end of 1950; to one hundred businessmen, together with · 300—500 British nationals of mixed parentage born locally, in May 1952; to a total figure of British commercial employees and dependents in early 1954 of 300. The London Missionary Society, for example, which had sixty-three members in China in 1949, cut its last links towards the end of 1952.[14]

Courses of action recommended to the government were many. They varied from a demand for retaliation by halting the purchase of Chinese exports, through to pressures on the British government to make concessions to allow the exchange of fully accredited ambassadors. But as Humphrey Trevelyan, chargé d'affaires in Peking from 1953 to 1955, pointed out later, there was little that Britain could do by way of retaliation. The only steps the British government could take might produce a 'mounting spiral of reciprocal brutality, a game which we were unlikely to win.'[15] It was not easy, in the atmosphere of the Korean War, to get the Chinese authorities to consider seriously the complaints being made by British businessmen. By 1952, the issue had boiled down to a British demand for compensation for property and assets requisitioned by the Chinese. Britain formally reserved all rights, and asked that compensation or rental be paid, except in cases where the owners of the property did not wish such action to be taken. The Note of April 1952, summarised the problems facing British firms. In May, China was informed that 'Nearly all, if not all, of the British companies in China, have come to the conclusion that this change of conditions necessitates a corresponding change in the nature of their organisations and in the scope of their activities . . . Consequently they feel that the proper course is for them to arrange for the transfer as going concerns, custody or closure, of their businesses.'[16] Ministers added in parliament that the government fully realised the gravity of this step, but felt that, having regard to all the factors, they could only endorse the decision which the firms had taken. A member of Jardine Matheson expressed the general view of many Britons: 'For some time past the trends in economic development under the Central People's government have indicated to us that the long-established organisations of foreign-operated commercial firms are not suited to present-day conditions in the country . . . It is therefore desirable that adjustments be made in a realistic manner.'[17]

Replying for the Chinese government, Chang Han-fu issued a statement in July. This simply asserted that 'the predicament of the British firms in China is the bitter fruit of the policy of trade control and embargo of the British government.' Companies had suffered as a result of 'the depressed state of the trade between the two countries, in addition to their bad management.' The People's Republic of China, he continued, had taken such measures as the advancing of loans and the supplying of raw materials in order to aid them. But the measures of trade control had 'not shown the least sign of relenting, and the resulting difficulties . . . have shown the tendency to become increasingly greater, instead of the slightest sign of abating.'[18] For the British side, the two issues were quite separate. A further British Note of January 1953, pointed out that many firms had been unable to make appreciable progress. A report carried by the *Sunday Times* in the same month, to the effect that since the diplomatic exchanges of the previous summer the majority of firms were carrying on business in improved conditions, was explicitly denied by the government. The flow of withdrawals from China had become irreversible. Some relaxation was experienced before and during the Geneva Conference in 1954, and there were reports of some improvements in conditions the following year. By 1956—7, however, the China Association's *Report* stated that, with the exception of a woollen mill operated by Messrs. Patons and Baldwins, all British industrial interests had withdrawn from China.[19]

There remained the question of what was the most appropriate way of handling trade *between* Britain and China. There seems to have been general accord both in Peking and London that such commerce, possibly restricted to certain types of goods and within defined limits, was of value to both countries. The Chinese, however, insisted that the traditional channels of trade were unacceptable and would have to change. British businessmen who visited China were made aware of Chinese views on the subject. China in the past had suffered unequal treatment from the 'old China hands.' These were now set in their ways, and were psychologically incapable of accepting the fact of the Chinese revolution; indeed, they were still practising inequalities. Some British merchants, it was maintained, had previously been politically active on behalf of the Kuomintang, and were still basically sympathetic to the Nationalist cause. A further Chinese complaint was that firms long established in the China trade would not go out of their way to obtain items needed by China, even goods which were not officially restricted under the strategic trade regulations. Hongkong traders, it was claimed, had broken many contracts with the

Chinese government; goods sent to China were often of poor quality; and merchants were still seeking excess profits 'as if China were still the old corrupt foreign colony.'[20]

The Communist authorities soon began to seek out alternative arrangements. The Moscow Economic Conference of April 1952, was seen as a step in the right direction. At the conference, agreements were reached between members of the British and Chinese delegations under Nan Han-chen and Lord Boyd-Orr for trade to the value of £10m. on each side. More specific Sino-British contracts were signed shortly afterwards in East Berlin. Some British traders continued on from Moscow to Peking to consolidate contacts.[21] The agreements, however, came up against the provisions of the strategic trade controls. Nevertheless, in his reply to Britain in July 1952, Chang Han-fu, a Vice-Minister for Foreign Affairs, emphasised that the private and state trading organisations of China had for more than two years signed contracts with foreign industrial and commercial firms in China. Any British companies and manufacturing firms might approach these bodies at any time, he added, establish contacts with them, and conduct specific business negotiations with them.

Implicit in Chinese statements, and often explicit, was condemnation of the strategic trade regulations on the China trade enforced by Britain and her NATO allies. This question is discussed separately in a later chapter. The system was blamed for the difficulties being experienced by British businessmen in China. The argument was put whenever possible that trading conditions could easily be improved, if only the British government would take the necessary steps to revise the regulations. This Chinese objective was not lost on British officials. The Foreign Secretary stated that the true purpose of the Moscow Conference was to organise popular pressure in non-Communist countries against the controls on strategic trade, and, further, against Western defence programmes in general.[22] The view was shared by the China Association, the Federation of British Industries, the Trades Union Congress, and the press generally. In the United States view, which was presumably put to Britain in exchanges on the subject, the Conference was also designed to split the United States from its allies.[23]

For a time, the old and the new patterns of Sino-British trade ran side by side. In its Note of April 1952, the British government reaffirmed its and the established China traders' view that 'there are numerous established British merchants in Shanghai and Hongkong who are well qualified to negotiate any such arrangements with the Central People's government or its representatives.' The traders themselves made the point frequently in meetings and statements to the press. Hongkong interests in particular were anxious about the possibility of being by-passed by the sort of trading methods being advocated and actively sought by the Chinese. There were worried or indignant references to the activities of the 'new traders.' Yet this side continued to develop. The Chinese state trading organisations set up a permanent office in East Berlin. It was visited regularly by British businessmen prepared to pursue trade with China on the terms laid down by the Chinese. In what was later seen as a pioneering trip by those sympathetic to this approach, a group visited Peking in July 1953, under the auspices of the British Council for the Promotion of International Trade. This was one of several such bodies established in various countries as a result of the Moscow Conference. This 'ice-breaker' mission, as it was known by its supporters, signed two-way trade agreements to the value of £30m. The *China Trade and Economic Newsletter* claimed that it firmly established the key principle that those who desired to export could not afford to disinterest themselves in imports; merchants and manufacturers in the party had been balanced by the inclusion of specialist importers of Chinese produce.[24]

Such methods were highly suspect in the eyes of the older trading organisations. But as early as 1952, there were reports that the Chinese might be interested in establishing a trade mission in London. The Foreign Office said that the British government would welcome such a move, while noting that Peking had contrived to make Anglo-Chinese trade almost impossible. In the diplomatic exchanges of that year, London mentioned 'a new form of organisation' better suited to the conditions of the time, which various British companies were contemplating setting up. It would take the form of an association of representatives of manufacturers and overseas buyers which would maintain direct contact with the appropriate Chinese authorities.

The breakthrough occurred in the spring of 1954. After

consultations with the Foreign Office, some British businessmen who had planned to join a group which was to visit Chinese trade officials in East Berlin decided not to go. The Chinese then postponed the scheduled meeting. This prompted speculation that the now well-established hard line was still operative: that all trade negotiations between Britain and China would have to take place under the auspices of the China Trade Committee of the British Council for the Promotion of International Trade. Yet, as the *Financial Times* noted, several British businessmen were already in Berlin acting independently of this body.[25] The Chinese were said to be concerned about the hesitations of British companies because of Foreign Office advice, discontented with the China Trade Committee's operations and commission, and willing to engage in more direct discussions. Whatever the reasons had been, the China National Import Export Corporation, the body set up in 1950 to handle trade with capitalist countries, eventually sent a letter of explanation and apology for postponing the Berlin meeting. It also sent a greatly expanded list of import requirements, half of which were free of strategic restrictions; and expressed a readiness to extend the talks to include other firms.[26] As a result, an enlarged British group that avoided incurring official disapproval, signed contracts to the value of £4m. in Berlin in April 1954.

It had by now become clear that the Chinese government had shifted its position quite substantially. In Geneva, Chinese officials openly declared their willingness to deal with the China Association and related bodies. In an interview with Harold Wilson, one of a group of Labour MPs who had been advocating greater East-West trade, Chou En-lai 'seemed anxious to develop all channels, including particularly direct trade through the shipping lines plying regularly between Britain and China.'[27] Meanwhile, in meetings in Geneva and in correspondence, British officials and traders urged the Chinese to establish a mission in London, particularly in view of the unacceptability of the channels used by the Chinese in the past to conduct trade. In June, it was announced that the Chinese government would be sending a chargé d'affaires to Britain. Soon after his arrival in the autumn, the China Association established contact with the new office and in particular with its Commercial Counsellor.[28] Peking also organised a trade mission which visited Britain during the summer. A more lasting result of the 1954 changes on the British side was the creation of the Sino-British Trade Committee, whose role will be discussed shortly. Progress even began to be made on the trying question of payments, which had for some time been a major British grievance. China's terms of payment called for the opening of a Letter of Credit for prompt payment on shipment from a Chinese port in the case of purchase of Chinese goods, and the provision of a Letter of Guarantee stipulating payment after arrival and inspection in respect of sales to China. The matter was raised during the Chinese visit, and officials apparently promised to make methods of payment more flexible.[29]

The 1954 arrangements thus mark a fresh departure in Sino-British trade. But all was by no means plain sailing in the years following. The newly-established Sino-British Trade Committee sent a delegation to Peking in November, and another in March 1955. In 1954 also, the Labour Party organised a delegation to China; the China Association contacted members of it before its departure. Many difficulties remained, both in terms of the procedures and mechanics of trading, and of the wider political background to Sino-British relations. In June 1955, for example, the Chinese government informed the Sino-British Trade Committee that they did not consider that further visiting parties from Britain would serve any useful purpose so long as the strategic regulations remained in force.[30] This, the China Association noted, was despite an agreement reached that spring on the desirability in principle of further visits. By 1956, greater use was being made of the so-called 'exceptions procedure' as a way of relaxing controls. The China Association expressed the hope that this might encourage the Chinese to change their attitude. It acknowledged, however, that contacts with the Chinese government trading organs were 'still far too difficult', and that every opportunity was being taken to impress on them the need for improved facilities in this respect.[31] London was also being affected by the increasing use made by China of bilateral trading agreements with non-Communist countries, since British trading interests had traditionally handled much of the distribution of Chinese goods to world markets.

An account of the 1949–54 period of Sino-British trade would not be complete without mention of the non-governmental bodies which came into existence on the British side. The China Association itself pre-dates Communist China. Its traditional role had been to promote the interests of those connected with the China trade by, for example, maintaining effective liaison with the Foreign Office and the relevant Chinese government officials both in China and in Britain; acting on behalf of individuals or member companies; keeping contact with interested MPs, and with trading and other organisations. Its member firms have included all the major ones connected with the China trade: Patons and Baldwins, Swire, Matheson, Shell Petroleum, British-American Tobacco, and others. Apart from periodic circulars, a monthly *Bulletin* was distributed to members until 1964. This provided information on developments connected with the China trade, and, at least in the earlier part of this period, expressed views shared by most member firms about developments in China which touched on members' interests. Its views on trade with China have tended to be consonant with those in official circles. That is, trade with China is not something to be sought at any political cost; in dealings with the Chinese, the political factors shaping the direction of China's international trade should be borne in mind; and traders', and Britain's, interests may often be best served by taking a firm line in negotiations.

The Sino-British Trade Committee was established in 1954 under the joint sponsorship of the Federation of British Industries, the National Union of Manufacturers, the London Chamber of Commerce, the Association of British Chambers of Commerce, and the China Association itself. Its principal aim at the time was described as being 'to promote, facilitate and rationalise trade between the United Kingdom and the People's Republic of China. In pursuance of this aim, the Committee maintains a close liaison with the Board of Trade and other government departments on the one hand, and with the Commercial Section of the Chinese Embassy in London and the Chinese State trading corporations on the other.' One of its main functions has been simply to introduce British firms to the Chinese corporations.[32] Its monthly publication, *Sino-British Trade*, took over in 1964 where the China Association's *Bulletin* left off. It has operated with the full approval of the British government, and ministers made this quite clear in parliament.[33] Its meetings, for example, are regularly attended by representatives of the Foreign and Commonwealth Office and the Department of Trade. Members of its staff have visited Peking every year, with the exception of the height of the Cultural Revolution period in 1967—9; and the attempt is made to arrange an industrial tour of Britain for the Chinese Commercial Counsellor at least once a year.[34]

The British Council for the Promotion of International Trade, set up as a result of the 1952 Moscow Conference, was, however, declared by the government in 1953 to be a Communist front organisation. In November 1955 parliament was informed that British firms had been 'constantly advised in this sense, and Her Majesty's government have recommended that they should not associate themselves with this organisation.' The decision as to its use by companies was left 'to the patriotic judgement of each firm or individual.'[33] As has been seen, the Council for a time enjoyed a dominant position in the China trade through its China Trade Committee, which worked in turn through the London Export Corporation. Chinese State trading organs in Peking, and the Chinese office in East Berlin, often dealt with British businessmen in 1952—3 only if they were acting under its auspices. It denied, naturally enough, the charges levelled at it. Its chairman in 1953, Lord Boyd-Orr, dismissed the characterisation of the Council as a Communist front organisation as 'nonsense.'[36] In the middle 1950s, it turned its attention increasingly to the strategic controls on Sino-British trade, which constituted the principal complaint from the Chinese side. Since 1955, it has published the *China Trade and Economic Newsletter*, which attempts a similar task, though from a different angle, to that of the publications of the Sino-British Trade Council.

The period 1949—54 was a formative one for the evolution of Sino-British commerce. By 1952, it had become clear to the vast majority of British firms operating inside China that their days were numbered. Yet the coming of the Communist regime represented more of a last straw for British entrepreneurs than a radical break with the past. Businessmen were already sorely pressed by the exigencies of civil war, inflation, the Nationalist blockade and bombing raids, and restrictions imposed earlier by the Kuomintang authorities. And in the light of the pessimistic expectations of some British observers in 1949, what was perhaps more surprising was the long delay before the actions of the Communist authorities made the continuation of all enterprise finally impossible. After 1952, the only real issue that remained was that of how commercial relations between the two countries should in future be organised. The issue was raised by the Chinese side, which put forward strong objections to the use of more traditional methods. The arrangements begun in 1954, however, seem to have satisfied honour on both sides. What still remained unsolved was the more important question singled out by Peking in exchanges with British traders, MPs, and officials: that of the regulations imposed by the British government to ensure that goods having potential strategic significance did not reach China. This is the subject of the next chapter.

6 Trade Versus Defence

In the early 1950s, the Chinese government never missed an opportunity to point out to British businessmen that the root cause of their difficulties was the system of strategic trade controls implemented by the British government. British opinion tended to respond that this was a separate and complex question. Within the limits set by these regulations, it was argued, a substantial expansion of Sino-British non-strategic trade was feasible. Especially after the end of the Korean War, however, criticism of the effects of the controls mounted in Britain. The protest eventually encompassed groups such as the China Association and the Sino-British Trade Committee, members of parliament on both sides of the House, and both the more specialist and the mass-circulation press. It focused on the differentially severe treatment of China within the array of controls on trade with Communist countries as a whole. In 1957, the British government bowed to this pressure and brought the China trade regulations into line with those applied to trade with the Soviet Union and Eastern Europe. It did so, however, against determined resistance from the administration in Washington.

Western strategic controls on trade with the Chinese Communists began to take shape before the establishment of the People's Republic in October 1949. The United States started to exercise control through licensing procedures early in that year, at the time of the southward drive of the People's Liberation Army.[1] Discussions on China trade policy in the event of a Communist regime being established were held between British and United States officials in London during the summer. By September, the two governments had agreed to ban the export to the then almost wholly Communist-occupied China of high-grade oils, heavy trucks, aircraft parts, copper wire, telephone and signal equipment, and a long list of machine tools. They also agreed to take steps to urge other Western powers to take similar action. By late October, United States controls had been extended to approximately one hundred additional items. At the end of November, the internationally agreed list included eighty-six items which were embargoed, two over which quantitative control was exercised, and nineteen which were on a 'watch' or surveillance list.[2] According to Secretary of State Acheson in Congressional testimony later, Britain was also co-operating with the administration and with the principal United States and British oil companies in restricting shipments of petroleum products to 'those types and quantities which are clearly intended for civilian use.'[3] In March 1950, United States export controls to China, as well as to all other parts of the world from which trans-shipment might take place, were made coextensive with existing controls on shipments to the Soviet Union and Eastern Europe. Residual gaps were plugged with the start of the Korean War. Soon after its outbreak, Washington revoked all current export licenses to China. In December 1950, following Chinese intervention in Korea, the administration instituted a complete embargo on all trade with the People's Republic of China.

Britain went some of the way along this route, but stopped short of a complete ban. Ministers emphasised repeatedly in parliament that it was not government policy to impose a total embargo on the China trade. However, a close watch was kept on the situation as soon as fighting began in Korea. In July, the agreed international controls then applying to the Soviet Union and Eastern Europe were applied also to China. In other words, a total prohibition was erected against 'all goods of military importance' and 'many other goods which might assist military operations.' Supplies of others were restricted to 'what we regard as normal quantities for civilian use in China.'[4] In the same month, Britain approved the addition of a wide range of petroleum products to the international embargo list. After Chinese intervention in Korea, this list was substantially extended in line with United States policy.

The effect of these measures was that by the end of 1950, Britain and other Western governments were in varying degrees applying stricter controls over shipments to China than they were over shipments to the Soviet Union. In May 1951, Britain supported the United Nations General Assembly resolution recommending the embargo of shipments to China of items of military value. Statutory export licensing control on all goods sent to China came into force in Britain at the end of June. Other checks were added in the months following. Various end-use checking methods were devised and implemented by Britain and other Western countries, intended to ensure that exports reached their legitimate destination and stayed there. As a result of talks held in Washington early in 1953 between Dulles and Eden, the government introduced a system of licensing British-registered ships so that they could not carry strategically significant materials from non-British sources to China. Additional steps were taken to ensure that no ships of any nationality carrying such cargoes to China could be bunkered in a British port.[5]

Despite Anglo-American consensus on the need for such controls in principle, London remained at odds with Washington over details. United States controls over strategic trade generally rested on a number of distinctions. Goods of primary strategic significance — where 'exports *in any quantity* would contribute significantly to Soviet war potential' — were distinguished from those of secondary importance, whose 'export *in large quantities* would contribute significantly to the war potential of the bloc.' The aim was stated as being to reduce 'the *rate* at which the Soviet bloc is able to build up its ability to wage war.' There was no intention of cutting off trade entirely, as this 'would harm our defense more than it harms the potential aggressor.' The one exception was 'in the case of military aggression', in which case a policy of complete embargo might be in order.[6] In the specific case of the China trade, the British government made similar distinctions. Thus a quantitative control for goods was erected where a total ban was not deemed essential, the limit for this category being set by the government's estimate of normal Chinese civilian needs. In sum, it was the British case that trade with China in non-strategic goods and services worked to the advantage of the West. It was 'wise to preserve a strong economic link between China and the West, in order to reduce China's dependence on Moscow.'[7] This governmental level of understanding was not always matched at that of public debate. 'Trading with the enemy' became a stock Congressional attack on Britain, particularly during critical stages of the Korean War.

Britain's controls on the China trade were thus one part of a wider network of arrangements devised by the NATO allies. International machinery relating to trade with Communist countries existed on a less formal basis from 1948. Strict secrecy was maintained, even down to the names of participating governments and announcements of meetings, at least until 1953. The key body was the Consultative Group, formed in Paris in November 1949. This eventually included all NATO signatories except Iceland, with governments being represented at Ministerial level. Two subordinate working committees performed the day-to-day task of co-ordinating controls, supervising enforcement, and recommending improvement measures. COCOM, conceived at the same time as the Group, began functioning in January 1950. CHINCOM was established in September 1952, upon Japan's accession to the Group. It dealt specifically with controls relating to trade with China, North Korea and North Vietnam. From this date, COCOM confined itself to trade with the Soviet Union and Eastern Europe. The lists of items regulated that are produced by the committees are confidential; Britain and other participating countries publish only their own generalised versions of the lists. Controls within each country are then supervised by inter-departmental committees. In the United States, these comprised the Departments of State, Defense, Commerce, and related agencies; in Britain in the 1950s, the relevant departments were the Board of Trade and the Ministry of Transport.[8]

A related factor was the Battle Act legislation of the United States.[9] Under this, the shipment to the Soviet Union and its allies of goods of direct military significance required the mandatory cessation of all United States assistance to the exporting country. The shipment of goods of secondary strategic significance required the cessation of aid unless the President directed its continuance. Still a further complication was the extension of American, as opposed to British, controls to subsidiaries of United States firms in Britain. Criticism from Labour MPs on this score mounted later in the 1950s. It was argued that the application of these regulations by parent companies severely hindered Britain's capacity to promote her exports to China. Cases were cited by indignant back-benchers in which the United States Embassy in London, and the

American parent company, had raised legal issues with British subsidiaries and prevented the implementation of contracts signed with Chinese officials.[10] One problem was that United States control of British industry was particularly great for goods which British businessmen wanted to export to China.[11]

So long as hostilities persisted in Korea, the China trade controls were not a major issue in British politics. Debate in the House of Commons was often animated, but more about specifics than about general principles. Even as criticism grew, there was understanding of the special American position, and appreciation of the reasons why the United States should wish to impose stringent controls. British traders, MPs, and officials, however, objected to the inclusion of the United Kingdom in a tough control system. For British opinion, the crux of the issue was the differential treatment of China. Two lines of attack were pursued. First, it was argued that the controls on balance had the effect of driving the Chinese further and more irrevocably into the Soviet orbit, and that the trade weapon was not being put to its best possible use as a means of trying to tempt them into a more independent stance *vis-à-vis* Moscow. Secondly, the case was developed that the British economy itself was suffering unnecessarily under the impact of the controls. A revision of the system, therefore, would contribute at least something to Britain's economic recovery (over-optimism with respect to the Chinese market was taboo), while at the same time inflicting no damage on the Western defence effort.

But the first, and most obvious, case for revision was the ending of the Korean War. At least in their final form, the trade controls were very much a by-product of war. Thus Lord Mancroft, speaking for the government in April 1953, thought that 'quite clearly it would be reasonable to say that the restriction . . . cannot possibly be extended to any general overall peace plan stretching far and away beyond Korea.'[12] It was the British case, *The Times* stated in 1957, 'that the conditions of the embargo set up in 1951 no longer apply.'[13] This was the central point made by members of the small group of Labour MPs and peers who urged relaxation of the China controls from 1953.

For this group, the control system was clearly more tied to

declared United States objectives with respect to China. Britain, it was claimed, was being dragged along by Washington and forced to implement policies aimed at goals which possibly included the ultimate overthrow of the Chinese government. Since Britain did not share such aims, it was inconsistent for it to employ the means for their fulfilment. But the problem was that, as the President of the Board of Trade put it in 1951, 'there is no generally accepted definition of "strategic controls." '[14] Any item could in theory be defended as falling in this category. Either it contributed directly to an enemy's military potential; or else it could be argued to do so indirectly by allowing diversion of resources within an adversary's economy. Parliamentary critics were thus afforded much scope for questioning the precise nature of the relationship between specific items, and China's military capability. During the second half of 1953, for example, the issue centred on the British government's restriction of the export of certain categories of pharmaceutical products to China.[15] It was further argued that the controls were manifestly failing to achieve what was evidently one American objective, that of retarding China's rate of economic growth. Both China traders and MPs observed that China's economy did not seem noticeably hampered by the controls. The Hongkong *South China Morning Post* suggested that the opposite might be true, 'just as defeat in war usually stimulates a nation's energy and enterprise.'[16]

More importantly, the particular nature of the controls seemed to run counter to what was a key component of Britain's own China policy. The China Association accepted that in fact China might very well be suffering economically as a result of the controls. This, however, was not necessarily desirable. What was happening, rather, was that costs were being entailed through forced reliance on expensive Soviet and East European supplies.[17] Goods were being shipped from the Baltic port of Gdynia to China. As much as 70 per cent of Poland's merchant fleet was engaged on the Far Eastern route.[18] Separate lists for China and the Soviet Union seemed futile, therefore, since Peking could get Western goods or Soviet substitutes from Eastern Europe. One example was given by the manufacturers of scientific instruments. Their association stated that not only were these items arriving in China via Eastern Europe, but the British originals were being copied and made in

East Germany.[19] There was disagreement, however, on the policy implications of these facts. Dulles, for example, admitted in May 1956, that items were procurable by the Chinese through the Soviet Union. But he went on to argue that that 'involves certain delay, certain additional expense. It involves questions of the availability of space on the roads, and the railroads.'[20] It was also suggested, in Britain as well as in the United States, that the increasing Chinese economic dependence on the Soviet Union was due less to Western economic policies than to fundamental Chinese foreign policy goals. The more generally held British view, and ultimately the decisive one for government policy, was indicated with a measure of understatement by *The Times* early in 1956: 'since China can get the goods quite legitimately from the Soviet bloc, the logic of having two different embargoes . . . has been questioned.'[21]

Indeed, as early as late 1953 critics were pointing to an apparent coolness in Sino-Soviet relations in the context of demands for revisions of the trade control system. In its 1954 Report, the Hongkong and Shanghai Banking Corporation argued that China had 'followed the Soviet road because there has been no other road to follow; that is why many of us think it would be wise for the democratic countries to open an alternative route.'[22] Early the same year, the China Association reported this consideration as that most widely shared in British thinking on the subject of strategic trade regulation. It still, however, found it debatable whether or not a reduction in the China controls to the Soviet level would ameliorate Sino-British political and diplomatic relations.[23] It was, then, the effect of the controls on Sino-Soviet relations that most seized the imagination of the government's critics. It was some time before it became part of the official view. In early 1956, Lord Reading thought that 'there may be something to be said for this argument', but it did not justify removal of the restrictions.[24]

Costs to the British economy formed a second basis of criticism. Few, by the end of the Korean War, held extravagant hopes for the future. The optimism of the *Statist* in 1949 could not survive the harsher climate of Communist rule: 'if the buying power of the Chinese multitudes were raised only moderately it would impart a magic stimulus to the commerce and industry of all quarters of the globe . . . China's natural wealth is capable also of adding enormously to the volume of the exportable commodities of international trade.'[25] But if the vista of limitless markets for British exports was dead, it did not follow that China could be disregarded with impunity.

Thus as the Chinese system of economic planning began to get under way in the early 1950s, China traders in Britain and their supporters pointed to the vast amounts of foreign capital and goods that would be needed to fulfil goals. Articles in the press on the potential of the Chinese market, and the value to Britain of Chinese raw materials and other items, appeared with increasing frequency in the mid-1950s. They had long been a feature of Communist reporting; a *Daily Worker* article of December 1949, entitled 'Ever eaten a Chinese egg?'[26] was typical of the genre. The group of MPs, including Wilson, Donnelly, and Silverman, and of peers, particularly Strabolgi and Elibank, who devoted themselves to the question of the China trade controls, took up the topic with renewed vigour in 1953–4. The low level of Sino-British trade was linked with specific cases of decline or serious problems in British industry. Chemicals, Lancashire cotton, rubber, edible oil processing, and motor vehicles, were each singled out for examination in this context. The traditional, long-standing, nature of Anglo-Chinese commerce was emphasised. As in 1949, others maintained that trade could be an important weapon in dealings with the Chinese. In March 1955, for example, the *Daily Telegraph* stated that trade could 'clearly be an important bargaining counter in any ultimate negotiations between China and the West.' The China Association recommended that strategic controls should not be given up 'without ensuring that we receive commensurate benefit in return.'[27]

However, there were a number of practical obstacles to an expansion of trade. Most attention in British political debate was given to the question of the availability of appropriate Chinese exports, and to the problem of the level of China's sterling reserves. How extensive the latter were was in doubt. Proponents of trade relaxation referred to the steady flow of exports to Sterling Area countries by China between 1952 and 1956, of £86m., £96m., £78m., £93m., and £118m., in successive years. By 1956, it was most commonly estimated that Chinese sterling balances were somewhere in the region of £100m., though the British government itself thought this figure exaggerated. Nevertheless, arguments about the figure formed an important part of the responses of British opinion to the question. There was enquiry into the impact of other factors on Chinese sterling reserves: China's capacity for rebuilding reserves from sales of gold; her conducting of a large proportion of her trade outside the Soviet bloc in transferable sterling; and the proceeds of sales of Chinese bonds to overseas Chinese. As a consequence of this almost continual monitoring by the British press and trading organisations, assessments became more modest. In January 1957, *The Times* reported a sharp reduction in holdings to an estimated £30–£40m.

Doubt was expressed whether China could increase these reserves through an expansion of exports to Britain. The *New York Herald Tribune* quoted British businessmen in 1956 as being of the opinion that Chinese potential exports consisted mainly of primary products for many of which substitutes had been found, or else supplies of which could readily be obtained in the non-Communist world.[28] The more sanguine of the traders believed that traditional Chinese exports could be expanded: soya beans, vegetable oil seeds, hog bristles, egg products, and so on. Some speculated that the Chinese could also provide a new range of goods, including canned fruit and meats, newsprint, and various chemicals. But this then prompted the objection that the question of strategic trade controls was not directly relevant. Expressing the government's view in January 1955, Thorneycroft said there was 'practically nothing that China can supply which she cannot freely export to this country.'[29]

As time went by, pressure for relaxation of the controls came to be motivated more and more by anxieties lest Britain be left behind in the race for the Chinese market. Japan, given its natural and historic trading ties, became an obvious target for British fears. Between 1953 and 1957, Japanese businessmen signed a series of well-publicised agreements with the Chinese State trading organs, events which did not go unnoticed in Westminster. They even raised the suspicion that Japan was becoming a vehicle for illicit United States exports to China. It was this prospect more than any other which signalled alarm. Many in Britain could not believe that the United States would continue indefinitely its total ban on trade with Peking, particularly with the ending of the Korean War, and the subsequent possibility of Californian and other Western businessmen putting pressure on Washington to revitalise trading links across the Pacific. One Labour MP warned in 1956 that 'if we are not very careful, we shall find that [China] has become another department of the trading unit of the United States.'[30] Meanwhile, in Europe, the growth of West German trade with China was viewed with concern, as was the increase in the number of French contracts being signed with Chinese officials. In 1955, the *Financial Times* noted also that Sweden and Switzerland — who were not bound by the strategic control system, though each had voluntarily agreed to limit their level of trade with China to that of 1948 — were exporting goods, such as generating plant, which the British government had banned for sale to China.[31] Other Western governments, it was claimed, were, with the exception of the United States, applying the controls much less strictly and consistently than was the British. The result was that contracts invalidated by the Board of Trade were being taken up by French, German, or Japanese rivals. But again, different opinions were expressed as to the policy implications of these developments. On the one hand, this 'fierce and growing competition', as Elibank was already calling it in March 1953, clearly indicated the need to ease regulations. On the other hand, it could imply the necessity for caution. China, the China Association argued, was 'past master in the art of playing off one nation against the other.'[32]

A closely related argument involved the costs to British colonial territories. Hongkong felt about the strategic regulations 'much as a man would feel if you were to give him a knife and tell him that it was in his interests to go and cut his own throat.'[33] The authorities had begun applying the agreed international controls in August 1950. The move was welcomed in Washington because of the close proximity of the colony to China, and its traditional role as a funnel for trade with the mainland. But the area also had to survive. A permanent block on normal trading relations would mean ultimately its commercial death. It raised the danger that Communism could prosper in Hongkong. It was no use having a military victory against Communism 'at the front door', the President of the Board of Trade declared in 1951, 'if Communism is infiltrating through the back door owing to economic, social and political difficulties.'[34] The Hongkong and Shanghai Banking Corporation had been especially critical of the extension to the colony of the Korean War controls. It was argued that they had disrupted contracts already negotiated, produced a good deal of uncertainty and confusion, upset the industry of the colony by depriving it of raw materials, and jeopardised the livelihood of workers and the functions of the port.[35] Hongkong did manage to develop alternate markets in Asia. But its problems continued to be raised by critics at Westminster, and the complaints of its businessmen channelled to London through the China trade network. In early 1951, for example, at the height of United States Congressional attacks on British and Hongkong trade with China, the China Association took care to maintain its contacts with the Hongkong General Chamber of Commerce.[36]

The strategic trade controls similarly had an impact on the Malayan economy. Rubber and tin products formed 84 per cent by value of the export trade of the Federation.[37] Though other factors than the China trade regulations were involved, the resulting progressive decline in the price of natural rubber was a matter of concern to the industry and to officials. Moreover, China was reported to be obtaining alternative supplies of rubber from Indonesia and Ceylon, and even to be receiving Malayan rubber re-exported from the Soviet Union. Eden wrote afterwards that the British government's concern over the China trade controls was 'not so much for ourselves, as for some of our colonies and other members of the Commonwealth.'[38]

This background of public debate in Britain ran parallel with official moves. The government was firm in its view that changes, when desirable, should take place only as part of a concerted decision on the part of the Western powers. It was only when every effort to secure such a decision had been exerted, and had led nowhere, that Britain took unilateral action in 1957.

The moves began with the end of the Korean War. In July 1953, the Foreign Ministers of the United States, Britain, and France, meeting in Washington, concluded that 'in existing circumstances, and pending further consultation, the common policies of the three Powers towards Communist China should be maintained.' Commenting in parliament, Butler said that Britain's strategic trade control policy would 'have to be reconsidered at the appropriate time after an armistice, but will not be automatically modified immediately on the conclusion of the armistice.'[39] Apart from some small changes in the China list during 1953, then, policy remained fixed. The official position was that Britain was in favour of trade with China in non-strategic goods; but that any expansion of Anglo-Chinese trade depended basically on the trading policy of the Chinese government, and there was little that the British government could usefully do. Little materialised from the Geneva discussions of 1954, which, as seen in the last chapter, brought about significant changes in the organisational pattern of Sino-British trade. In March, Ministers expressed some hope that the Conference would open the way to a reconsideration of the controls. In July, however, Amory re-stated British policy with vigour, adding: 'I am afraid that there is no question whatever of our unilaterally altering the China list.'[40]

Indeed, what changes there were in 1954 had the effect rather of widening the differential between the Soviet and the Chinese lists. They resulted from discussions between British, United States, and other Western officials within the NATO committee framework. Controls were strengthened by means of fresh enforcement measures, while Soviet bloc trade became freer. The position just before this agreement was that there were 266 items on the embargo list, ninety-two on the quantitative control list, and 102 on the 'watch' list. Afterwards, the figures were, respectively, 170, twenty-four and sixty-two. No discussions took place with regard to the China lists.[41] In Britain, the China Association was quick to criticise the decision. It was clearly against Britain's interests, it stated, to facilitate the Soviet Union's being able to continue supplying China with machinery and other goods. Britain should aim instead at making it specifically advantageous for China to trade with her instead of with Soviet bloc countries.[42] United States sources recognised some truth in the British analysis. The official report of the 1954 revisions said that 'it had to be recognised that as the differential in Western controls between destination Eastern Europe and destination Communist China became even wider, the possibility of evading the China embargo through reshipment of goods from Eastern Europe to Communist China would grow.'[43]

The 1955 Geneva meetings produced no change in the

situation, and in the following April the United States effected a further relaxation and simplification of trade with the Soviet Union and Eastern Europe. But several participating CHINCOM governments began, from the latter part of 1955, to express concern at the size and the expansion of the differential. Public criticism of the China trade regulations grew in Britain. Finally, in January 1956, the government announced that the scope of the China trade controls was under study in consultation with the United States authorities. Eden raised the question with Eisenhower in Washington the same month. He was unable to make a dent in the American position. The communique merely affirmed 'that trade controls should continue and should be reviewed now and periodically as to their scope, in the light of changing conditions, so that they may serve the interests of the free world.'[44] This masked the degree of urgency felt in official circles in London. According to Macmillan, the trade question had been the government's 'chief concern' in September 1955. A decision had been postponed then only because of difficulties arising elsewhere.[45] United States officials were by now fully aware of the British position. The Ninth Battle Act Report stated that

> those who favoured a substantial easing of the China embargo argued that the Korean armistice had been signed; that the USSR and other Eastern European Communist nations could purchase goods which were under embargo to Communist China; that those items could therefore be re-exported to Communist China despite the added transportation and other costs; and, finally, that the effect of the embargo was to force Communist China into a greater economic dependence on the Soviet Union.[46]

With Washington adamant during the 1955–6 talks, and with encouraging noises coming from other Western European governments and Japan, Britain during 1956 explored other possibilities. In May, it was announced that the government would henceforth make greater use of the control system's exceptions procedure 'to permit reasonable exports in appropriate cases to China of goods which are not on the Soviet lists.'[47] CHINCOM would, however, be kept informed of the use made by Britain of the procedure. The first test of the new approach came in June. It was then applied in the case of a contract signed by British businessmen for the supply of tractors to China. Congressional reaction was immediate and unfavourable. The Foreign Office and the British Embassy in Washington stated, in defence of the British action, that no strategic goods would be sold to China; that the move was strictly 'procedural'; that this step had been urged by the British government for many months; and, finally, that any increase in Anglo-Chinese trade was likely to remain 'quite minor.' For his part, Dulles also played down the significance of the move, which seemed to some to indicate that the administration had now accepted the inevitability of a gradualist, unilateral British revision of the China trade controls.

There now followed a series of British departures from the earlier, more rigid, system. In June 1956, the governments of Malaya and Singapore both announced that exports of natural rubber to China would henceforth be permitted 'in reasonable quantities' under license. This represented the culmination of several months of effort by the Malayan and Singapore authorities to secure removal of the embargo, which had included a visit to London by Tengku Abdul Rahman.[48] Reports that the United States had agreed to this decision following representations by Eden were, however, denied in Washington. The Foreign Office stated that no policy decision was involved; the export of rubber to China flowed logically from the general policy announced in May. Increasing use was made of the exceptions procedure in subsequent months. Licenses were approved for the export to China of British steel, tractors, trucks, and some machine tools. Renewed pressures were brought to bear on Washington by several Western governments. In March 1957, during the now heated public debate in Britain, the Sino-British Trade Committee urged that the China controls should either be abolished, or at least that trade should be put on the same footing as that of trade with the Soviet bloc.

It was clear, however, that there were limits beyond which Washington would not budge. British use of the exceptions procedure to allow more non-strategic goods to be exported to China was acceptable; tinkering with the control system itself was not. Early in 1957, for example, there were signs that the United States in fact wished to tighten controls on Western trade with China. Details were not made public. In February,

Dulles merely made reference to a 'disposition to try to tighten up somewhat the provisions of the COCOM' following Hungary, adding that 'the same may be true about the CHINCOM.'[49] Macmillan brought up the issue with Eisenhower in March at the Bermuda meeting. Early the following month, Britain made changes with regard to the restrictions in force for trade with North Korea. This swelling movement of revision now prompted the United States to put fresh proposals on the table. Under them, 'certain items for peaceful use' then embargoed to China would be removed from controls and placed on the same basis as that applying in the Soviet case. Also, 'certain other items' would be transferred to the Soviet list but under a lesser degree of control. But, finally, the proposal 'would involve a tightening of the "exceptions procedure" now in use.' The State Department confirmed that the United States had been 'repeatedly pressed' by 'some of its allies' to relax China controls, but that it was and had been 'unwilling to agree to any relaxation which would result in an increased flow of strategic goods to Communist China.'[50]

The American proposals received a mixed, and on balance unfavourable, reaction in Britain. *The Times*' diplomatic correspondent argued that the effect of the envisaged changes in the exceptions procedure might be to reduce trade between China and the West.[51] This was not, incidentally, greatly different from the view of the Peking *People's Daily*, which described the planned move as 'a strategy of advance that looks like retreat.' Trade opinion in Britain remained sceptical. Reservations were expressed by the Sino-British Trade Committee and by the London Chamber of Commerce. These criticisms were later seen to be well founded. It became known that the fifty or so items which the United States intended amalgamating with the Soviet list were precisely those on which British hopes of an expansion of trade with China had rested.

The CHINCOM meetings of May 1957, failed to produce results. Before the Committee were the United States proposals, some from Japan, and others drawn up by the French government. These latter had been submitted to other Western governments before the Bermuda exchanges. The fundamental obstacle persisted. As one official United States account put it, the problem was 'one of trying to reconcile the retention of a significant differential with the insistence on its complete elimination.'[52] By this date, the division between Washington and other governments had become too great to be papered over. The United States delegation put forward what it saw as a compromise proposal. The French delegation, with British support, refused an American request to withdraw its proposals; whereupon the Canadians suggested a further compromise position, which was likewise unsuccessful.

The meeting of 27 May thus ended in deadlock. After it, the British delegation issued a 'solemn declaration' setting out the government's intention unilaterally to relax the China restrictions. This had been on the cards at least since April, before the last-minute CHINCOM round. The possibility was perhaps the crucial factor in persuading the United States to develop its proposal of April and May. On May 30, the Foreign Secretary repeated in the Commons that 'in future, we shall adopt the same lists for China and the Soviet bloc.' This would mean no change as regards items embargoed for both areas. Rather, 'certain items now embargoed for China will either be transferred to the quantitative control list, or to the watch list, or completely freed.' The British Embassy in Washington issued a lengthy defence of the decision. Abolition of the differential was declared to be fully consistent with the United Nations resolution of May 1951; morally justifiable after Hungary; defensible since the signing of the Korean truce because of the anomaly of maintaining two separate controls; and an expression of the strong political and commercial pressures in the United Kingdom for its abolition. Trade controls, it continued, had to be based on clear strategic grounds. Any more stringent controls than those applying to the Soviet Union could only be justified as a measure of economic warfare. The British government did not believe

> that any such measure, designed to retard the industrialisation of China, can be justified — even if their objective could be attained in practice . . . A postponement or partial solution of this problem would satisfy no-one. It would merely serve as a continuing source of friction, and lead to further anti-American feeling in the United Kingdom and in other European countries.[53]

The United States was officially 'most disappointed' at the British action. It was nevertheless followed by similar moves on the part of other participating CHINCOM governments. Meetings were held in Paris during the summer of 1957 to work out new quotas for the quantitative control list. The decision was welcomed in Britain. The China trade organisations expressed a cautious expectation that the question of the channels of trade would become more amenable to settlement, and that the longer-term prospects for trade would improve. A Commercial Secretary was shortly afterwards appointed to Peking; in November, the President of the Board of Trade visited China, and a Chinese trade mission came to Britain.

Chinese commentary on the trade controls during this period was blended into Peking's general analysis of the nature of the relationships between capitalist states. Thus the focus was on American policies, and the purposes behind them. One of these was to use the trade controls 'as an instrument to push forward the "cold war" and the "policy of strength" in an effort to slow down and strangle the economic development of the Soviet Union and the People's Democracies.' The other was 'to monopolise the markets of the capitalist world, in order to make the other capitalist countries economically more dependent on the US.'[54] Britain's own economic difficulties were hence very much of her own making. She, and other Western countries, was cut off from the huge markets of the democratic world, and therefore had to sell her goods to the United States, who, 'as a big purchaser . . . uses every pretext to force down prices and raise customs duty to inflict great losses on those countries whose economy is dependent on exports.' Not surprisingly, opposition to the strategic control system was continuing to grow in Britain and Western Europe among both governments and businessmen. Moreover, with 'the tremendous economic development of the Soviet Union and China', British trade with these countries 'would have very big prospects.' It must not be forgotten, though, that there was 'keen competition among capitalists' for the China market.[55] In sum, then, the embargo, while hurting Western countries, had in no way impeded China's reconstruction.[56]

The issue of relaxing the China trade controls in 1957 thus involved far more than technical commercial arrangements. It went straight to the heart of British thinking on China, and turned on the crucial difference between London and Washington on the whole question of China policy. It had since 1949 been Britain's contention that Western policy towards China should be directed towards facilitating a more independent stance on the part of Peking, and in particular that China should not be forced into a corner from which closer ties with Moscow appeared the only way out. In the specific case of trade, the British case was thus that, by being differentially more severe against China than against the Soviet Union and Eastern Europe, the strategic control system in the particular form that it had emerged out of the Korean War was inconsistent with those objectives. Other factors were important, particularly the adverse effects of the controls on the economies of British colonial territories with interests in the China trade, notably Hongkong and Malaya. The principle of imposing controls, however, was not questioned, nor was it by the majority of the government's critics.

Apart from its substantive importance, the 1957 case is also of interest for the light it throws on the ways in which domestic pressure could on occasions exert influence over government policy. Between 1955 and 1957, the issue became an intensely political one in Britain. It aroused the worst fears of critics who maintained that American policy was damaging to British interests, in this case in so far as British export potential in the China market was being inhibited. The mounting wave of criticism enveloped all shades of trading opinion, and the traders' supporters in the Commons and Lords and in the press, particularly the *Financial Times*; and came to outweigh the government's predilection for joint Anglo-American action, as expressed in earlier statements that a unilateral British departure on the China trade controls issue was not possible.

7 Between Washington and Peking

It was not entirely unreasonable in 1955 to speculate that the future historian would attribute the cause of World War III to a quirk of Chinese geography. The peculiarity in question is the location off the coast of the Chinese mainland of one major island, variously called Formosa or Taiwan, a nearby group of islands, the Pescadores, and several much smaller groups scattered along Fukien and Chekiang provinces. During the final crucial stage of the civil war, Chiang Kai-shek fled the mainland and took refuge on Formosa. In the early months of 1950 it was widely believed, even among knowledgeable circles in the United States, that this last Nationalist stronghold would shortly fall in the face of advancing units of the People's Liberation Army. With the outbreak of the Korean War in June of that year, however, President Truman made the decision to contain the progress of the Chinese civil war at this penultimate stage. Formosa and the offshore islands thus became a permanent thorn of potential counter-revolution in the side of the new regime in Peking.

The immediate problem was not so much Taiwan itself — though the Nationalist presence on the island soon became a unifying symbol on the mainland — as the smaller islands very close to the coast. Quemoy and Matsu in particular were located in highly sensitive positions within intelligence-gathering and bombardment range of Communist China. Other islands garrisoned by Chiang's forces took the Nationalist grip of the coastal zone further north towards Shanghai. In a nuclear age, the dangers inherent in this situation were obvious. Given the strength of Nationalist and Communist feeling, local hostilities could easily break out by accident, miscalculation, or design. Given the appropriate mixture of global circumstances, the Soviet Union and the United States could then find themselves being drawn in on opposing sides in a confrontation in which the actual use of nuclear weapons was a distinct possibility. It was precisely this consideration that shaped British policy in the two offshore islands crises of the 1950s. The first, in 1954-5, is the more important of the two. It was during this crisis that British policy on China as a whole finally crystallised, possibly for the first time since the Communist seizure of power in 1949. And it was also during this crisis that Washington and Peking, with British encouragement and assistance, took the first tentative steps towards establishing the groundwork for a dialogue. These steps led eventually to the amelioration of Sino-American tensions during President Nixon's term of office from 1968.

The roots of the Formosa conflict lay deep in the diplomacy of World War II. The island had not been under Chinese rule at any time during the twentieth century. It had been ceded to Japan by the Chinese government in 1895 by the Shiminoseki Treaty. Experience of Japanese rule, grafted on to a long history of separation from the mainland and cultural distinctiveness, helped to foster the growth of Formosan nationalism. The major concern of the allies, however, was not that the island should achieve independence, but that the whole of China should be liberated from Japan. The Declarations of Cairo and Potsdam therefore included important commitments. It was the purpose of the allies, according to the wording of the 1943 Cairo Declaration, 'that Japan shall be stripped of all the islands in the Pacific which she has seized or occupied since the beginning of the first world war in 1914, and that all the territories that Japan has stolen from the Chinese, such as Manchuria, Formosa, and the Pescadores, shall be restored to the Republic of China.' The intention was reaffirmed at Potsdam in 1945.[1] Chinese forces did indeed return to Formosa in September 1945; but the legal tangle remained. Cairo referred simply to 'the Republic of China.' Could the Communist government which was created six years later be regarded as the rightful heir to this legacy?

United States policy was the crucial factor here. Yet American attitudes towards China in 1949-50 were far from stable. Hard-line support of the Nationalist cause took a significant length of time to emerge. Indeed there are signs that the Administration in Washington might even have welcomed a

Communist seizure of these territories during 1949 or the early months of 1950. It would have made final the cutting of the entanglements of the 1940s, and facilitated the start of new policies more relevant to the 1950s. In addition it would have averted an awkward situation for the Western powers in their handling of relations with the new China.

But at the same time the Administration was coming under increasing fire from the rising tide of pro-Nationalist sentiment in the Congress. Steps were taken late in 1949 to ensure that the expected occupation of Formosa by units of the People's Liberation Army would not signal a renewed onslaught on President Truman's China policy. State Department officials, on a directive from Acheson, drew up a memorandum intended to prepare public opinion for the final blow. The loss of Formosa, it stated, was 'widely anticipated.' In public statements, therefore, great emphasis should be given to the notion that the island, 'politically, geographically, and strategically, is part of China in no way especially distinguished or important.' Historically it had been Chinese. Politically and militarily it was strictly a Chinese responsibility. Efforts should be made to counter the 'false impression' that Formosa's retention would save the Nationalists; that the United States had any special interest in the island; that its loss would seriously damage the interests of the United States or other anti-communist countries; or that the United States was responsible for or committed in any way to act to save Formosa. The memorandum also set out clearly the likely consequences of further commitments to the Nationalists. Seeking American bases on Formosa, supplying arms, or similar action, it argued, would accomplish no material good for China or for the Nationalists. Moreover, it would serve Russian propaganda interests, and would involve the United States 'in a long-term adventure producing at best a new area of bristling stalemate, and at worst possible involvement in open warfare.'[2]

The forecast is a remarkably accurate one of the situation that had arisen by the mid-1950s. British opinion was moving along similar lines. The best indication of this can be seen in the tone of resignation that pervaded the conservative press. At the end of 1949, the *Daily Telegraph* declared that 'the Communist conquest of China is a fact, and by no possible stretch of the imagination can it be supposed that Chiang Kai-shek's precarious foothold in Formosa will provide the nucleus for an alternative regime.'[3] Events seemed to be moving rapidly towards the final end of the Chinese civil war. The People's Liberation Army stated that liberation of Taiwan was one of its major tasks at the beginning of 1950. In April, the relatively large island of Hainan was occupied, and some smaller islands the following month. Chinese Communist forces were mobilising amphibious and other assault vehicles for the final push on Formosa itself. By May, it was generally expected in Britain that this would be launched from Fukien province some time in July.

The prospect was not viewed with any great dismay by the Foreign Office. Government statements were framed cautiously and legalistically. The Chinese government, it was stated, had 'assumed the administration of Formosa pending the conclusion of a Treaty of Peace with Japan.'[4] There was little feeling, either in government or outside that something should be done about the situation in the Far East. The only exception to this was over the plight of the Formosans themselves. Considering traditional attitudes, Japanese rule, resentment at the influx of Nationalist Chinese from the mainland, unrest with Kuomintang mismanagement and deteriorating economic and social conditions, and above all the massacre, looting and mass imprisonment suffered at the hands of Nationalist troops in 1947, *The Economist* predicted that deep suspicion and hostility towards all Chinese mainland authorities would be characteristic of the Formosan population for a long time to come.[5] Some kind of United Nations trusteeship or neutralisation scheme for the island was put forward in some quarters as a solution that might accommodate American, Chinese Communist, and Formosan sensitivities. The State Department, however, was opposed to such schemes. A Formosan plebiscite, officials argued 'would be almost universally interpreted in mainland China and widely interpreted throughout Asia as an attempt by this Government to separate Formosa from China'. The Administration did not wish 'to create a Formosa irredenta issue, about which the Chinese Communists could rally support within China and with which they could divert attention from Soviet actions in the North.'[6]

As it happened, the People's Liberation Army did not move on Taiwan in the summer of 1950. Following the outbreak of

war in Korea in June, President Truman announced that the
United States would prevent an attack across the Taiwan Strait
by either party to the Chinese civil war.

The State Department's reference in 1949 to a bristling
stalemate should just such a move be taken proved an accurate
one. Liberation of Taiwan became the major rallying cry of the
Communist government, and a prominent issue in exchanges
with foreign governments on the establishment of diplomatic
relations. Korea, however, absorbed much of the energy of
Peking. It was not until September 1954, after the Geneva
Conference had reached a settlement on the Korean and
Indo-Chinese situations, that Formosa and the offshore islands
seized the attention of Western leaders.

At the beginning of that month, units of the People's
Liberation Army began the bombardment of Quemoy. A
variety of explanations for this turn of events were put forward
in Britain. First, it was seen as a tactic designed for strictly
domestic consumption. *The Times* argued that 'Revolutionary
regimes welcome, as a cohesive and energising force, any appeal
to genuine national emotion.'[7] It was suggested that Peking was
trying to divert the attention of the Chinese people from local
adversities, such as floods, or else trying to conceal failures in
the Chinese economic plan. International developments were
seen as a second possible explanation of Communist motivations. China, that is, had responded to Western appeasement
policies in the same way that Germany had done before World
War II. Her leaders had become strengthened in the conviction
that the West lacked the determination to resist aggression. The
settlement reached at Geneva, moreover, had freed Chinese
resources, and particularly air power, for use elsewhere; and on
top of this there was evidence that Soviet military and
economic assistance had been stepped up.

A third hypothesis, however, was that the Chinese government was responding desperately to a series of threatening
Western gestures. This outlook on the situation played a major
part in the deliberations of Attlee and the Labour Party. Even
discounting Eisenhower's 'unleashing' of Chiang Kai-shek in
February 1953, American policies towards China had become
much more dynamic under Secretary of State Dulles. Negotiations between United States and Nationalist Chinese officials

on the subject of a defence treaty began in August 1954. There was loose talk in Washington about the creation of a North-East Asian equivalent to the South-East Asian Treaty Organisation, incorporating Formosa, South Korea, and Japan. All this, it was argued, engendered anxieties on the part of the Chinese Communist leadership about the 'encirclement' of China by a hostile coalition of both traditional and newer enemies. The Chinese, a *Times* correspondent maintained, feared that American intentions were such that Formosa's status would soon be decided in a way which would put it permanently out of reach, except at the price of a world war with all the western powers.[8]

The British government was in a far from easy position. To urge acquiescence in Chinese Communist demands to the full would have meant not only the destruction of the Nationalist Chinese, but would also have constituted, if the United States went along with the idea, an unacceptable setback for Western interests throughout Asia. The consequences of the resulting expansion of Chinese Communist prestige, for example on the situation in Malaya, were incalculable. Yet the existing situation was just as intolerable. Three intertwined British policies are clearly discernible during the crisis, particularly as tension mounted in the early part of 1955. First, it was a fact of life that the United States was committed to defend the Nationalist Chinese regime. Any interim settlement would therefore have to recognise the security of Taiwan as an entity separate from the Chinese mainland. And further, if both sides renounced the attribution of rebel status to the other, or at least the use of force in the pursuit of what each considered its legitimate objectives, then the way could be prepared for the co-existence of the two Chinas. Secondly, however, Chiang Kai-shek would have to be kept under a tight rein. Global peace could not be left in the hands of a group of men defeated in a civil war five years earlier. Nationalist troops, in the British view, would have to be evacuated from the islands closest to the Chinese coast if any lasting settlement were even to be thought about. Later, British opinion became hazy about the necessity for Chiang's evacuation of all the smaller islands including Quemoy and Matsu, but this shift of ground will be discussed in a moment. Thirdly, it was seen to be essential in London that Washington and Peking raise their blackout on direct and mutual communication. It was not, as yet, realistic to talk in terms of an exchange of ambassadors between the two countries; but this did not mean that all forms of contact were to be ruled out. There were strict limits, though, on British mediatory activity. In the background to the offshore islands crisis was a growing British feeling that Anglo-American solidarity ought, at all times, to be preserved and publicised. The Defence White Paper for 1953—4 had stated that it was 'clear that one of the principal Soviet aims is to weaken the strength and cohesion of the Atlantic Alliance.'[9] Before the crisis unfolded, Sir Roger Makins, the British Ambassador in Washington, wrote in *Foreign Affairs* that one means the Soviet Union would use would be to play 'on every difference, real or imaginary, between the British and American approach to our common problems in this sensitive area.'[10] Indeed there was some speculation in the autumn of 1954 that the crisis had been deliberately precipitated as a tactic for promoting Anglo-American dissension, and top-level Sino-Soviet consultations in October were suggested as evidence to support this interpretation.

That the British government appreciated the need to secure Taiwan emerged slowly. The first indication came in December 1954 in a television interview given by Anthony Nutting in New York. In reply to questions about the situation in the Far East, he stated unequivocally: 'A Chinese Communist attack on Formosa is an attack upon a member of the United Nations and would no doubt call for collective action by the United Nations, in which we would, of course, be involved as a member of the United Nations.' The Chinese Communists, he went on, 'certainly should be on notice that if they start to attack anybody they will involve the United Nations.'[11] The remarks were surprisingly incautious. Whatever the legal intricacies of the situation, Formosa was not a Member of the UN. Nutting may have been deliberately testing the wind for reactions; but judging by the Foreign Secretary's reaction of immediately demanding a verbatim transcript of the relevant passages of the interview, this seems unlikely.

The Parliamentary Labour Party were quick to demand an official explanation. 'Was not there an implication', Attlee wanted to know, 'that this country, in circumstances which were not fully discussed, was bound to come to the assistance of the United States in the event of an attack being made upon that country when it was engaged in possible intervention in a civil war in China?'[12] Turton, speaking for the Government, at first insisted that Nutting had done no more than to set out the facts of the case. In response to persistent questions from the Labour benches, however, he concluded with the generalisation that 'any form of aggression is a matter for consideration by members of the United Nations', an interpretation which Opposition spokesmen found more acceptable. Reports continued to appear in the press, on both sides of the Atlantic, that the British government's commitment to the defence of Taiwan was greater than had originally been supposed.

However, the nearest officials got to making this explicit was in clarifying the government's view of the international law relating to the status of Formosa. There could of course be no question of formal recognition by Britain of the authorities on the island. British officials there were accredited not to the Nationalist Chinese government but to the Chinese province of Taiwan. Speaking in the Commons in January 1955, Eden laid emphasis on the differences between Formosa and the rest of China. It had not formed part of China throughout the whole of the twentieth century. Moreover there had been important developments in the 1940s. The Cairo Declaration of 1943 was simply a 'statement of intention' that Formosa should be retroceded to China after World War II. The retrocession had not taken place 'because of the difficulties arising from the existence of two entities claiming to represent China, and the differences amongst the Powers as to the status of those entities.' Formosa's occupation by Chinese forces in 1945 did not involve any change of sovereignty. Nor was the situation resolved, in the British Government's view, by the Peace Treaty of April 1952, by which Japan formally renounced all right, title and claim to Formosa. In conclusion, then, Formosa and the Pescadores were 'territory the *de jure* sovereignty over which is uncertain or undetermined.'[13] If the government could not be fully explicit about the strategic and diplomatic importance of the status quo, public opinion was less inhibited. As the *Daily Telegraph* put it, there was 'no reason whatever . . . for surrendering this important strategic base, together with its millions of anti-Communist Chinese, to Mao and Chou.'

Liberal opinion was in general agreement. There might be a good case, the *Guardian* argued, for saying that Formosa was an integral part of China. But 'in present circumstances an attempt to capture it by force would be met with force by the United States', and China's threats 'would therefore cause a revival of the tension in Asia which since Geneva has been falling.'[14] All this put the Labour Party in a situation of acute embarrassment. It could not afford to be seen as a convert to the Chiang Kai-shek camp, but at the same time Attlee and his front-bench colleagues were well aware of the dangers of handing Formosa back to the government in Peking. Attlee stated the Opposition's view in an interview published in the *Daily Herald* on January 31, 1955. His verdict was that since Formosa had such strategic importance for both Peking and Washington, it 'should for a period of years be administered under a neutral control.' This would continue 'until a fair plebiscite can be held, so that the Formosan people themselves can decide their own future.' Chiang Kai-shek and his colleagues, meanwhile, would go into exile. This scheme had the advantage of avoiding the bloodshed which all agreed would be the result if the Chinese People's Liberation Army were to try to seize Taiwan. In an equally well publicised interview in the *News Chronicle* two weeks later, Attlee defended his proposals by pointing out that he had not suggested 'that the Formosans should be handed over to Communism irrespective of their wishes.'[15] Kenneth Younger, a former Labour Minister, explained the technicalities of the Opposition's view of the international law on the subject in correspondence to *The Times*.

While this two-Chinas policy was gradually taking shape in Britain, Chinese Communist officials were becoming increasingly hostile to both the government and the Labour Party. Press reports of Britain's commitment to the defence of Taiwan late in 1954 were taken as confirmation that London had fallen in with the plans of 'the American aggressive group.' Nutting's television interview, and the government's explanation of it, were taken as further proof of Britain's real intentions. Detailed criticisms of the legal arguments raised in Britain, whether by Eden and other ministers in parliament, or by politicians and international lawyers in the correspondence columns of *The Times*, appeared regularly in Chinese publications. The Peking

People's Daily condemned Eden at length and in strong language. 'Just as Chamberlain exerted great pressure on Czechoslovakia in order to force her to cede the Sudeten area to Hitler, Eden now spares no effort to try to coerce the Chinese people to accept . . . the American seizure of Taiwan.'[16] But the Chinese were just as critical of the kinds of ideas then gathering momentum within the Labour Party. In a veiled attack on Labour's thinking on the Taiwan question, the *People's Daily* insisted that no one who held that Taiwan could be neutralised could be considered as respecting China's sovereignty in regard to Taiwan. This was 'as simple and clear as that no stand for the neutralisation of Wales could be regarded as respecting British territorial sovereignty.'[17]

Despite the strength of this Chinese Communist reaction, hammering out a consistent position on the issue of Taiwan's status in international law was not the government's chief preoccupation during the crisis. On a straight military calculus, there was no possibility of Peking's being able to launch a successful thrust against the island. The more urgent task was to make sure that Chiang Kai-shek did not start a world war.

To this end British officials urged on Washington the desirability of Nationalist evacuation of the more provocative of their island outposts. The Foreign Office's view was that there was a clear distinction between Taiwan and the smaller islands off the coast of the mainland. These islands, Eden maintained, 'undoubtedly form part of the territory of the People's Republic of China.' This did not mean that the British government would be content to watch Chinese Communist forces occupy the islands. Any attempt by Peking to assert its authority over them by force 'would, in the circumstances at present peculiar to the case, give rise to a situation endangering peace and security, which is properly a matter of international concern.'[18] What the government was really after was agreement on the part of Chiang unilaterally to withdraw. Bringing pressure to bear on Washington was not necessarily the best means of achieving this, for United States influence over its ally was not always decisive, but in the circumstances it was the only course for Britain. British officials in London and Washington viewed the situation in early 1955 with growing anxiety. In a memorandum to the United States government,

Britain expressed 'fears that during the next two or three years the United States may, through impulsiveness or lack of perspective, be drawn into a Chinese war.' As Eden wrote later in his memoirs, 'no great power could seriously want to fight' about the offshore islands, but they 'could be a cause of war, just the same.'[19] These two planks in the British platform were summarised in a letter which Churchill wrote to Eisenhower early in 1955. 'As a matter of honour', he argued, 'the United States must not permit its loyal ally Chiang Kai-shek to be liquidated and massacred and scuppered by the Chinese Communists.' However, from this 'overriding purpose', he also urged the Americans to disentangle one which he believed secondary — holding the offshore islands as a bridgehead for a Nationalist invasion of the mainland. To Chiang Kai-shek, the United States 'should give the protection of its shield but not the use of its sword.'[20]

As these transatlantic exchanges continued during the winter of 1954—5, tension mounted in the Far East. Units of the People's Liberation Army began air operations against the Tachen Islands, off Chekiang province, on January 10, 1955. A week later, Chinese Communist forces seized the tiny island of I-Chiang. The British government's position was clear: the United States should force Chiang to pull back his troops and, as *The Times* expressed it, 'put a hundred miles of salt water between the two sides.' Washington did not follow British advice wholly, but neither did the administration fully reject it. American policy was finally decided, according to Eisenhower, at a top-level meeting on 20 January. At this meeting, Dulles argued in favour of two moves: Nationalist Chinese evacuation of the Tachens, but at the same time a public American commitment to the defence of Quemoy and possibly Matsu. Four days later, the President sent a message to Congress seeking authority to use American forces 'for the specific purpose of securing and protecting Formosa and the Pescadores against armed attack, this authority to include the securing and protection of such *related positions and territories of that area now in friendly hands* and the taking of such measures as he judges to be required or appropriate in assuring the defence of Formosa and the Pescadores.'[21]

The wording was ambiguous, probably deliberately so in order to keep the Chinese Communist leadership in the dark about actual American defence commitments in the area. But in general the move was welcomed in Britain. The Foreign Secretary lent his support in the Commons, and declared the government's conviction that the object of the administration had been to reduce the risks of any extension of the fighting. One of the reasons for British confidence appears to have been the defence treaty between the United States and Nationalist China, then before Congress, some of the provisions of which could be interpreted as instituting an American check on Chiang's counter-revolutionary zeal. Indeed towards the end of January and the early part of Febraury, there was much discussion in the British press of the major transformation which it was felt had taken place in America's China policy since the period of Chiang's 'unleashing'. President Eisenhower, *The Times* thought, was moving sensibly and cautiously towards acceptance of the two-China stabilisation plan being urged by the British government.[22] There was even speculation that American policy was leading logically in the direction of diplomatic recognition of Peking and support for Chinese Communist participation in the United Nations. Though some in Britain were uneasy about the ambiguities of the American position, it fell to Congress itself to provide the most outspoken critics of the administration's new policy.

Evacuation even of the Tachens group did not prove an easy task. There was a delay of several days, while Chiang apparently tried to bargain for firmer American commitments to the defence of Quemoy and Matsu. The withdrawal was finally completed, with the aid of a massive display of United States armed strength, in mid-February.

But there now arose the question of Quemoy and Matsu. British opinion had not usually distinguished between various categories of offshore islands. The only distinction that counted, in the British view, was between Formosa itself and the islands off the mainland coast. Nationalist Chinese withdrawal from all of these continued to be advocated with some urgency in Britain. Labour back-benchers took to comparing them with the Isle of Wight, the Scottish islands, or some American equivalent. Strachey, for example, after hearing the Foreign Secretary's detailed exposition of the government's view of the legal status of the offshore islands, wondered what Eden would think of a foreign statesman who, at the time the Germans were in occupation of the Channel Isles, had said, 'Of course these Channel Isles undoubtedly belong to Britain, but Britain will be guilty of causing a war if she attempts to occupy them.'[23] The Labour Party seems on this question to have come closest to articulating the public mood in Britain at the time. Chiang's forward positions were seen as unquestionably provocative to the Communists, and as avoidable risks in a dangerously volatile nuclear age.

Ministers and officials, on the other hand, were made increasingly aware of Washington's reasons for keeping some at least of the islands firmly under Nationalist Chinese control. For one thing, this may have been the only practicable option. Eden acknowledged later the difficulties of persuading Chiang to see reason: 'We were not always able to get our friends to do what we wanted.'[24] There is some evidence that Britain was at least able to persuade Washington to refrain from making public any commitment to Quemoy and Matsu. It was reported at the time that these territories were in fact specifically mentioned by Eisenhower in an early draft of his message to Congress as ones that the United States would help Chiang to defend, but that, under pressure from Britain — and also from the Canadian government — these references were deleted in the final version. Beyond this, British officials appear to have made no headway. They would certainly have been made aware of the American view that further evacuation would have a serious effect on Nationalist Chinese morale and therefore on internal sercurity in Formosa; that there would be repercussions throughout South-East Asia and a general undermining of the determination to resist the spread of Communism; and finally that complete withdrawal would constitute another Munich — with the difference that the Chinese Communists were refusing to make even the promises about future non-aggression which Hitler had made.[25] Further, the debates in the United States on the military value of the islands were widely reported in the British press. There was some appreciation, how much depending on the political ideology of the observer, of the strategic significance of Quemoy and Matsu in particular, which screened military activity in the ports of Amoy and Foochow, two of the main bases for any invasion of Formosa. Probably the Cabinet did not go this far. Macmillan writes in his memoirs that the islands were 'of no great military significance', but they were 'of considerable psychological value.' He and the Government 'did not altogether agree' with Eisenhower's case on Quemoy and Matsu, but he found it 'powerful, well-argued and persuasive.'[26]

Anglo-American diplomatic exchanges during this period were cloaked with secrecy and declarations of common purpose. But it appears that evacuation of the remaining islands continued to be advocated. The general impression is that the British government was hinting that it could come much closer to some agreed form of commitment to the security of Formosa, provided that Chiang be persuaded by Dulles and Eisenhower to evacuate Quemoy and Matsu. This was denied by the Foreign Secretary when Labour members suggested that the government was holding back only because of the forthcoming British elections. There was 'no truth whatever in our having entered into such an engagement', Eden stated categorically, 'or having contemplated entering into such an engagement, or having been asked by anybody to enter into such an engagement.'[27]

The third strand of British policy in the crisis was to promote more direct communications between United States and Chinese Communist officials. If Chiang Kai-shek and his armed forces were to stay where they were, then at the very minimum Washington and Peking should be able to talk to each other when future threats to the peace arose. Three possible means to this end were pursued: Communist Chinese participation in United Nations Security Council deliberations on the existing crisis; the convening of an international conference on the subject, at which both America and China would be present; and, finally, the opening of more permanent channels of communication between the two capitals.

The United Nations option had been raised as early as September 1954, in discussions in London between Eden, Dulles, and the New Zealand High Commissioner. The Foreign Secretary was apparently an enthusiastic supporter of the idea, but it was then shelved by the Americans. It came to light again in January. On the 19th, Eisenhower said that he would 'like to see the United Nations attempt to use its good offices.' Close consultations began immediately between the United States, Britain, and New Zealand, whose delegate was that month President of the Security Council.

Britain took a major part in developing the UN initiative. Approaches were made by British officials to both Moscow and Peking to ensure its reception would not be hostile. The overtures to the Soviet Union came at a time when British opinion was coming round to the view that the Kremlin was itself willing to take on a mediatory role in the crisis. Macmillan, for example, wrote later that 'the only encouraging signs appeared to be in Moscow, for it was clear that the Russians did not want a war in the Far East which it might not be possible to limit.' He went further and noted that 'Indeed, both Moscow and London are working (somewhat paradoxically) on the same lines and trying to restrain their friends.'[28] On 28 January, Sir William Hayter, the British ambassador in Moscow, expressed the British Government's hope 'that the Soviet government would feel able to urge restraint on the Chinese', and its view of the importance of avoiding any incidents which might lead to general hostilities. Molotov was also informed of the proposal to invite Peking to send a delegate to New York. It was explained that Britain hoped it would have the cooperation of the Soviet government in the Security Council, 'and that in particular the Soviet government will urge on the Chinese government very strongly that they accept any Security Council invitation to attend the council when it is made.' The Foreign Secretary took the matter up a few days later with the Soviet chargé d'affaires in London.[29] Also on 28 January, the British chargé d'affaires in Peking contacted the Chinese government on the matter of the UN initiative.

Yet it must have been clear before the Security Council discussed the situation that Chou En-lai was unlikely to respond favourably. Denunciation of any scheme for a cease-fire was the basic raw material for all Chinese Communist commentary. And the Indian government, through its officials in Peking, was convinced that any invitation to Peking to attend the Security Council would be flatly rejected. This view was put to British officials in the intensive round of consultations that preceded the meetings of the Security Council, both in New Delhi and in London. It was repeated by Nehru himself when he arrived in London to attend the Commonwealth Prime Ministers' Conference. And in the event, the People's Republic of China did remain determinedly hostile to the UN's deliberations in New

York. The Security Council itself was hardly conducive to a harmonious atmosphere. From the outset the air was charged with accusations and recriminations. The Soviet delegate proposed the expulsion of the Nationalist Chinese representative, and proceeded to detail Chinese Communist charges of American aggression; and the passages in the British and New Zealand speeches which received most press attention were those most firmly pro-American and anti-Soviet. At the conclusion of the 31 January meeting, the proposal to invite a representative of the People's Republic of China to participate in the discussion of the New Zealand agenda item was passed by nine votes to one, with the Soviet Union abstaining.[30]

As forecast by Indian officials, Peking refused to attend. On the day the Security Council met, the *People's Daily* declared the New Zealand initiative to be part of United States aggression. Its supporters were 'peddling the line that the rights and wrongs of the Taiwan question should be shelved for the time being and that the cessation of military operations should take priority.' The British government was condemned as an advocate of this line. On the next day, the *Kwangming Daily* further attacked the 'United States resolution', introduced 'with British backing.' If Britain and New Zealand were truly interested in lessening international tension, they should 'demand that the UN halt United States aggression against China and that the United States pull its armed forces out of Taiwan.'[31] These points were reiterated in Chou En-lai's reply to Secretary-General Hammarskjoeld's letter informing him of the Security Council decision. The purpose of the New Zealand resolution was 'obviously to intervene in China's internal affairs and to cover up the acts of aggression by the United States against China.' China was 'firmly opposed' to the proposal, could not send a representative to New York, and moreover all decisions taken in the Security Council on questions concerning China would be illegal and null and void.[32]

The Foreign Office was 'deeply disappointed' at this reply. China had 'not merely slammed the door,' one official was quoted as saying, 'she has locked it, thrown away the key and stuffed the keyhole with a rude diplomatic Note.'[33] Fears were expressed that Chou's attitude would only serve to promote the cause of those American extremists who wanted to use military force against China. Indian officials repeated that British and

Western opinion had completely misread the attitude of Peking. There were never any grounds for supposing that Chou would agree to send a representative to the Security Council. The idea of settling the crisis through the United Nations progressed no further. There was some American support for New Zealand introducing another resolution in April 1955. But by then, the British government was more appreciative of the drawbacks inherent in this kind of initiative, and advised against it.

The second avenue, an international conference outside United Nations auspices, at least had the merit of being less likely to degenerate into a mutual propaganda onslaught. Nehru was more favourable to the idea of a conference on the grounds that the Chinese would feel less threatened in such surroundings. During the Commonwealth Prime Ministers' Conference in London, he raised this possibility with Eden. The idea also cropped up about the same time in Anglo-Soviet exchanges. Molotov sent for the British ambassador in Moscow on 4 February and proposed that, since the position of the Chinese government would make discussion in the Security Council impossible, 'a conference should be called this month in Shanghai or New Delhi' to consider the situation. The participants would be Britain, the United States, the Soviet Union, France, the People's Republic of China, India, Burma, Indonesia, Pakistan and Ceylon. In his reply of 9 February Hayter objected to the composition of the conference, which 'did not appear to be representative.' In particular, the Foreign Secretary explained afterwards, 'we noted that the Chinese Nationalist authorities in Formosa were to be excluded.'[34]

This was not necessarily an insuperable obstacle. Presumably the question of composition could have been open to further negotiation; presumably also Moscow was not too serious in its suggestion of Shanghai as a possible location. The United States, however, was adamant in its refusal to view a conference as realistic. A spokesman for the State Department said that he found it difficult to believe that anyone who had been at Geneva would wish to repeat the experience. Dulles confirmed later that the Soviet proposal was 'quite unacceptable.'[35] The British government persisted in its efforts nevertheless. In mid-February, for example, Eden announced in the Commons that exchanges with the USSR on the subject were 'not yet closed.' But it seems a reasonable conclusion that British interest in a full-scale conference was more of a medium- or longer-term one. Such an event might be conceivable after a cease-fire in the Straits, and after a great deal of diplomatic preparation, but not before. In the meanwhile, though, it did no harm to nurture constructive contacts with the Soviet Union. A more active pursuit of a conference was undertaken by the Indian government. Officials in New Delhi were of the opinion that Moscow could be persuaded to drop its insistence on Chiang Kai-shek's exclusion. Indian and Soviet officials met regularly in Moscow during February. Shortly afterwards, Eden discussed the matter with the Prime Ministers of Burma and India during the course of his Asian tour. 'After these talks,' he told parliament on his return, 'and on the basis of the information about the attitude of the Chinese Government which reached me from Peking, I came reluctantly to the conclusion that the necessary conditions for progress do not yet exist.'[36]

The conference proposal persisted though. At the beginning of March 1955, the British Embassy in Moscow again established contact with Molotov after a gap of nearly three weeks. There were also signs in that month that Peking might be prepared to sit round a table with Chiang's representatives. Though he himself denied it, Indian officials working in London claimed that the Chinese chargé d'affaires there had let it be known that the People's Republic would not now object to the Nationalists being represented 'in some way' at a conference.[37] These leads do not appear to have been taken up however.

Given these setbacks to British diplomatic probes, the third option of direct Sino-American bilateral talks appeared more and more attractive. There was talk in February of an 'Eden Plan' comprising secret conversations between the United States and the People's Republic of China, contact between the officials of each government being maintained by the British. The Trieste understanding of October 1954, preceding which British and American officials in London acted as channels of communication between Italian and Yugoslav officials, was suggested as a precedent. As a preliminary to more direct links, the British government sought formal declarations by both sides not to use force. That the Americans would be interested in such a declaration from Peking had been made clear by Dulles in mid-February; presumably the argument was put to Eden by the Secretary of State at the SEATO meeting in Bangkok shortly afterwards. In a full account of British thinking, Eden pointed out to the Commons on 8 March that Peking had refrained from attacking Quemoy and the Matsus. The British government, he continued, trusted that they would continue to exercise this restraint 'and that they will make it apparent that while maintaining intact in all respects their position in regard to Formosa and the Pescadores they will not prosecute their claims by forceful means.' It was 'equally desirable' that the Chinese Nationalists do two things. 'We would like to see them withdraw their armed forces from the other coastal islands. We would also hope that they would let it be known that they too, while maintaining their claims, will not prosecute them by forceful means and will abstain from all offensive military action.'[38] Making public in this way British advocacy of Nationalist evacuation is interesting. It may be indicative of a realisation by the Foreign Office that this objective was unattainable, but that frankness was necessary to add credibility to British overtures to Peking.

Bringing Washington and Peking together in some kind of mutually acceptable diplomatic forum now became an important goal of British diplomacy. As Macmillan wrote later, 'we did our best to get some negotiations started.'[39] In March, it was reported from New Delhi that the Chinese were willing to talk with the United States. The main difficulty was their reluctance formally to renounce the use of force as a means of settling their differences with Chiang Kai-shek. On 23 April, Chou En-lai announced at the Bandung Conference his government's willingness 'to sit down and enter into negotiations with the United States Government to discuss the question of relaxing tension in the Far East, and especially the question of relaxing tension in the Taiwan area.' The immediate American response was cool, but Dulles took care to close no doors. Chou's statement was welcomed in Britain by the Foreign Secretary, and the British chargé d'affaires in Peking was instructed to discuss the question further with Chou. The chargé was also acting as a channel of Sino-American communication on a separate question: the fate of a group of American pilots sentenced by the Chinese in mid-November 1954 to long terms of imprisonment for espionage. It was the British view that the release of the pilots would go a long way towards clearing the ground for Sino-American talks. At the end of May, and after intervention by the United Nations Secretary-General, it was finally announced that some were to be released. British efforts ran parallel with the activities of some Asian Commonwealth governments. In particular, Krishna Menon, leader of the Indian delegation to the United Nations, was engaged in an almost feverish round of diplomatic contacts.

The breakthrough finally came in July 1955. On the 11th, Washington proposed to Peking, through Britain, the commencement of Sino-American talks. Eden, now Prime Minister, took the opportunity of the summit meeting in Geneva to promote the idea. In talks outside the formal conference framework, he did everything he could 'to persuade those present, and absent, of the peaceful intentions of the other side.'[40] On July 25, after the conclusion of the summit, the State Department announced that 'as a result of communication between the United States and the People's Republic of China through the diplomatic channels of the United Kingdom,' talks at ambassadorial level between the two countries would begin on 1 August in Geneva. Welcoming the announcement, the Foreign Office expressed the hope 'that this fresh contact on practical matters will assist towards the alleviation of tension between China and the United States. We are glad to have acted as intermediaries.'[41]

The 1954—5 crisis acted as a catalyst for shaping British policies. When fighting broke out again in 1958, it sparked off little more than a replay of the earlier events. The major difference seems to have been that the British government was far less prepared to give even the slightest appearance of conflict between London and Washington. Certainly so far as public statements were concerned, there was virtual unanimity. And private overtures over Chiang's continued occupation of the offshore islands have the appearance of advice given 'for the record,' without there being any serious conviction of its being taken or of the desirability of its being taken.

Chinese Communist units commenced shelling the Nationalist-held islands again in August and September 1958. By this date, the United States was less inhibited in its public declarations about their strategic value. Dulles stated on September 4 that 'the securing and protecting of Quemoy and

Matsu have increasingly become related to the defence of Taiwan.' He thus made explicit the link that was ambiguous in Eisenhower's message to Congress in January 1955. For the Republic of China, moreover, Quemoy and Matsu had 'a great significance, comparable to the significance of Berlin to the West.'[42] The British governmment had also shifted over to a more hard-line position than Eden had taken in the earlier crisis. Government statements often focused exclusively on the fact that Peking was using force to achieve its objectives. Selwyn Lloyd, the Foreign Secretary, declared the government's objective as being 'to secure general international approval of the contention that the status of these islands and of Formosa should not be settled by force.' It was 'one way of preventing the use of force' to 'give in to the other side;' but this kind of appeasement could be very dangerous.[43] All this, it is true, formed one element of Eden's multifaceted policy in 1954—55. However the government then had also attempted to ease tensions by soothing anxieties on both sides of the confrontation. No such efforts were prominent in 1958. Nevertheless, in reply to critics, Lloyd maintained that his policy was fully in tune with that of 1955. In particular, he pointed out that Eden too had completely repudiated the use of force for altering the situation.

Communications from London to Washington similarly do not have the ring of urgency in 1958 that they had in the earlier crisis. Writing to the President in September, Macmillan quoted Churchill's view of 1955 that 'a war to keep the coastal islands for Chiang would not be defensible' in Britain. He also summarised the 'rather negative attitudes' that he anticipated from the various Commonwealth countries, and, according to Eisenhower's own account, suggested a demilitarisation of the offshore islands. This scheme, he felt, might be advanced by the British government either in the UN or in a bilateral approach to the Soviet Union.[44] One minor incident suggested that in practice the government were reconciled to the United States view. On 11 September, Randolph Churchill wrote in the *Evening Standard* that he had been with the Prime Minister the previous evening. As a result, he was 'happily in the position to tell the world that Britain will stand by the United States in the Far East.' Macmillan was 'loyal to his allies and would be very unlikely to rat on them ... we ain't going to let the United

States down over Quemoy and Matsu.' Though the statement
was immediately repudiated by Downing Street, many in
Britain believed that there was more than an element of truth in
the story. Gaitskell, for example, argued that Churchill was
well-informed and 'would be most unlikely to invent such a
story.'[45]

Nevertheless, the British government was not totally im-
mobile. It was obvious that if the United States were in fact to
become involved in the fighting, then Britain would be faced
with an extremely difficult situation. However, the importance
of the British role in the moves to re-establish Sino-American
communications (talks had broken down when the American
Ambassador was transferred to another post) is difficult to
judge. At the end of October, the Foreign Secretary stated that
the government had to try to produce an atmosphere in which
some agreed *modus vivendi* would be possible. Up till then,
however, there had been 'complete inflexibility on the part of
the Peking Government.'[46] While in New York in September to
address the UN General Assembly, Lloyd appealed to the Soviet
Union to use its influence in Peking. The Soviet response was
said to be not encouraging. Some steps were also apparently
taken along with Menon with a view to raising the level of the
Sino-American talks in Warsaw at least to that of Under-
Secretary. Sino-American communications were in fact resumed
in mid-September. There was some speculation that the matter
might be brought before the United Nations. Indeed Khrush-
chev made such a proposal in public correspondence between
Washington and Moscow, but the suggestion was rejected by
Eisenhower. In all of this diplomatic activity, close consultations were evidently maintained between London and Washington, for example on the occasion of Dulles' visit to Britain in
late October.

So far, the pattern of government statements and exchanges
seems fairly closely modelled on that of 1955. One significant
difference in 1958, at least as far as the British government was
concerned, was that Hongkong took the centre of the stage for
a time. Anxiety over the security of the colony had been
expressed in Britain during the 1954—5 crisis. After all, if the
interpretation was valid that the Peking government was trying
to consolidate its position by drawing attention to the
machinations of foreign barbarians, then Hongkong was at least

as good a target as Quemoy and Matsu. But it was not until the 1958 episode that these fears seemed to have a more solid basis. The crisis in the autumn over the offshore islands coincided with a particularly heavy propaganda barrage from the Communists against British occupation of Chinese territory. Two Notes were handed to the British chargé d'affaires in Peking. These complained, respectively, about the flight of British aircraft over China and about incidents involving Chinese schools in Hongkong.[47] These protests by the Chinese received scant attention in Britain. To the extent that they were, they tended to be dismissed as propaganda or as tactics connected with the Chinese Communist campaign against Quemoy. But on 4 September, the People's Republic took the more serious step of laying claim to a twelve-mile limit as China's territorial sea. This move was more unequivocally aimed at Britain, though *The Times'* view was that it was aimed primarily at inhibiting American naval aid to the Chinese Nationalists. The Foreign Office, however, found the Chinese announcement 'no surprise.' It was pointed out that Britain did not recognise territorial waters of more than three miles, and that this had been explained to the Chinese government when the issue arose in diplomatic correspondence as far back as 1951.[48]

If the British government was calmer about the situation, public opinion seemed much more agitated than during the 1954–5 crisis. Partly this was due to the growing appreciation of the nature of nuclear weapons, especially on the part of the Labour Party Opposition. American support of Chinese Nationalist tenure of Quemoy and Matsu was fiercely criticised. Nothing had been done since 1949, when the People's Republic was established, *The Times* complained, 'to disburden the world of an untenable commitment and a risk which is likely to bring it periodically to the brink of war and one day perhaps over it.' A forceful strategic argument to support this position was given by Sir John Slessor in corresponence to the *Daily Telegraph*. A cardinal point in Western policy should be 'to avoid by political action the possibility of being committed to use force in an issue which is not vital, but which still involves any chance, however remote, of our being faced, if things go wrong for us, with the alternatives of local failure or general war.'[49] Such remarks did not spring from naivete about Chinese Communist motivations. Indeed there seemed to be a cool appreciation of

Peking's grasp of the principles of *realpolitik*. There was
speculation that the People's Republic was pursuing the
objective of splitting Britain and America. Alternatively, and
with events in the Middle East still fresh in mind, it was thought
that the Communist world as a whole was engaged in a series of
global probes, testing Western determination first at one point
and then at another. And it was still thought likely that the
Chinese Communist leadership was using foreign adventures as a
means of distracting the Chinese people from troubles at home.

The Labour Party for its part sketched in the details of an
alternative policy to that being implemented by the Foreign
Office. A crucial consideration, in the thinking of Gaitskell and
his colleagues, was nuclear technology. The use of nuclear
weapons, the Opposition Leader insisted in a letter to the Prime
Minister, would be 'sheer lunacy.' The point was driven home
by Bertrand Russell in correspondence to the *Guardian*. In a
series of speeches, key Labour Party figures formulated their
critique of the government. Gaitskell itemised the main points
in a speech on September 16. It was the belief of the
Opposition

> (1) that the Peking Government should now be recognised as
> the Government of China and take its rightful place in the
> United Nations; (2) Formosa and the Pescadores should for a
> period be placed under United Nations administration;
> (3) Chiang's Government should accordingly withdraw;
> (4) after a period the people of the islands should be free to
> make their own decision, without intimidation, either to be
> independent or to join China.[50]

This is in line with the position arrived at during the 1954—5
crisis by Attlee. There was, if anything, still less chance in 1958
of their being adopted as realistic courses of action by the
British and United States governments. This too was acknowledged. In his letter to Macmillan, the opposition leader
understood the government's reluctance to publicise differences
between allies, but added: 'we regard the situation as far too
serious for this consideration to be decisive.' Nobody could say,
he continued, 'whether the Government have quietly acquiesced
in American intentions or are trying to stop them going to
war ... "My ally right or wrong" may have some emotional
appeal but it is not the principle on which the Atlantic Alliance

is based.' The point made little impact on the government. The Prime Minister told TUC leaders who came to Downing Street to lend support to the Shadow Cabinet's proposals, that it was much better to keep the crisis at the level of private consultations and diplomatic negotiations rather than make public declarations.

The impact of all this on Peking is interesting. In contrast to 1954–5, when the Chinese Communist media expended a good deal of energy responding point by point to almost every analysis of the Far Eastern situation coming out of Britain, Peking now, in 1958, resorted far more to slogans in its condemnation of most shades of British opinion. The Foreign Secretary was simply 'parrotting Dulles' in his public statements. The Labour Party was singled out for no special treatment, but was simply dismissed out of hand in Peking's denunciations of the 'Dulles–Lloyd–Attlee line' to create two Chinas. Britain, in other words, had at least revealed her true colours for what they were. As the *People's Daily* put it in December 1958, 'a gang advocating the creation of "two Chinas" has long made its appearance in British ruling circles. In the past those out of power shouted more vigorously than those in power. But now the British Government has come out in the open and is behaving more blatantly and viciously than at any other time.'[51]

The two offshore islands crises of the 1950s — there was further tension at intervals in the 1960s — may be viewed as a final attempt by Peking to contest the emerging reality of two Chinas. If this is true, the effort failed. During the first of the crises, in 1954–5, Western policies, both British and American, reflected a growing presumption that there *were* two Chinas in existence. The realisation involved a compromise with earlier views on the part of both London and Washington. It implied, for the United States, some degree of acceptance of the *de facto* position: that, no matter how undesirable the fact of Communist control of China might be, nevertheless the fact was there and was unavoidable. It was this reasoning that had played a large part in the British decision to extend diplomatic recognition to the People's Republic in 1950. Moreover, if the status quo in China was to be accepted as a fact, then it was imperative for the interests of Western security that Chiang

Kai-shek be prevented from trying to return with glory to the mainland. The commencement of talks between Washington and Peking, and the passing through Congress of the United States treaty with Nationalist China, together signalled the 're-leashing' of Chiang after his brief spell in the open.

The British government too moved from its earlier position and went some way during the 1954–5 crisis towards meeting Washington. Nothing like a formal commitment to Formosa emerged from London during this period, nor would that have been conceivable in the circumstances. But at the same time the government, ever pragmatic, appreciated well the fact of Nationalist rule on Taiwan. It took no real steps to try and persuade the United States or other NATO allies of the desirability of changing the Formosan status quo. Real efforts were made, however, on the separate question of the smaller islands, Quemoy and Matsu in particular, which London felt properly belonged to Communist China and which in the British view constituted a perennial threat to world peace. This opinion persisted into the 1958 crisis. But by then, after the trauma of Suez, Britain was far less predisposed to depart from the United States line. The Far East was an area of crucial United States rather than of British interests.

8 Towards Normalisation

British recognition of Peking in 1950 did not produce worth-while results. The fact was often commented on in other countries when they assessed their own future relations with the People's Republic of China. An exchange of ambassadors did not finally take place until 1972. This normalisation emerged, ironically, out of one of the lowest points in Sino-British relations. A wave of arrests of British subjects, and even physical assaults on diplomats, accompanied the heat of the Cultural Revolution. In settling these questions, the British government refused all demands from public opinion for retaliation against the Chinese; and exchanges between British and Chinese officials gradually merged into the broader question of establishing at last full diplomatic relations. In 1971, as part of these moves, Britain also voted for Peking in the Chinese representation question at the United Nations, and after the 1970 vote stood opposed to proposals that the issue be treated as an 'important' one that required a two-thirds majority. In the aftermath of these events, Sino-British cultural and trading ties were further consolidated, and ministerial visits exchanged. Factors external to Sino-British relations had now become decisive. In particular, British membership of the EEC came to be seen in Peking as a valuable contribution to the creation of a solid anti-Soviet bloc on Moscow's western flank. Moves towards normalisation also ran parallel with a much wider Sino-Western rapprochement, of which the improvement of Britain's relations with Peking was one facet.

The reverberations from the Cultural Revolution had been felt in Hongkong in 1966, but the main impact came the following year. There were a number of indications that Britain was being singled out as a special target. In February, Britain was accused of plotting with the USSR against China during

Kosygin's visit to London. In May, Chou En-lai appeared at a major anti-British rally in Peking. Two British diplomats were kicked and smeared with glue, and a strike was staged of all Chinese employed by the British mission. In June, Red Guards stormed the building in protest against British involvement in the Middle East war. In July, two diplomats were pelted with tomatoes, Chinese troops surrounded the British mission, and tighter restrictions were placed on the movement of officials. Finally, on 22 August, the mission was sacked. British staff were forced to evacuate and operate from temporary premises. The following month, the Shanghai Revolutionary Committee took over the Shanghai office of the British mission. Official complaints were lodged by the Chinese government concerning the violation of Chinese air space by British aircraft and helicopters based in Hongkong. There were periodic accusations relating to the use of Hongkong by United States warships. A number of Britons were also detained by the authorities; and this became the focus of British official and public attention during the next two years.

The more immediate task for Britain, of getting diplomatic links back to pre-Cultural Revolution normality, proved not too difficult. The Prime Minister, who returned from holiday to London specially to deal with the August violence, noted drily later: 'We did not retaliate in kind against the Chinese in Portland Place.'[1] However, the movement of Chinese officials in London was restricted. Enforcement of the Order in Council by the police led to an attack on them by staff of the Chinese mission in which axes and other weapons were used. This stage of mutual diplomatic restrictions did not last long. In November 1967, the government began to lift the restrictions on Chinese diplomats, and the police cordon round the legation was lifted. This was done, the Foreign Office let it be known, in anticipation of a resumption of closer relations. Also in November, British staff in Peking returned to the embassy building, and the Union Jack was raised. At the end of the month, the Chinese in turn eased movement restrictions on British officials, and a trickle of exit visas started. The situation improved still further after April 1968, when the British government lifted all remaining restrictions placed on the staff of the Chinese chargé d'affaires in London. But he was informed at the same time 'that we expect full reciprocity in the lifting of restrictions and the rapid issue of outstanding visas for our staff to leave China.'[2] It was not until August, however, that a visa was issued for the chargé d'affaires in Peking, Sir Donald Hopson; after his departure, only a skeletal British staff remained for the time being.

The British handling of the question of diplomatic restrictions now set the tone for the government's approach to the much more difficult issues posed by Chinese detentions of British subjects. It refused to accede to the often vociferous public demands for some form of retaliation against China. Whenever possible, moreover, the Foreign Office tried to avoid dramatising incidents, and to persuade critics of the value of quiet but vigorous diplomatic representations to Chinese officials in Peking and London. It was believed that the present situation in China was essentially temporary. The fervour of the Cultural Revolution could not last for ever. One important consequence was thought to be a breakdown of authority between the centre in Peking and outlying cities, notably Shanghai and Canton as far as British interests were concerned. It would, therefore, be unwise to inflict sanctions against Peking when local extremists outside its control indulged in anti-British actions. Not only might patience be rewarded in the long run by a return to normality; the immediate situation might well be worsened if hotheads in China were able to point to public outcry in Britain as evidence that hard-line policies were effective in dealings with British imperialism. Thus in mid-August 1967, the Foreign Secretary merely 'regretted' China's attitude to Britain. In a letter to the Chinese Foreign Minister at the end of the month — after the sack of the British mission — Brown 'sought his cooperation to bring the situation back to normal and to set both countries on a better course in their relations.' It was confirmed in November that 'we stand ready to do everything possible to improve relations if the Chinese on their side are ready to cooperate with us on this.'[3]

However, public indignation could not be contained, particularly over two cases. Anthony Grey, the Reuters correspondent in Peking, was put under house arrest in July 1967. All outside communication with him was cut the following month. It gradually became clear that his detention was in retaliation for arrests of pro-Communist activists in Hongkong. George Watt, working for Vickers-Zimmer, Ltd, on a contract to erect a plant at Lanchow, was arrested in 1967 and sentenced to three years' imprisonment for espionage in March 1968. The latter case was further complicated by its being used for wider purposes by the Chinese. The 'unearthing of the British spy case' was held up as 'a tremendous success in the Great Proletarian Cultural Revolution and a great victory for Mao Tse-tung's thought.' The charge against Watt was that he had 'engaged in espionage activities directed against the People's Republic of China and rendered active service to the British imperialist policy of aggression.' More specifically, he 'stole by means of spying important intelligence about China's military, political, and economic affairs and the Great Proletarian Cultural Revolution, and stealthily took large numbers of photographs of prohibited areas in China.' The various stages of the case were accompanied by denunciations of the activities of 'the British imperialist intelligence organisations.'[4]

The British Government's response was cautious. First, persistent representations were made, mainly in Peking but also in London, with the object of gaining consular access to detained Britons, and of acquiring information on any charges being brought against them in Chinese courts. Secondly, Chinese behaviour was condemned in public statements. The treatment of Grey was described variously as 'indefensible', 'deplorable', 'inhumane and entirely contrary to accepted international practice', 'disgraceful', or 'scandalous'. And thirdly, public clamour was checked as far as possible. Thus at first the Foreign Office advised against publicity in Grey's case, though this course was dropped later. Similarly, a representative of Vickers-Zimmer, explaining in March 1968, why no details had been released of Watt's arrest the previous September, said: 'You can play this two ways. In conjunction with the Foreign Office we decided to keep things quiet. We felt this was the best course.'[5]

Chinese intransigeance soon rendered this latter policy temporarily unworkable. Parliamentary and public pressure concerning Grey gathered momentum from early 1968. Douglas-Home, for the Opposition, regarded the various detentions as 'a serious matter.' The government should 'make the strongest possible representations to the Chinese because this is a situation which cannot be tolerated and there must be some retaliatory action taken if this is to go on.' The chairman of the all-party Commons committee on Hongkong demanded steps to reimpose restrictions on the movement of New China News Agency correspondents in London. Indignation on both sides of the House led to an adjournment debate on detained British subjects in China in June.[6] The *Daily Telegraph* kept up throughout this period a sustained attack on government policy. 'The British Government's reaction has been predictably wet ... who are we trying not to offend?... If the Foreign Office thinks that diplomatic pleadings impress the Chinese, it is living in cloud-cuckoo-land. The only effective move would be an embargo on British trade with China.'[7] Other moves being called for at this time included closing the Peking mission entirely once British staff had acquired exit visas; not supporting Peking's candidature for the United Nations seat; some form of collective international protest; and the denial of privileges to Chinese diplomats and news agency staff in London.

There are indications, however, that the Foreign Office's arguments had some effect. In June 1968, Rodgers stated that 'we have, of course, considered frequently and with the very greatest care whether there were measures we might take which would bring effective pressure to bear on the Chinese authorities.' But he urged against 'striking attitudes which, frankly, would yield no results. We must remember that China today is a unique case where none of the normal rules appear to apply.'[8] The dilemma was that all schemes for retaliation ultimately implied a greater degree of isolation for Peking. It was the government's view that this isolation was itself one of the chief factors making for Chinese hostility to the outside world. Thus in November 1968, the Foreign Secretary refused on these grounds to institute sanctions in connection with the issue of Chinese representation in the United Nations. After leaving his post in Peking, Hopson emphasised that 'there are clearly important reasons for maintaining relations with the most populous nation and one which is becoming a nuclear power.' The Chinese government, he thought, wanted to return to more normal diplomatic relations.[9]

These arguments seem to have convinced the press of the lack of scope for British manoeuvre. 'Unfortunately,' the *Telegraph* acknowledged in September, 'there is very little Britain can do to encourage the Chinese to behave in a grown-up way instead of acting like schoolboy gangsters.' Reprisals would only make matters worse for Britons in China.[10] And during 1968, Grey's situation marginally improved. In April, he was permitted a visit by the British chargé d'affaires. One factor making for British restraint was a belief that Grey would be released at the end of the year. The Chinese had reiterated that he had been detained in reprisal for the Hongkong arrests of 1967, in particular that of one Hsueh P'ing. He was due for release in the middle of November. 'In the circumstances,' Stewart told the Commons two days later, 'we must hope for the speedy release of Mr. Grey.'[11] Guarded optimism was also expressed by the Prime Minister.

This expectation proved unfounded. Hongkong Communist sources made it known, first, that only Grey's case was open for negotiation; and, secondly, that he could not be released until all the arrested Chinese 'journalists' in Hongkong had regained their liberty. Late in December, Peking launched a renewed attack. In order 'to mislead public opinion and divert the resentment of the people at home,' the government had made use of Grey 'to fan up an anti-China outcry.' The real source of the problem it declared, was the repression and brutality of the Hongkong authorities. British officials had themselves visited Grey and admitted that he was being treated leniently, which was 'a forceful slap in the face of their superior.' In conclusion, since 'the Hongkong British authorities continue to keep the 13 patriotic Chinese journalists in jail, the Chinese Government is fully justified in continuing to restrict Grey's freedom of movement.'[12]

Public protest, already gathering force at the end of 1968, grew in strength during 1969. The press itself came to be much more actively involved. The General Secretary of the National Union of Journalists, also now in touch with the Foreign Office, argued that a constant barrage of publicity was the best weapon. The International Press Institute protested to Chou En-lai in October 1968; Reuters lodged an appeal the following month; the International Federation of Journalists, on the request of the British union, asked for full publicity; and Fleet Street journalists unsuccessfully petitioned the Chinese mission in London. Almost daily coverage was given the Grey case. *The Economist* urged the government to 'show a tooth', and demanded the closure of the Chinese news agency office in London. The *Guardian* suggested that the BBC expand its foreign-language coverage of the case. The most extreme, if ambiguous, sentiment came from the *Daily Express* in May 1969: 'The question that should be considered now is how much longer any Chinese citizens should be tolerated in this country.'[13] Apart from the comparatively rare suggestion in the Commons that Grey was the victim of Hongkong's policy of arresting troublemakers, there were no widespread demands for concessions. The *Guardian* argued on several occasions that the Hongkong arrests and the Grey case were not comparable, and that the principle of reciprocity did not apply. The Opposition leadership refrained from pressing for a vigorous programme of retaliations. Douglas-Home, however, argued that it was 'very important that our restraint should not be misunderstood overseas.'[14]

The Communist press also took up the question. The *Morning Star* stated that by freeing Grey, Peking would increase China's standing in the world, and that the move would be welcomed by progressive people in Britain. Its staff signed the Fleet Street petition presented to the Chinese mission at the end of 1968. This was not, however, so important a development as it might have been in the 1950s. In the Chinese view, the Communist Party was too pro-Soviet. Contacts were maintained rather with Reg Birch as head of the Central Committee of the Communist Party of Britain (Marxist-Leninist). Other organisations sympathetic to China refused to join the movement. The Society for Anglo-Chinese Understanding, for example, turned down a request from the relatives of another detained journalist to dissociate itself from the Chinese action, on the grounds that their distress was being used by the British government for anti-Chinese propaganda.[15]

The Foreign Office continued its representations to the Chinese authorities, while emphasising the virtues of quiet diplomacy. But it clearly could not enter into negotiations on Chinese terms. This would involve questions of political interference in the judicial process. The government consistently maintained that 'as regards the Chinese prisoners in Hongkong, they were arrested and sentenced in the courts to terms of imprisonments for their part in the violent disturbances in the Colony in 1967 and are in no way comparable to the British subjects detained in China.'[16] This 'solemn pretence', as the *Sunday Times'* Hongkong correspondent called it, was essential in the context of exchanges between Hongkong and London. In Hongkong, it was being emphasised that early releases for political reasons would create a dangerous precedent; would cause serious grievances among ordinary convicts; and would outrage a public still smarting at the 1967 violence. However, a steady flow of releases continued during 1969. An under-standing between British and Chinese officials seems finally to have been reached during the markedly improved diplomatic atmosphere of the summer. (In June, for example, the chargé d'affaires went on a tour of Chinese cities, the first time this had been allowed since 1967.) The date for the release of the last Hongkong journalist was set for 3 October. Grey was summoned to the Chinese Foreign Ministry the next day and informed that 'since the Hongkong British authorities had already released all the patriotic Chinese journalists', he was now free.[17]

By October 1969, then, two important steps had been taken to lift Sino-British relations out of the depths of the Cultural Revolution phase. Chinese and British officials had been freed of the additional restrictions on their movement imposed by each government in 1967; and the release of Grey and the Hongkong journalists had gone a long way towards separating the affairs of the colony from issues in Sino-British diplomatic relations. From now on, a different approach to common problems emerged. Despite arrests of more Britons, British officials continued to point to evidence of a Chinese softening. The Foreign Office's policy of extreme patience was exem-plified in various incidents during 1970. In March, the Chinese released the ship *Glenfalloch* after British representations; Britain argued that it had been detained as a result of overzealousness by local Shanghai officials. In the case of the arrest of two merchant navy officers the same month, the government drew attention to the uncertainty which existed about harbour regulations in Shanghai, and suggested that accusations of a violation of Chinese regulations had arisen from a misunderstanding. At the same time, 'vigorous pressures'[18] were put on Hongkong for still more releases of prisoners, particularly after the embarrassment caused by the death of a Communist in a Hongkong jail in December 1969.

The upshot of this sensitive interim period was a further

improvement in relations in 1970. In Britain, Chinese officials began attending social functions, including Ascot and a Buckingham Palace garden party. The improvement was noted with approval by the Prime Minister: 'it was, at this point, only at the level of gestures; but in Peking gestures are not accidental — they included a long and friendly talk which Mao Tse-tung chose to have with our chargé d'affaires at a diplomatic reception.'[19] A message of greeting was sent the same month on the occasion of the Queen's birthday. The way was thus prepared for talks aimed at raising relations to a level of normality going beyond that of the pre-Cultural Revolution years.

That more was potentially at stake than the immediate issues had been implicit in the British approach from the outset. These hints grew in 1970. Thus in his exchanges with Chinese officials over the arrests of the merchant navy officers in March, Thomson took the opportunity to ask for a 'real improvement' in Anglo-Chinese relations; emphasised that the level of trade between the two countries had risen sharply; and pointed to the recent improvement in the diplomatic climate.[20] By August, *The Times* thought that relations were already back to the pre-Cultural Revolution level. In October, a British official returning from Peking referred to the Chinese government's continued detention of six Britons in terms of the obstacles this posed for an improvement in Sino-British relations. An added spur was the change now fully evident in United States thinking. By the winter of 1968—9, it was already clear what the future evolution of Washington's China policy was likely to be; though at the time there was scepticism on the part of British officials on the chances of America being able to pull off a successful rapprochement. In contrast to 1949, however, only minimal efforts at a concerted Anglo-American approach were made, though each side was kept well briefed of the other's actions. The second incentive was provided by evidence that the Chinese themselves, in the aftermath of the height of the Cultural Revolution, and given the continued high tension in Sino-Soviet relations, were interested in promoting contacts with the West.

Prior to, and side by side with, official Sino-British talks went a series of unofficial exchanges and partial agreements. These are discussed more fully later. All were important, however

marginally, for contributing to the atmosphere of a willingness
to tackle and solve outstanding problems that was the chief
characteristic of this period. In 1970, for example, discussions
were held on the institution of a direct telephone service
between London and Peking. This had ceased functioning in
1949; it began again in April 1971. Late in 1970, a BBC
Television *Panorama* team was allowed into China; parcel post
between Hongkong and China was resumed; and the Chinese
announced that they would release the last remaining Briton
held who was not a permanent resident, the last of those, that
is, for whom the British government considered it had a moral,
as against merely a juridical, responsibility. This particular
release was widely interpreted as conclusive evidence of a new
approach on the part of Peking, since it was taken apparently
on China's initiative, and not as part of the painfully slow
tit-for-tat that had been a feature of earlier developments. In
this situation, the arrest of another merchant navy officer who
not only admitted to spying on Chinese warships, but added
that he had been approached for this purpose by the Royal
Navy, caused acute embarrassment in Whitehall. However, the
officer later retracted his statement, and no harm was done to
Sino-British relations.

Formal talks on the exchange of ambassadors commenced in
Peking early in 1971. Three major issues arose: the question of
Chinese representation in the United Nations; the status of the
British consulate at Tamsui on Formosa; and the question of
the British government's view of the legal status of Taiwan. The
British chargé d'affaires was elevated from *ad interim* to *en titre*
status.

Other questions lay in the background, but did not impinge
on the negotiations. Soon after they began, Peking indicated
that the Chinese government would bear the full cost of
rebuilding the British mission damaged in the 1967 violence. In
March, Chou En-lai expressed his regrets to the chargé d'affaires
at the incident: it had happened against the wishes of the
Chinese government and the Communist Party; the crowd in
Peking had been angered by the arrest of Chinese newspaper
workers in Hongkong, but it was 'bad elements' which had
incited it to attack the building.[21] Detentions and arrests were
not an issue. In April 1971, the Chinese furnished information

for the first time on Britons still detained. In January 1972, the British government refused to raise the case of one of them in the context of the negotiations, since this would help neither the individual concerned nor the prospects of success in the talks. Similarly, the situation in Hongkong, though of periodic concern to the Chinese, does not seem to have figured in the negotiations. Its status was, however, increasingly not described on the British side as a colony, out of a wish to accommodate the Chinese view that it was part of Chinese territory under British occupation. The matter remained sensitive. During the Foreign Secretary's visit to Peking in 1972, there was visible tension at one slip of the tongue by Douglas-Home when referring to Hongkong; it was, however, quickly passed over by Chou.[22]

Considering the backlog of obstacles, the talks themselves proceeded with reasonable speed. Both sides were keen to reach agreement. Royle afterwards quoted Chiao Kuan-hua's comment: 'Problems are big or little depending on the efforts made to solve them.'[23] Various extraneous factors influenced their course and duration. Early in the summer, Britain appears to have accepted an American request to tread water for a time so as to give United States officials time to complete arrangements for President Nixon's visit to Peking. After this trip had been announced, delays were evident in the Sino-British talks. They were attributed variously to problems in the Chinese hierarchy, or to China's own setting of improved relations with the United States as a higher priority. A more serious problem arose following the successful vote in the autumn of 1971 on Peking's entry into the United Nations. A slowdown in Chinese momentum, and some hardening of Peking's position on Taiwan, became noticeable. As a result, Britain allowed the talks to lapse for a time. They were resumed for a final successful burst in February.

In contrast to 1950, the question of Chinese representation in the United Nations raised no major difficulties. In 1961, Britain had begun to vote for Peking. She maintained, however, that the question was an 'important' one, requiring a two-thirds majority for the passage of a resolution. This continued until 1970. In that year, the Albanian resolution supporting Peking's admission secured for the first time a simple majority in the

General Assembly. Britain then decided in future to vote against the resolution declaring the question 'important'; otherwise, 'the result could be to keep Peking out merely by a procedural motion.'[24]

This policy change came at the end of a public debate stretching back several years. Questions about Peking's participation arose with almost monotonous regularity from the Labour back benches. Successive governments, whether Labour or Conservative, had been criticised for acquiescing in the 'procedural wrangle' designed by Washington to postpone indefinitely Peking's admission. Ministers at first merely repeated the government's belief that the question was important, in both the common-sense and the Charter meanings. Asian conflicts strengthened Labour demands. Wilson's approach to a settlement of the Vietnam war in May 1970, included the statement: 'the whole House recognises the undeniable very much wider fact, which overlies all conflict in Asia, that the conflict of South-east Asia . . . cannot be decided on a world scale without the representation on a world scale, in the United Nations, of the Chinese Government and the Chinese people.'[25] The general argument was shared by most shades of opinion in Britain, however; though Conservatives tended to draw rather more attention to the presence on the Security Council of two Communist vetoes, the unlikelihood of Peking's participation modifying Chinese policies in Asia or elsewhere, the obstructionist attitude likely to be adopted by its delegates in United Nations debates, and, finally, the dangers of excluding the representatives of pro-Western Chinese and native Formosans on Taiwan.

The last point prompted a measure of support for some form of two-Chinas solution to the representation issue. The *Guardian* in 1970–1 advocated Peking's taking the Security Council seat, while Taiwan retained a place in the General Assembly. Jeremy Thorpe, the Liberal leader, also expressed support for the view that both Chinas should be members of the UN.[26] Whether or not the government itself toyed with the idea, it was apparent that dual representation was not practical politics. The two-Chinas solution, the government argued, was 'superficially attractive, but it does not take into account the fact that neither Peking nor Taiwan is willing to accept that there could be a two-Chinas solution, since they both claim to represent the whole of China.' In these circumstances, the British government took the view that 'the exclusion of the 14 million inhabitants of Taiwan is a lesser evil than the continued exclusion of the representatives of 750 million people in China.'[27]

If the situation at the United Nations posed no obstacle to Sino-British diplomatic relations, the question of Taiwan did. The Chinese insisted that Britain 'cut off its tail' on the island. Two questions were closely related. The first, the retention by the British government of a consul stationed at Tamsui, was more important in 1971 than it had been in the 1950 exchanges. At the earlier date, the expectation, on both the British and the Chinese sides, had been that the island would fall under Communist jurisdiction at some point during that summer. By 1971, the Nationalist authorities were firmly entrenched, and had established themselves as a rival Chinese government enjoying a wide measure of international recognition. The presence of a British consul in these changed circumstances was therefore unacceptable. In 1971, Douglas-Home repeated the British view that the consul was accredited not to the Nationalist authorities *qua* government of China, but rather to the provincial authorities of the Nationalist regime responsible for administering Taiwan's affairs.[28] During the negotiations in Peking, the British position came to be that if an agreement on an exchange of ambassadors were reached, then Britain would be prepared to withdraw the consulate. There was, that is, no suggestion that such a step could be made prior to an agreement. The cutting of the last official link with Taiwan was thus announced at the same time as the agreement on the exchange of ambassadors between London and Peking.

The final, and immeasurably more important, issue related to the British view of the legal status of Taiwan. The British government's position was particularly difficult because of the stand taken in 1955 that the status of the island had not finally been determined. This had to be reconciled with the simple Chinese view: that there was only one government of China, and that Taiwan fell under its jurisdiction as a province of China. All positions diverging in the slightest from this had in the past been denounced as two-Chinas plots. As in the resolution of this problem in the agreements reached between China and other states around this time, the key was largely semantic, though not the less important or difficult to arrive at for that.

On 1 August 1971, Army Day statements in Peking included criticism of the 'fallacy that "the title to Taiwan remains to be settled." ' This was taken by observers as an attack on the British government's own position. It was also seen as indicating a harder line in Peking on the question following the announcement of President Nixon's forthcoming visit to China. The question arose more stubbornly after the successful vote on Peking's entry to the United Nations in the autumn. In December, Chou declared that Britain 'must correct' the anomaly in her attitude to China, and abandon her support for Taiwan. The Prime Minister shortly afterwards confirmed in the Commons that China regarded the attitude of the British government towards the future of Taiwan as the major stumbling block to the alteration of diplomatic relations.[29] And it was on this point that the talks got bogged down towards the end of the year. Britain, it seems, was being treated differently from other states, partly because of her own history, and partly because of the subtly changed outlook in Peking following the Kissinger talks and the UN vote. The *Financial Times* pointed out in August that the agreement between Turkey and the People's Republic of China on the establishment of diplomatic relations had made no reference to Taiwan at all. There were hopes that a semantic compromise might be worked out along the lines variously described as 'the Canadian formula' or 'the Belgian formula'. The Chinese government, that is, would state its position on Taiwan's being an inalienable part of Chinese territory; and the recognising government would 'take note' of the Chinese position. This optimism came to nothing when it appeared that in Britain's own case such phraseology was not acceptable.

The issue was not finally resolved until the following year. Britain's new chargé d'affaires, Sir John Addis, arrived in Peking and held talks with Chinese officials in early and mid-February, and again during the first week of March 1972. The new year also brought a fresh round of opposition criticisms of government obstructionism. Healey contrasted the Foreign Office's view with Nixon's earlier statement on Taiwan, and accused the government of continuing 'a legalistic quibble' on the status of the island.[30] By February, though, it was clear that both sides were prepared to solve the question by a judicious choice of phrasing. The compromise was contained both in the terms of the final agreement, and also in remarks made at the same time in the Commons by the Foreign Secretary.

The communique of agreement, signed by Chiao and Addis in Peking on 13 March, stated that

> both confirming the principles of mutual respect for sovereignty and territorial integrity, non-interference in each other's internal affairs and equality and mutual benefit, the Government of the People's Republic of China and the Government of the United Kingdom have decided to raise the level of their respective diplomatic representatives in each other's capitals from chargé d'affaires to ambassador as from 13 March 1972.

The British government, 'acknowledging the position of the Chinese Government that Taiwan is a province of the People's Republic of China, have decided to remove their official representation in Taiwan.' It also 'recognised the Government of the People's Republic of China as the sole legal government of China.' For its part, the government of the People's Republic of China 'appreciated the above stand of the Government of the United Kingdom.' Speaking in the Commons the same day, Douglas-Home said that both the Government of the People's Republic of China and Taipeh maintained that Taiwan was part of China. 'We held the view both at Cairo and at Potsdam that Taiwan should be restored to China. That view has not changed. We think that the Taiwan question is China's internal affair to be settled by the Chinese people themselves.'[31] The first part of this remark is a selective interpretation of Britain's past positions on Taiwan; the second part goes further towards meeting Peking's view than had Britain on any occasion hitherto.

In the months following, Sino-British relations were expanded and consolidated. Ministerial visits were exchanged on a level and frequency surpassing earlier contacts. Royle's visit to Peking in June 1972, made what one British official described as 'a real breakthrough' in relations.[32] The talks centred on two main topics. First, Britain and China agreed on a number of specific ideas to be pursued later by their respective embassy staffs on cultural exchanges, in particular theatrical and orchestral visits and exchanges in the field of art and sport. This side of the talks led eventually to the staging of the Chinese antiquities exhibition in London in 1973. Secondly, trade relations were reviewed, particular attention being given to Chinese interest in purchasing British civil aircraft. Developments in Sino-British trade relations are discussed shortly. Then at the end of October, the Foreign Secretary arrived in Peking. Douglas-Home had already, as early as August 1971, said that he would 'very much like to visit China at some time, if that were convenient to the Chinese.'[33] The continuing official exchanges on cultural links were discussed, and a programme of student exchanges approved. Agreement was also reached on the appointment of Defence Attaches in each country's Embassies. Finally, it was agreed that two-way ministerial visits would continue over the next few months. Britain and China, the Foreign Secretary stated, 'should acquire the habit of consulation at Government level ... We need to know your thoughts on many issues which face the world ... this is still a world of high risk.'[34] He also made reference to Britain's hope of making an 'effective and distinctive' contribution to relations between the EEC and the rest of the world, including East Asia. The Chinese, both formally and informally, were by now increasingly drawing attention to the value of a European Community based on what was seen to be Britain's 'sound' attitude towards the Soviet Union. The two sides also had wide-ranging discussions on world problems, including Vietnam and the affairs of the Indian sub-continent. As recently as December 1971, the latter situation had brought forth a sharp attack from Chou En-lai on the responsibility of British colonialism for conflict in the region. The Chinese Foreign Minister paid a return visit to London in mid-1973.

But for the exigencies of British politics prior to the first 1974 General Election, these exchanges would have been crowned by the first visit of a British Prime Minister to the People's Republic of China. During the Cultural Revolution, a number of Labour back-benchers had tabled questions asking if the Prime Minister had plans to visit China, as part of their advocacy of fuller contacts between China and the West. These continued sporadically until June 1973, when Heath announced that he had accepted an invitation to visit Peking. It finally took place in May 1974, after two postponements caused by British economic and political problems. By this latter date, however, Heath was once more Leader of the Opposition. It is a telling comment on the importance attached by the Chinese to a strong EEC grouping including Britain, that the invitation remained with Heath personally rather than with the Prime Minister of the day. A Chinese official had been quoted in 1972 as saying that Heath and Mao had a lot in common in their fears of both the United States and the Soviet Union.[35] According to *The Times'* account, the only observable difference between the protocol for Heath's visit and that for a head of state was the absence of the Peking diplomatic corps at the welcoming ceremony, other than officials from the British embassy. The visit included a meeting with Mao Tse-tung. Heath was praised by Teng Hsiao-ping for attaching importance to the development of Sino-British relations, and for standing for the unity of Western Europe. He responded in like terms: 'It is right that you in China and we in Europe and many other countries across the world should have our say — and that when we speak the superpowers should listen.'[36]

Even before the commencement of talks on the exchange of ambassadors, cultural and other exchanges between China and Britain were beginning again. From 1972, these increased both in number and variety. Talks on cultural exchanges were initiated by Royle in his visit in June. In 1973, a programme of exchanges was agreed upon between China and the British Council together with the Great Britain–China Committee. The two-way visits of this period cannot be summarised briefly; but some indication at least can be given of their scope. China kept up its now traditional contacts with sympathetic Communists. In the 1970s, this meant the Communist Party of Britain (Marxist-Leninist). The Communist Party itself was unwelcome. In April 1974, for example, the Chinese authorities refused a visa for Michael McGahey as leader of a National Union of Mineworkers' delegation, thus forcing its cancellation.[37] Other trade union delegations did visit China, though; and the Society for Anglo-Chinese Understanding resumed its programme of visits.

These kinds of older links were considerably augmented in the early 1970s. Well-publicised sporting exchanges preceded the agreement to exchange ambassadors; a British table-tennis team visited Peking in April 1971, and was received by Chou; a Chinese team, received by Heath, came to Britain in December. More significantly for longer-term relations, British news media began to enjoy greater access to China. A second BBC–television team went in 1971. The national dailies sent their own correspondents to cover the visits of the British table-tennis team and of the Foreign Secretary and Heath later. In October 1972, *The Times* established an office in Peking, and Lord Thomson visited China. The Norwegian journalist reporting for *The Times* and the *Sunday Times* had been expelled in 1967; in November 1970, the only representatives of the Western press corps in Peking were the correspondent for the Toronto *Globe and Mail,* and two working for international agencies.[38] Visits were paid by delegations of medical specialists and of the Royal Society. In 1973, the London Philharmonic Orchestra toured China. More difficulties were encountered on the more sensitive questions of student exchanges and Western tourism. Negotiations on the latter began in the spring of 1971 (British tours planned in 1967 had been cancelled by the Chinese), and arrangements were finally reached some three years later.

Political and parliamentary links were established or strengthened. A parliamentary delegation travelled to China in the autumn of 1972; another went in November 1973, under the auspices of the Anglo-Chinese Parliamentary Group. During 1971–3 various members of the Labour Opposition front bench met with Chinese officials, though this relationship suffered somewhat as a result of the party's lurch towards anti-Europeanism. Benn visited Peking in September 1971, and put forward a five-year programme of exchanges; these included plans for the greater encouragement of Chinese language teaching in Britain, the 'twinning' of British and Chinese cities, and continued links in the sporting, cultural, trading and other fields.[39] Finally, this upsurge of interest was matched on the Chinese side by visits of scientists, journalists, and other specialists; and by the sending of Chinese students to study in Britain. In 1974, the London and Peking zoos exchanged giant pandas and white rhinos, and the Chinese staged an industrial and handicrafts exhibition at Olympia. The high point of Chinese cultural diplomacy was reached in the spectacular exhibition of art treasures and antiquities opened in London by the Prime Minister in September 1973.[40]

Mention was made in an earlier chapter of the various
organisations in Britain which emerged in the 1950s to handle
trade relations with China. This survey can now be completed.
One outcome of the 1972 agreement was the establishment of a
Great Britain–China Committee, with official British support,
'to promote contacts of all kinds between Britain and China.'
Malcolm MacDonald and Lord Trevelyan, both distinguished
former British officials in the Far East, became respectively
President and Vice-President of the new body. It changed its
designation to a Centre in July 1974, upon taking a permanent
staff and office in London, and encouraging public membership.
It operated 'with the encouragement of Her Majesty's Government for the purpose of promoting on an unofficial basis
understanding between the peoples of the United Kingdom and
the People's Republic of China, by fostering closer cultural,
social and economic contacts between them. It is non-political
in character.'[41] The Foreign Secretary's speech in opening it was
indicative of the good relations then existing between Britain
and China. Over the last few years, Callaghan said, 'we see the
growing flowering of relations between our two countries. I
wouldn't say that they have reached full bloom yet. I hope that
they will do so and we must go on hoping that as nature
progresses, so the bud will open to a flower, and we shall really
feel that we have a lovely bouquet to share.'[42]
More specifically, its role was:

(a) to serve as a non-official channel for contacts between
Chinese and British people interested in China. (b) to make
its premises available as a meeting place in London for
Chinese visitors . . . and British people interested in China.
(c) to hold small receptions for Chinese visitors and for
British people returning from China . . . (d) to organise lec-
ture meetings and seminars. (e) to facilitate in so far as
possible visits to China either by groups or individuals when
these are not catered for by other organisations. (f) to
publish a periodical newsletter for the information of
members.

The Executive Committee of the Centre included a representative of the Foreign and Commonwealth Office, as well as

former officials in their own right, and senior members of the two major political parties. A rule was also adopted that not less than five members of it were required to be MPs.[43]

Other bodies, some of which have been mentioned already in passing, have nonetheless continued functioning. The Society for Anglo-Chinese Understanding grew initially out of a dissatisfaction on the part of a number of individuals sympathetic to China with the overtly ideological bias of the Britain—China Friendship Association in the early 1950s. Its aims, as stated in 1967, were:

> (a) Opposition to our government's policy of hostility to China which has brought Sino-British relations to their present deplorable state; (b) A vigorous programme of spreading knowledge, dispelling misconceptions and countering misrepresentations — focussed on issues that are of key importance to the British people in the present situation; (c) a determined effort to make known the phenomenal progress of the Chinese people since 1949.[44]

Its attraction of a membership much broader than the left in British politics in the mid-1960s must be attributed at least in part to the stature of its leading founder, Joseph Needham. Internal dissensions grew later. Some members complained of too great a readiness on the part of the Society to adopt the Chinese line on international questions and on issues affecting Sino-British relations. The refusal in 1969 to denounce China's detention of a journalist has been mentioned earlier. Other examples included a congratulatory message to the Chinese government on the occasion of China's explosion of its first H-bomb; silence during the 1967 violence in Peking and London; and condemnation of the British government's 'subservience to US anti-China policies' in the period before the successful United Nations vote. These and other events prompted a series of well-publicised resignations by members such as Professors Hugh Trevor-Roper, A.J. Ayer, H.W. Thompson, and Nicholas Kurti, who cited as grounds the Society's becoming merely an agent for Chinese Communist propaganda.[45]

There has been no Nationalist Chinese lobby in Britain. However, some support has been voiced for the argument that British interests would be best served by promoting relations with the Republic of China on Taiwan. During parliamentary debates and questions in 1971–2, a small number of Conservative MPs advocated such a course. The view has received backing through bodies like the Friends of Free China Association. Its objective, as stated in 1968, was:

(1) To make plain to the British public that the freedom of the Chinese people is indispensable to a free Asia and that [this] is necessary to the existence of a free world. To that end we support the free democratic government in Taiwan. (2) . . . that the Chinese Communist government is an integral part of the International Communist Movement whose object . . . is world domination. (3) . . . that [it] has proved by its unparalleled inhuman atrocities to be utterly unworthy of the support of civilised people. (4) . . . that [it] was not elected by the Chinese people and that Communism is entirely alien to the Chinese people.[46]

Finally, the nineteenth-century background of private and university-based scholarship has been sustained. The small China Society, established in 1906, continued its work of encouraging the study in Britain of Chinese language and culture. Centres of academic study have flourished in Oxford, Cambridge, London, Leeds, and other universities. There were some signs during 1971–2 that British sinologists were being left out of the general expansion of contacts, presumably because of Chinese suspicion of their motivations or sources of finance; however, a group of six China specialists did visit China in November, 1974.[47]

The Cultural Revolution came at an unfortunate juncture for British traders. British interest picked up again in 1963–4, after the earlier push of 1957–8 mentioned in a previous chapter. The President of the Board of Trade visited China in 1964, and a British Industrial Exhibition was staged. In the two subsequent years, an ICI exhibition in Peking and a Scientific Instruments Manufacturers' Association exhibition in Tientsin were organised. Around this time also, the Sino-British Trade Council recruited a full-time secretariat, and moved into permanent offices in the building of the Confederation of British Industry in London.

This momentum was hit hard by the Cultural Revolution. Its effects, though, were not felt evenly by all British traders.

The year 1967 saw a general slump in trade, which continued into 1968. Nevertheless, some sales were made by British businessmen, and these continued to be publicised in the commercial and financial press. The Chinese reopened their trade office in London in January 1968, after a closure lasting less than four months. Chinese officials assured a group of British traders in May 1967, that China was willing to increase trade with Britain.[48] (Similarly, officials pointed out in 1974 that the anti-Confucius campaign was entirely internal, and would not affect trade with Britain.)[49] However, during the height of the Cultural Revolution period, it was the '48 Group' of traders rather than those acting under the auspices of the Sino-British Trade Council that was able to keep up its connections. Difficulties were compounded by the strategic controls. In particular, the sale of a £500,000 advanced computer to China by International Computers and Tabulators, Ltd., was the subject of strong objections from the United States from the spring of 1966. United States opposition also halted delivery of a large KDF-9 computer from English Electric.

British political debate on Sino-British trade continued along a now well-trodden path. Labour MPs urged British initiatives to promote it, particularly on the grounds of the weakness of the British economy. The party's 1970 election manifesto argued that trade and technological links might help to bring China into the community of nations. On the other hand, Chinese actions against British subjects stimulated calls for sanctions against Peking. In 1968, the *Daily Telegraph* questioned the morality of Sino-British trade in view of the likelihood of potentially strategic items reaching North Vietnam. 'The current passion for trade with Communist countries smacks of precisely the sort of greed and stupidity which the old Bolsheviks always predicted would lead to the West's downfall.'[50] The government itself stated that there was little that could be done in the circumstances to expand trade.

The first signs of change came in the summer of 1969. The Chinese government appointed a commercial counsellor to London; and British officials began to express confidence that trade was on the increase, and had considerable growth potential. In July, the Bank of China instituted transactions in futures of yuan in London, available only for deals between

China and Britain. By the end of the year, trade had reached almost double the level of that in 1968.

This development was given an official push in 1970. In January, the government lifted quota restrictions on three categories of goods imported from China. In March, a trade minister drew attention to the increase in trade, and expressed the hope that it would continue, despite difficulties over shipping. And towards the end of the year, the *Board of Trade Journal* published a major article by the British commercial counsellor in Peking. Commenting that the Chinese market had been neglected because of the Cultural Revolution, he emphasised China's growing economy and foreign trade, and discussed both the prospects for particular categories of British exports and the ways in which the Export Services Division and the Commercial Relations and Exports Division of the Board of Trade could assist traders.[51] In London, the Chinese commercial counsellor and his staff became more accessible; a number of delegations visited British factories in the north of England. Chinese missions visiting Britain indicated a special interest in machine tools and civil aircraft. In October, the first collective British mission for some time was organised by the '48 group'. It was followed by a visit by John Keswick, President of the Sino-British Trade Council. As a result of his talks with Chinese trade officials, it was agreed that there should be more frequent exchanges of trade missions.

During 1971, the British government took a series of measures to assist trade expansion, partly because the 1970 figures had not kept up the momentum of the previous year. They included encouragement for two-way missions; a reduction of the administrative and quantitative restrictions on imports from China; a strengthening of British commercial representation in Peking; the taking of an initiative to propose the staging of a major British exhibition in Peking; and continued support for the work of the Sino-British Trade Council.[52] In particular, administrative arrangements for imports from China were brought into line with those for imports from the Soviet Union and Eastern Europe. An additional factor was the easing of Sino-American relations. 'As far as Britain is concerned,' the Secretary-General of the Sino-British Trade Council said, 'it means that we have another competitor and a very powerful one at that.'[53]

During his 1972 visit to Peking in the follow-up to the March agreement on the exchange of ambassadors, Royle discussed in particular the sale of British civil aircraft to China. The Foreign Secretary later drew the attention of his Chinese hosts to Britain's ability to supply sophisticated engineering, electronic and other equipment. Early in 1973, the Chinese Minister of Foreign Trade visited London for talks. The British Industrial Technology Exhibition held in Peking in March—April 1973, under the sponsorship of the Department of Trade and Industry in association with the Sino-British Trade Council, represented a high point in post-Cultural Revolution relations. It received official Chinese blessing in the form of a visit from Chou, and provided an opportunity for British ministers — Walker and Heseltine — to probe civil aviation prospects further. The two governments agreed to draw up a two-year programme of trade missions; it was also agreed that there should be more exchanges of information about economic developments in each country to assist exporters. In the months following, plans got under way for a major British Machine Tools and Scientific Instruments Exhibition in Shanghai.

Throughout this period, British export hopes had centred on capital-intensive projects. The major categories of trade continued, however, along fairly traditional lines. British exports included textiles, chemicals, non-ferrous metals, transport machinery, and scientific instruments; imports included foodstuffs, oil seeds and nuts, vegetable oils and fats, metal ores and scrap, and hides, skins and furs. Even so, bilateral trade was running at a high level: China was Britain's third Communist trading partner after the Soviet Union and Poland. British speculation about Chinese interest in purchasing aircraft had been given a boost by a Chinese visit to the 1970 Farnborough air show. In 1971, China ordered six Hawker-Siddeley *Tridents*, a further fourteen in two orders in 1972, and fifteen more at the end of 1973. A related development was the signing of an agreement, after long negotiations, for the start of scheduled BOAC flights between London and Peking. There was even hope, despite the strategic barriers, that the Chinese might be interested in purchasing Harrier VTOL fighters. And every effort was made to keep alive Chinese enquiries about *Concorde*.

The strategic issue had not disappeared; it had simply been

pushed further into the background. Though less stridently than in the 1950s, the Chinese continued to point out that British policy was 'not helpful' to the development of trade. Officials apparently took a tough line with British machine tool manufacturers during the 1973 exhibition because the controls had prevented the sale of some products. Li Hsi-fu, Vice-Chairman of the China Council for the Promotion of International Trade, explained the Chinese view in an interview with the *Financial Times* in April 1973. He expected that the rapid expansion of Sino-British trade would continue. But this would depend not only on the 'physical conditions,' which he described as good, but also on the 'attitude' shown by the United Kingdom. It was up to Britain, in particular, to take 'positive and active measures' to settle the embargo problem.[54] The issue was raised periodically by Labour MPs in the context of aircraft and other specific items. The government denied that it constituted a real problem. After his 1973 Peking visit, Walker commented that 'as for strategic limitations, certainly in matters of trade upon which I had discussions with the Chinese, and a whole range of industries, I do not see any particular problem of a strategic nature.'[55]

British traders in general were appreciative of the problems involved in trying to develop trading links. These included the limits imposed by China's own needs. Observers pointed out that China, as a developing country, did not need Western consumer goods; and that she already possessed adequate capability as regards ordinary technology. Other obstacles were the political direction of Chinese foreign trade, which in the early and middle 1970s just happened to be towards Britain because of China's overall foreign policy goals at that time; the Chinese predilection for achieving a rough balance in bilateral trading relations; and the reluctance of Chinese trade officials to buy on credit. Within these parameters, optimism was felt to be justified. 'Clearly,' Walker wrote in 1973, 'the world's most populous country must be a trading partner of great significance for this country and indeed the whole western world.'[56]

The 1972 agreement clarified further Britain's relationship with both the People's Republic of China and the Nationalist authorities on Taiwan. In a sense, Britain had practised a mild form of two-Chinas policy ever since 1950. Links with Taiwan, however, have been at a comparatively low level. As mentioned previously, a consul was maintained on the island after recognition of Peking in 1950. He was, however, accredited to the provincial rather than the government authorities there. British officials tried, with little success, to use this channel as a means of bringing pressure on the Nationalists in connection with attacks on British merchant ships. Yet Nationalist officials let it be known at the time of the transfer of relations that they fully expected to continue doing business with the British in the future. Trade in subsequent years remained steady, but marginal in terms of Britain's overall foreign trade; British annual imports and exports often fell below the £1m. level.

The British government responded cautiously to the realisation that Chiang Kai-shek's regime would not in fact fall to the Communists. The Board of Trade kept in touch with trade developments and opportunities for British exporters, and provided a regular service of commercial intelligence with respect to the market. In the early 1950s, the government itself, through the Ministry of Food, made purchases of sugar and other products from Nationalist Chinese traders. And in 1957, officials of the Board of Trade's Exports Credits Guarantee Department visited Taiwan. Yet British traders themselves seemed in no hurry to tackle the market, or to exert pressures on the government in favour of more ambitious promotion schemes. Many difficulties resulted from the complexity of trading regulations administered by Taiwan; and the absence of formal diplomatic relations did not assist British businessmen. In a report written in 1956, the British Deputy Consul at Tamsui acknowledged the validity of many of these grounds for complaint. He added, however, that manufacturers from other countries found it profitable to do business there. There was 'no reason why, given the requisite effort, far more British goods should not be exported to this country than has been the case in recent years.'[57]

The problem for government policy was to ensure that such commercial transactions as were taking place did not reach a point — either in volume or in the nature of the contacts they entailed between Britain and Taiwan — where they might conflict with the British government's recognition of Peking. The Foreign Office tended to the view that British trade with Taiwan was not in itself inconsistent with the maintenance of official relations with Peking, and that in any case the overall size of the trade was negligible. Nevertheless, a close watch was kept on trading developments with this consideration in mind. Replying to a questioner sympathetic to closer ties with the Nationalist authorities in 1968, the Minister said that he was aware that some members of the Commonwealth differed from Britain in recognising Taipeh. However, 'we do not accept this claim and there can therefore be no question of granting recognition to the Nationalist authorities. But in the same way as some Commonwealth countries nonetheless trade success-fully with mainland China, this country trades with Taiwan.'[58]

But in any case, broader public support for a consolidation of these links, and their elevation to a political and diplomatic level, has been minimal. At the time of the United Nations votes on Chinese representation in 1970 and 1971, public opinion was receptive to the notion that both Chinas be represented. Some Conservative MPs were steadfastly opposed to an ex-change of ambassadors with Peking. One gave as his reasons the inhumanity of Peking's rule, and described Mao as 'perhaps the greatest tyrant the world has ever seen.'[59] After the 1972 agreement, the *Daily Telegraph* argued that Formosa must not be forgotten: 'British trading and other contacts with the island must continue to be nourished as best they can.'[60] The agreement, however, meant that the British government lost whatever official contact it had previously had with Taiwan. British interests on the island were subsequently looked after by the Australian government.

9 Britain and China 1949-74

What does anybody here know of China? Even those Europeans who have been in that empire are almost as ignorant of it as the rest of us. Everything is covered by a veil, through which a glimpse of what is within may occasionally by caught, a glimpse just sufficient to set the imagination at work and more likely to mislead than to inform.

Macaulay, House of Commons, 7 April, 1840.

China has often been seen through glass more of the observer's than her own making. Even before 1949, misjudgements of the situation in China could arise from a sheer lack of information. It was even more in the interests of a Communist government to impose clamps on the ability of outsiders freely to scrutinise the affairs of the Middle Kingdom. Foreign visitors to the new China had — or, more importantly, were thought to have had — a picture distorted by its being based on a fragment of the whole.

The People's Republic of China raised infinitely more difficult problems of interpretation than were thought to exist for the Soviet Union. By the late 1940s, what differences of opinion there had earlier been in British politics about the nature of modern Russia had largely been resolved. Opponents had found their views vindicated by the excesses of Stalinist rule; sympathisers had for the most part been outraged by a sense of having been betrayed. Such a consensus did not emerge in the case of Communist China. After 1953, United States opinion became gradually more entrenched in the view that Peking represented on balance a greater danger than did Moscow. The regime was held to be more repressive internally, at a time when there was evidence that the Soviet Union was beginning to move out of the Stalinist era. And its frequently proclaimed commitment to the cause of global revolution came to contrast alarmingly with the noises coming out of Moscow. Yet, even of those in Britain who shared this perspective, only a tiny minority went on to advocate a Western policy of isolation and embargo. The view persisted that Chinese Communism was of a different species from Russian Communism. It was perhaps as morally reprehensible. But its roots were held to be so firmly implanted in Chinese conditions and history that long-term collaboration with the Soviet Union seemed impossible. Thus a conciliatory approach to Peking did not imply a weakness of resolve. It was held to be one element in a consistent policy towards the Soviet Union. If at all possible, China should be made to appreciate the existence of alternatives other than an alliance and trade pact with the USSR.

British attitudes to the People's Republic of China grew out of the lessons of the previous two decades. China's future, it was felt, would be an intensely nationalist one. Its nationalism, moreover, would be of a strongly anti-western kind. There would be some role for Western capital, but it would be a very much restricted one. And this momentum neither Britain nor the United States could halt. The hostility of the People's Republic of China was thus anticipated by British opinion. It was not of itself taken as evidence that the Communist leadership was under the sway of the Kremlin.

Beyond this point, however, the evidence seemed to conflict. Some, mainly in the Labour Party, saw a clearly discernible pattern in Asia in the 1940s. The rising tide of nationalism, focused on anti-colonialism and land tenure reform, was seen also to permeate the support of the Chinese peasantry for Communism. In addition, China's middle classes had been attracted by the call of a movement which seemed to offer real alternatives to the corruption, inefficiency and weakness of Kuomintang China. Others thought the evidence of Soviet intrigues after Yalta too great. This sometimes led in turn to the conclusion that the West could ill afford being distracted by Asian conflicts, unless there were clear proof of Soviet manipulation. There was some suspicion that the Korean War itself was part of a diversionary strategy designed by Moscow to force NATO strength into Asia by playing on known American sensitivities with respect to the Far East, and thus leave vulnerable the approaches to Western Europe. British opinion faced a further dilemma. The views of the United States and the governments of the Asian Commonwealth were poles apart on China, so much so that Nehru was found genuinely incomprehensible by many Americans. Britain needed to keep a foot in both camps. The choice was often stark in the early 1950s. To refuse to deal with Peking would alienate India, and threatened a racial cleavage in the Commonwealth. On the other hand, too great a willingness to approach China rubbed deeper the nagging thorn in Anglo-American relations. Sino-Indian conflict in the 1960s removed an important impetus to Britain's own China policy. At the same time, though, it reinforced another aspect: the belief that Asia's affairs could never be settled satisfactorily until China's isolation were ended.

There have been other changes. In 1950, British policy rested on the view that Peking would sooner or later grow restless under Soviet supervision. This did not mean that short-term dangers posed by the alliance could be ignored. But it implied that Western policy towards China should be evaluated against the criterion of whether it promoted or undermined Sino-Soviet friendship. It was on this criterion that Britain objected to the form taken by Western strategic controls on trade with China. Sino-Soviet tension in the 1960s, mounting to the possibility of war in the 1970s, did not, however, cause Britain to sit back. Within limits, good relations were sought with both. The Soviet threat to Europe, though diminished, was felt still to be a factor. It seemed reasonable, therefore, at least not to object when the possibility of Moscow's having to divert its own strength to the Far East had arisen. And it was the Sino-Soviet split that ultimately, after the upheavals of the Cultural Revolution, persuaded Peking of the virtues of a European connection. The exchange of ambassadors with Britain in 1972 was one consequence. This also fitted neatly into British views about the European Community's role in world affairs. The other major change occurred in Washington's own relations with Peking. A belief in the wisdom of a Sino-American rapprochement had been a constant in British thinking from 1949. For many in the Labour Party, indeed, it was America's failure to come to terms with Chinese realities that lay at the root of instabilities in Asia, through the support which Washington felt obliged to give to the forces of reaction in South-East Asia. The shift apparent in the American approach to Peking from 1968 removed a final obstacle to the vigour with which Britain could pursue her own relations with China in the 1970s.

A final change took place in British views of internal Chinese politics. Moral considerations were not decisive in 1950. Conservatives could at the same time denounce Maoist totalitarianism and support diplomatic recognition by Britain. Later events, such as the development by China of a rudimentary nuclear weapons capability, added to the conclusion that China's isolation did not serve the interests either of Western security or of world peace. It was in this context that trade between Britain and China could, it was felt, be legitimately pursued; trade was justified since it was consistent with prior definitions of Western security interests. The moral repugnance of the Chinese regime remained an article of faith for some in Britain. By the mid-1970s, however, centre opinion had made a return to the arguments of 1950. China was seen as having a form of government different from those of the liberal democracies of the West. Ethical and political judgements drawn on the basis of these had dubious validity in the Chinese context. And in any case, there was thought to be evidence that the regime was one that met with the approval of the Chinese people, and, further, one that permitted participation at local levels.

Despite the rancour of much public and Parliamentary debate in Britain, the structure of official thinking stayed fairly constant. Aspects were changed to meet altering circumstances. But a basic core remained intact, to be shelved temporarily rather than taken to pieces when events threatened to render it unworkable. Domestic construction and economic growth were held to be the major priorities of the regime. Anti-Western propaganda was to be seen in the light of the domestic function it performed, rather than as an indication necessarily of aggressive intent. Peking did, however, have external ambitions. These were thought unlikely to include direct aggression, except in the case of tension on the borders of China which got out of hand. A greater danger was subversion; but the tendency here was to argue that China's interest in, and capacity for, spreading unrest in the Third World could easily be exaggerated. Her longer-term goal was not to dominate Asia. Rather it was, first, to minimise and ultimately to eradicate Western influence in the states on her immediate perimeter, and to ensure that another great power — Russia or Japan — did not take the place of the United States. In this situation, and given Peking's latent or visible animosity towards Moscow, the best course was a policy of recognition, limited trade and contact, and acceptance of Peking's representatives in the United Nations. Moreover, since for much of the period after 1949 the United States was burdened by the weight of its commitments during the Chinese civil war, it was seen as Britain's role, as the more detached NATO ally, to inject some element of realism into Sino-Western relations. As one aspect of this, Britain could play a useful though limited mediatory role when relations between Washington and Peking threatened to become dangerously tense. Finally, within this wider framework, an expansion of Sino-British trade would serve British and broader Western interests; and Hongkong's security could be protected — though in the final analysis it was militarily indefensible — and its economic prosperity assured.

The evolution of policy, however, proceeded slowly. Central to British thinking was the belief that approaches to Peking should not be precipitate. The repercussions of actions on the United States and on Commonwealth countries had to be considered. A rebuff by Peking could damage Western interests by undermining British prestige. Thus decisions to initiate moves on the diplomatic relations, United Nations, or trade fronts were shaped, on occasion preponderantly, by considerations of timing. It was twenty-two years before the basic diplomatic mechanics came into being. Peking was recognised in 1950; a Chinese chargé d'affaires was appointed to London in 1954; Britain began to vote for Peking's admission to the United Nations in 1961; and the two governments exchanged ambassadors in 1972, a few months after the People's Republic of China had finally taken China's United Nations seat.

What, then, were the sources of Britain's policy towards China? A search for origins may as well start with the three verdicts reached by various critics of the government. That each is wrong because too simple can be concluded quickly. However, by probing their limitations, we may come up with a more constructive answer. In each, there is a scapegoat for supposed errors committed by Britain. First, China policy has been attributed to the dominant influence of traders in Britain and

Hongkong; secondly, to that of the United States; and thirdly, to that of the Foreign Office. The theories were characteristic, respectively, of Republican critics in the United States Congress during the Korean War, of Labour Party critics in the House of Commons for much of the 1950s and 1960s, and of public opinion during the Cultural Revolution.

The first problem with the view that pursuit of commercial self-interest has been paramount in Britain's approach to Communist China is that there has not been one single and coherent body of trading opinion. In 1949, the bulk of British businessmen in Britain, Hongkong and China were undoubtedly in favour of recognition. But there was a wide divergence of expectations about the future. Few expressed great optimism. Some later regretted British recognition: first, because it antagonised the Nationalist Chinese, and in 1949–50 traders were probably more anxious about the effects of their actions, particularly through the blockade of the Chinese coast and bombing of mainland installations, than about Communist intentions; and secondly, because no obvious benefits accrued. A significant minority believed that the only virtue in having official relations with Peking was that it allowed the British government to negotiate satisfactory terms for the withdrawal of all British interests from China. By 1952 at the latest, there was agreement at least that foreign, including British, capital could not prosper in China.

But the issue that arose then had the effect of dividing British traders into opposed camps. Some sought out the trading channels preferred by the Chinese; those, that is, established as a result of the 1952 Moscow Conference. This activity met with the active disapproval of the British government, which denounced the organisations handling trade on the British side as Communist fronts, and advised British businessmen in the national interest not to let themselves be used by them. Since the 1954 developments, this earlier pattern has continued side by side with arrangements supervised by organisations receiving official encouragement and support. Within the latter framework, a high degree of mutual understanding has emerged as between traders and officials. Trade organisations have not pushed for trade at any cost. They accepted fully the broader principles of British foreign policy, including the need for strategic controls on trade with Communist countries. It was a comparatively long time after the end of the Korean War, for example, before a consensus emerged on the need for Britain to take unilateral action to relax the China trade controls.

This is not to deny that official policy has been influenced by the demands of trading groups. On some occasions, the Foreign Office acted simply as a vehicle of expression for businessmen's complaints: in the representations to the Nationalist authorities in 1949–50; or in the list of grievances presented to China in 1952; or even, to some extent, in the representations to Washington on trade relaxation in the mid 1950s. But trade was not viewed, either by officials or by merchants, as the end towards which all instruments of policy should be directed. Thus traders may have supported diplomatic recognition on grounds of expediency, or have expressed concern at Sino-American rapprochement later because of the competitive threat this posed to Britain's trade with China. But traders' advocacy of moves to end China's isolation owed more to the wider background of public debate in Britain. In this debate, the traders were only one group. Nor, finally, has public opinion in Britain been universally sympathetic to Sino-British trade, even within the strategic limits. In the contexts of the Korean War, the Vietnam War, and the detention of Britons during the Cultural Revolution, there has been vociferous criticism even of any commercial contacts between Britain and China.

The British government, then, in the post-1949 period as in the early 1900s, had a set of priorities in which the promotion of trade held a place, but in stiff competition with other considerations. In the final analysis, these other considerations were primary. This brings us to the second verdict: was the government so sensitive to the implications of countering the Soviet threat that it allowed the United States to have a dominating voice in the formulation of its own policy towards China? Certainly the British government was appreciative of the vulnerability of the Anglo-American relationship to conflict over China policy. Despite the friction of the 1950s, British and American policy rested on a broad measure of agreement. This declined in the early 1950s from the level of understanding reached in 1949. Then, a joint policy resting on the twin foundations of recognition of Peking (the timing of which was acknowledged to be more difficult for Washington) and a more vigorous programme to combat the spread of Communism in other parts of Asia, was hammered into shape in response to People's Liberation Army victories in China during the year. Not all issues were resolved by any means; differences remained, for example, over the best methods of containing Communism. These grew later and came to a head in Anglo-American clashes over SEATO and the Geneva Conference in 1954.

The Administration's refusal, or inability, to proceed with recognition in early 1950 according to British expectations, opened the way for more serious divisions between London and Washington. United States influence over British policy, as opposed to 'agreements to differ', tended to be of two kinds. There was, first, a dampening effect on the implementation of policy options derived from British analyses of the Far East. An early example, not important in itself, was the delay instituted in the momentum towards British recognition of Peking in November 1949. Until 1961, the tenacity with which the American position was held made Britain pause before pressing its case at the United Nations; and for another decade, the government continued to vote simultaneously for the United States view that Chinese representation was an 'important' question requiring a two-thirds majority in the General Assembly. Yet British unwillingness to arouse American fears did not lead to a permanent rejection of preferred options. Rather, courses of action thought desirable were put to one side until such time as circumstances – including at least American acquiescence and some likelihood of a positive response from Peking – altered, and they stood a better chance of success. These kinds of considerations were important for judging the timing and manner of trading initiatives in the early 1960s, and in preparing the ground for the Sino-British talks on an exchange of ambassadors from 1970.

Secondly, policies derived more from American than from British thinking were agreed to by London. Examples are United States pressure on Britain and other Western allies to secure the passing of the United Nations resolution declaring China an aggressor in Korea early in 1951; and Washington's insistence on the commencement of moves for the establishment of SEATO before the 1954 Geneva Conference. In each case, the move was resisted. The reason given in London was that such steps might inhibit the likelihood of success of diplomatic talks. The government's acquiescence prompted parliamentary criticism that the timing of the proposed moves had been chosen carefully in Washington with a view to ensuring that such talks did indeed fail. On such occasions, British ministers defended the steps taken partly on the grounds that they would not hamper the diplomatic route originally planned.

Influence did not, however, always succeed. Britain was able to secure American acceptance of her need to depart from Washington's line on some issues. This is one possible interpretation of the exchanges preceding British recognition of Peking in 1950. Similarly, the United States acknowledged the desirability of Britain trading with China in non-strategic items. Britain resisted American representations in connection with her voting changes in the United Nations on the Chinese representation issue. American objections did not, for example, prevent the British government from embarking on a fresh initiative in the few days immediately preceding the outbreak of the Korean War. Still fiercer United States pressure was unsuccessful in 1957 when Britain made it clear that she would be forced unilaterally to relax the China trade controls unless Washington were prepared to make concessions. British trade officials, for example in the 1966—7 computer cases, sometimes mounted strong objections to American interpretations of the strategic regulations on trade.

More positively, the British government tried, particularly in the period up to 1955, to move United States policy in the direction of a greater realism on China questions. British diplomacy may have been decisive in bringing about the Sino-American ambassadorial talks in Warsaw from 1955. However, in the offshore islands crisis which preceded this agreement, British influence seems to have been minimal. Some Nationalist troop withdrawals were staged from the smallest islands along the Chinese coast. But these probably owed more to exchanges between Washington and Taipeh, and to American definitions of her own national security interests, than to British pressure. And while the British government resisted all suggestions that it make a greater commitment to the defence of the territorial integrity of Taiwan, it was at the same time unable to counter the growing American commitment which culminated in the 1954 Treaty between the United States and the Republic of China. It came to argue instead that such a treaty might be a useful way of restraining Chiang.

Britain was not constrained so much by the United States as by the accepted norms of the Anglo-American alliance. In the final analysis, restraints were accepted voluntarily because of the importance of the relationship. The norms ruled out, for example, any publicly voiced criticism of American policy. This course was strongly suggested by the Labour Opposition during the 1955 and 1958 Quemoy-Matsu crises. A limit was perceived beyond which British attempts to exert pressure would be inappropriate. The Far East was primarily the responsibility of the United States. Before 1956, there was some expectation that British support in that region would eventually rebound in the form of United States backing for British interests in other parts of the world, particularly in the Middle East. In the following decade, the American military involvement in Vietnam, British withdrawal east of Suez, and her growing concentration on European affairs, consolidated United States resistence to suggestions from Britain on China policy.

On behalf of the third theory, it can at least be said that British policy towards China drew much of its nourishment from traditional Foreign Office diplomatic virtues. A refusal to recognise the fact of Communist power in China was never seriously considered. Neither was a final withdrawal of whatever official contacts existed in Peking during the low points in relations during the Korean War and the Cultural Revolution. This laid the government open to the charge that it was sacrificing real British interests for the dubious benefits of keeping up the pretence of a functioning British presence in Peking. The government's justification for retaining this link also ruled out in practice retaliatory action against China when British interests were under attack. The argument in 1951–3 was the same as that in 1967–9. Retaliation by the British government would not be an effective way of bringing pressure to bear on the Chinese authorities. Any spiralling round of sanctions could not be won by Britain. Reprisals might be taken by the Chinese against British nationals or property. Many threats that Britain could make would simply not be credible. More importantly, all schemes for retaliation — such as a refusal to support Peking's credentials in the United Nations before 1971, or a cutting of trade, or measures against Chinese diplomats or news agency officials in London — implied a belief in the desirability of China's isolation in world politics. This belief the Foreign Office did not share.

More is involved here, though, than a professional aversion to pandering to the emotionalism of a temporarily indignant public. In several instances, China policy seems to have emerged out of deliberations within the Foreign Office, and to have altered little in passing through the Cabinet, if indeed it reached that level. This appears to have been the pattern prior to diplomatic recognition in 1950. It does not imply that Foreign Office opinion was unanimous. For example, occasional lapses by officials in China who described the country, or areas of it, as 'liberated' were frowned on by London unless the term were inserted between quotation marks. Officials handling relations with Washington were presumably not eager to support too overtly a friendly approach to Peking. The main argument in 1949—50 was between those close to the situation in China — whether officials, traders or journalists — who tended to contrast the Communist authorities favourably with their Nationalist predecessors, and those removed from it who tended to set such considerations against a wider global perspective that hinged on a fear of Soviet aggrandisement. This conflict was present within the Foreign Office. On the other hand, diplomatic recognition itself raised no strong objections from more cautious officials.

The authority of the Foreign Office's view was helped by several factors. China was a field for the specialist. The Foreign Office had, before the civil war, maintained a large establishment in China. China officials, moreover, enjoyed a tradition of independence which arose from their having successfully navigated the linguistic barrier, their distance from London, and their daily contact with a country that was an immensely old civilisation. The Confucian tradition of being both scholar and official was kept alive into the 1970s. China specialists were in this sense akin to the Foreign Office's Arabists, though not necessarily with a similar degree of influence on policy. The fact that the Foreign Office had within its ranks a corps of such officials, having on their tours of duty at least some contact with Chinese officials, was itself a source of divergence of British from United States policy.

The other side of this was the relative absence of a sustained push from Cabinet level on questions of China policy. Of post-war British Prime Ministers, only two — Eden in his earlier academic studies to some extent, and Wilson in his pursuit of Sino-British trade in the 1950s — and of Foreign Secretaries only Eden, could be said to have had anything amounting to a personal interest in China before taking office. All, however, from Attlee and Bevin in 1949, to Heath and Douglas-Home, and Wilson and Callaghan in 1974, were engaged at times in different aspects of China policy. But in only a few cases did a coherent line on China emerge independently of the course being advocated by the Foreign Office: from Churchill in his belief in the proper role in world affairs of great powers; Eden in the vigour with which diplomatic solutions were sought to the succession of problems of 1954–5; Wilson through the backlog of Labour Party thinking in Opposition on Indo-China, trade, and China's rightful place in the United Nations; and to some extent Heath, in the implications of his conception of the European Community's external role. Chinese sensitivities could too easily be pricked by inadvertent references to Taiwan or to Hongkong using the wrong phrasing: Bevin brought a welter of Chinese indignation on himself in 1950 for failing to refer to the new regime by its proper designation. In these circumstances, it was natural that more than the details and methods of policy should fall to the Foreign Office. In crises, the Prime Minister might be involved, as was Macmillan in the 1958 offshore islands crisis, or Wilson in the Cultural Revolution violence of August 1967. But with the exception of Eden in 1954–5, the pressure of events was then such as to add weight to Foreign Office advice relative to the independent judgement of senior ministers. China has not figured as a major item of government business, with the exception of the drives to establish relations in 1949 and 1971. And on these occasions the initiative was kept in the hands of the Foreign Office. Other areas of British policy were of more pressing concern to the Cabinet. China policy, finally, did not give rise to inter-departmental conflicts of a kind that needed Cabinet resolution. Thus while a large number of ministries with potentially divergent interests were involved in the move towards recognition in 1949, none questioned the need for this step. Separate lines of policy have, however, run parallel. And once a decision had been made in principle, in consultation with the Foreign

Office, that such moves were appropriate, trade ministers, such as Walker in 1973, could then be personally active in taking a lead in the formulation of policy.

China was not a Cabinet priority in part because it was not one for the public or the major political parties. The parties faced the problem that any foreign policy plank was unlikely to be decisive in swaying voters in their direction. Labour cornered the middle ground of criticism of government policy during the 1950s. MPs advocated an expansion of Sino-British trade, a relaxation of the strategic controls, pressure on Washington, and active steps designed to bring Peking into the United Nations. The party's 1970 manifesto argued that trade and technological links between China and the West could help bring about China's re-entry into the world community. Labour had had a tradition of thinking about China, at once sympathetic to her resurgence and critical of the policies of foreign powers, dating at least from the 1920s. Yet the interpretation of Chinese Communism in the 1940s as an indigenous variant of Asian nationalism did not lead the party to oppose British involvement in the Korean War, though it prompted often severe criticism of the United States' handling of operations. Nor, apart from a minority on the left, did the party oppose SEATO as a device for the hostile encirclement of China. From the late 1960s, opposition to government policy came more from the Tory back benches. The Conservative leadership, even during the Cultural Revolution, was not fundamentally at odds with the government. In office in the early 1970s, it followed a course that, had it been implemented by a hypothetical Labour administration in the 1950s, would have been greeted with warm approval by the *Tribune* group. The Labour Party tried at the same time to put forward programmes, such as that of Benn, for the more speedy improvement of Sino-British relations. But by then, the initiative was firmly in the hands of the government of the day. And Labour was suffering the Chinese costs of its anti-Europeanism.

Finally, the Foreign Office was not constrained by the Cabinet's having to respond to public or parliamentary clamour. Public feeling rose to something approaching the pitch of American public opinion on only two occasions; during the 1954–5 offshore islands crisis, and during the Chinese detentions of British subjects in the Cultural Revolution. And only in the second case did it begin to have an effect on government policy. Proposals for retaliation were rejected on the grounds cited earlier. Similar considerations were held to apply in the case of too great a public outcry. Public pressure was such, however, particularly in the Grey incident, that the earlier attempt to restrain popular indignation was dropped. It also seems to have been instrumental in persuading the government of the merits of engaging in talks with the authorities in Hongkong on the question of concessions. Yet this policy was not always followed. British businessmen in the early 1950s were sometimes reluctant to take up official offers to publicise their plight, on the grounds that this might trigger reprisals by the Chinese. In general though in Britain, China policy was not made in an atmosphere of sustained and heated public debate. Critical opinion, moreover, was often in the difficult position of objecting not to the government's thinking, but rather to its apparent willingness to allow Washington an undue influence over its actions. A further difference with the United States was the absence of pressure groups capable of mobilising opinion against certain policy options. The unofficial organisations that have existed — apart from the various trading groups operating with government approval — have exerted no influence on policy; and seem to have played a negligible role even in the moulding of broader public attitudes. The Society for Anglo-Chinese Understanding, for example, was unable to resolve the dilemma in the 1960s of expressing support and admiration for modern China, without at the same time giving the appearance of being an instrument of Communist propaganda. Finally, there has been no active Chinese community in Britain. Nationalist Chinese officials and businessmen who remained after 1949 became assimilated into British society; while retaining a cultural identity, they had for the most part no interest in making any political impact. The Nationalist-Communist propaganda rivalries in the Chinese communities, which reached a peak during the Cultural Revolution, similarly had no consequence for external policy.

The press itself was unanimously in favour of diplomatic recognition in 1950, though with reservations from the Conservative side. Coherent arguments against aspects of government policy were in subsequent years most fully developed by the *Guardian* and the *Daily Telegraph,* and of the weekly press by the *New Statesman* and *The Economist.* A steady stream of news and commentary about Chinese developments has been maintained. This is despite the often difficult problems of gaining access to information. The Cultural Revolution brought about a final break of direct contacts maintained by the British press, and led to the explusion of the journalist reporting to *The Times* and the *Sunday Times.* Judging by the amount of coverage given China in *The Times* it would appear that the peak of British interest was reached in the period from late 1948 to 1950. After this period of upheaval, there seems to have been a general decline in the amount of space devoted to Chinese news, with periodic jumps for crises internal or external to China. In one case, that of Grey's detention in 1967–9, newspaper and journalists' organisations forged a common front to arouse public opinion in Britain and in other countries, with some success. And the press has played some role, varying with circumstances and issues, in the subtle and complex processes by which public and parliamentary attitudes came to be formed. Thus news and editorial opinion from *The Times* was often cited by MPs in parliamentary debates on China; while the *Financial Times* maintained a close and well-informed watch over developments with respect to Sino-British trade.

We can therefore exonerate each of our three would-be scapegoats. Britain's China traders operated within a framework shaped largely by factors other than commerce; the United States was neither wholly successful in putting pressure on Britain, nor immune from reciprocal influence; and the Foreign Office has not functioned in an atmosphere free of public, Cabinet or allies' concerns. Each of these, of course, has been important in the formulation of policy. But so, generally in lesser ways, have others. Consensus on China policy at the official level tended to emerge in ways that defy simple summary. Participants included ministries in addition to the Foreign Office, allies in addition to the United States, and publics in addition to the China traders. Also involved were Asian Commonwealth governments, the authorities in Hongkong, those in Malaya for a time, the United Nations Secretariat on some occasions, the press, and those MPs and peers who avoided extreme positions for or against Mao but who kept a close interest in British policy towards China. The influence exerted by each of these was not uniform over the period since

1949, nor identical for all kinds of issues raised in Sino-British relations. Each of the three central characters could occasionally set the scene, but none could shape the subsequent dialogue or its outcome.

We have so far assumed, for the sake of argument, that there has been something rotten in the state of Britain's policy towards China, and that if we probed deeply enough a culprit would sooner or later be uncovered. This was merely a device to assist discussion. It is time now to examine this assumption itself more closely.

There are, unfortunately, major problems in evaluating British policy. A central conclusion of the last few pages is that Britain's options after 1949 were often far fewer than critics on either the left or the right were prepared to admit. Two powerful kinds of constraints loomed large. First, Britain was no longer a great power as far as the Far East was concerned. She was prepared to adapt to Chinese nationalism, and later to the transition to Communist rule, because in the final analysis the British government appreciated that it lacked the capacity to influence these events. The suspicion that, given greater determination on the part of Chiang Kai-shek and a more ambitious programme of anti-Communist resistance on the part of the Truman administration in the late 1940s, the changes in China could have been checked or reversed, continued to dog American thinking for fully two decades after the establishment of the People's Republic. Britain was often, therefore, ready to negotiate with China from a position of what appeared in the United States to be weakness. In 1950, Britain and the United States responded quite differently to Chinese seizures of consular property belonging to their respective governments. During the Cultural Revolution, British officials reacted to Chinese arrests of British seamen, or detentions of British ships, by first considering the possibility that such actions had arisen from misunderstandings or from the over-zealousness of local minor officials. It was not, that is, automatically assumed that anti-British actions were necessarily a product of a hostile attitude in Peking. When there was evidence of a concerted anti-British operation, as in 1967, the possibility that it might have been instituted entirely for domestic consumption served to undermine the attractiveness of diplomatic sanctions.

A second constraint arose from Britain's relations with other powers in the 1950s. India wanted a positive response to China: an appreciation of the virtues of the Communist authorities, a readiness to believe the best of Peking's intentions, and a refusal to take the kinds of defensive measures in Asia that might arouse the fears of the Chinese government. The United States emphasised the dangers to Western interests and world peace of the revolutionary ambitions of the Chinese Communist leadership, and stood opposed to Western policies that might, by being misinterpreted in Peking, contribute to Chinese intransigeance and aggressive intent. Britain was caught in the middle. The dilemma of how best to deal with Communist China was already present in British official and public debates. It was made acute by the fact that two governments, its relations with each of which London valued highly, appeared to take the opposite ends of the argument to unrealistic extremes. This conflict, keenly felt by Britain over recognition of Peking and over the complex of Korean and Indo-China issues in 1954, diminished later in the decade, and disappeared, at least in the form it had begun to take in 1950, with the emergence of Sino-Indian tensions at the beginning of the 1960s. Yet its disappearance was anticipated in the evolution of British policy. In her effort to steer a reasonably consistent middle course, it was perhaps inevitable that Britain should suffer the costs of appearing to rebuff both India and the United States. In the final analysis, however, if a choice had to be made, antagonising the Asian Commonwealth was thought a lesser evil. Regret that recognition of Peking had opened the way for Anglo-American friction in the 1950s, proved greater than disappointment over Indian condemnation of SEATO in 1954. This setting of priorities arose not only from considerations of European security and of traditional Atlantic links. The British government also thought it essential that the administration in Washington not be forced into a situation where it saw its alternatives polarising into either rash military action in Asia or a withdrawal into isolationism.

This dual constraint of a decline of British power and a conflict of views on the part of friendly governments left its mark on British actions. But even within the slim margins allowed for manoeuvre, the government did not always take the steps most likely to tip the balance in its favour in Peking. The significance of diplomatic recognition in 1950 was played down to head off a charge of appeasement. Yet this accentuated the Chinese predisposition to believe that Britain was merely seeking trading concessions, and that the *Amethyst* incident represented the true face of British imperialism. In the Quemoy-Matsu crises, British insistence on maintaining a public front of Anglo-American unanimity helped to confirm the Chinese belief that the British government was one instrument of Washington's policy, and to undermine the chances of success of British conciliatory approaches to Peking.

Sino-British animosity was in part a product of misunderstandings engendered by the lack of smoothly functioning diplomatic relations. A perennial British, and Western, difficulty has been that of interpreting Chinese Communist statements. Sympathy for the struggle of the British people to free themselves from the yoke of capitalism, and condemnation of the brutality of the Hongkong authorities, could be readily interpreted as being simply a part of the daily diet of the Chinese in mobilising their resources for economic construction. But not all statements could be dismissed so lightly. At some point they spilled over into definitions of foreign policy objectives threatening to British interests in Asia. A more precise identification of this point could not be made in the absence of good Sino-British official relations. On occasions, such as during the Cultural Revolution in 1967 or the anti-Confucius campaign of 1974, Chinese officials emphasised that China's problems were internal ones which should not be construed by British businessmen as having deleterious consequences for Sino-British trade. This kind of suggestion at a more official level would have been a valuable contribution to the shaping of British policy from 1950, even if it were not to be taken necessarily at face value. Chinese views, too, have been determined in part by the kinds of contacts established with Britain. A reasonable conclusion for the Chinese to draw in the early 1950s, on the basis of exchanges with Britons, would have been that the Communist Party represented the true aspirations of the majority of British citizens. Links were kept up with another Communist party in the 1970s. But by then, these were balanced by a regular flow of contacts at official level with Britain, and exchanges with unofficial groups of a non-political character. While such relations were not present, the actions of each served to confirm the worst fears of the other. And initial expectations were not optimistic. Debate inside both Britain and China during 1949 turned against those who had argued that mutually beneficial relations with the other were both desirable and practicable. The actions taken later by each side were often such as could be interpreted by the other as continuing proof of the wisdom of this earlier shift, even though in large measure the constraints on both countries' policies were extraneous to the Sino-British relationship.

The fragility of the new link of the 1970s was acknowledged by British opinion. It was vulnerable to the many pressures that impinge on any East-West relationship. Renewed tension could arise from international problems where Chinese and British interests did not coincide, as in the affairs of the Indian sub-continent. The factors that brought it into being could change. China might find herself in a situation where a rapprochement with the Soviet Union was thought necessary to tackle a feared Japanese threat; or she might grow restless with the British and West European penchant for talks on matters of common interest with Moscow. But there was a more solid footing too. No longer, from the British point of view, could the collapse of the 1950 talks be held up as a salutary warning to all who would attempt the folly of trying to deal reasonably with Peking. As expected by the British government in 1949, China had been unable to live harmoniously in tandem with the Soviet Union. As predicted, China had emerged from the Cultural Revolution more intent rather than less on seeking more normal relations with the Western powers. The approach of 1949 seemed finally to have been vindicated. Patience, the virtue of Middle Kingdoms, had been rewarded.

Notes

Chapter 1

1. Sir John T. Pratt, *China and Britain* (London: Collins, 1946) pp. 123—4.
2. P. O'Donovan, reporting to the *Scotsman*, cited in *China Association Bulletin*, 37, 20 June 1949, p.1.
3. E. V. G. Kiernan, *British Diplomacy in China, 1880 to 1885* (Cambridge University Press, 1939) pp. 2—3.
4. A. S. Lawrence, *The Origin of Chinese Hostility to Great Britain* (London: Labour Party, 1927).
5. W. C. Costin, *Great Britain and China, 1833—60* (Oxford: Clarendon Press, 1937) p. 1.
6. Kiernan, op. cit., p. 307.
7. Ibid., p. 310.
8. Bradford A. Lee, *Britain and the Sino-Japanese War, 1937—39: A Study in the Dilemmas of British Decline* (Stanford University Press, 1973) p. 4.
9. Irving S. Friedman, *British Relations with China: 1931—39* (New York: Institute of Pacific Relations, 1940) pp. 3—9.
10. *The Foreign Office List and Diplomatic and Consular Yearbook* (London: Harrison and Sons, annually).
11. Ann Trotter, *Britain and East Asia, 1933—37* (Cambridge University Press, 1975) p. 4.

Chapter 2

1. Quoted in *House of Commons Debates*, vol. 459, 9 Dec 1948, col. 566.
2. R. C. Rose, 'The Relation of Socialist Principles to British Foreign Policy, 1945—51', D.Phil. thesis (Nuffield College, Oxford, 1959).
3. K. G. Younger, 'Britain and the Far East', *The Dyason Lectures, 1955*, no. 2 (Melbourne: Australian Institute of International Affairs, 1955) p. 16.
4. Francis Williams, *A Prime Minister Remembers: The War and Post-war Memoirs of the Rt. Hon. Earl Attlee . . .* (London: Heinemann, 1961) p. 60.
5. *China. Exchange of Notes constituting an Agreement between the*

Notes 183

Government of the United Kingdom and the Republic of China for the Transfer of Certain British Naval Vessels to China..., Cmd 7457 (1948).

6. Bevin, *House of Commons Debates*, vol. 459, 9 Dec 1948, col. 566.

7. Evan Luard, *Britain and China* (Baltimore: Johns Hopkins, 1962) p. 73.

8. The Earl of Avon, *The Eden Memoirs*, Vol. 3: *Full Circle* (London: Cassell,1960) p. 7.

9. *Winnipeg Free Press*, 17 Oct 1949.

10. China Association, *Annual Report 1948–49*, p. 3.

11. Mayhew, *House of Commons Debates*, vol. 450, 3 May 1948, cols 890–1.

12. *The Times*, 1 July 1949.

13. *House of Commons Debates*, vol. 533, 22 Nov 1954, cols. 87–91.

14. Hongkong and Shanghai Banking Corporation, *Annual Report 1949*, pp. 13–14.

15. *House of Commons Debates*, vol. 464, 5 May 1949, col. 1348.

16. China Association, *Annual Report 1949–50*, p. 7.

17. Lindsay, 'The New China', *Sunday Times*, 4 Dec 1949.

18. Gammans, *House of Commons Debates*, vol. 456, 15 Sep 1948, col. 167.

19. *House of Commons Debates*, vol. 475, 24 May 1950, col. 2081.

20. *House of Commons Debates*, vol. 464, 5 May 1949, col. 1341.

21. *House of Commons Debates*, vol. 459, 9 Dec 1948, col. 658.

22. Cooke, reporting on opinion in Washington in the *Manchester Guardian*, 11 Oct 1949.

23. *Report of the United Kingdom Trade Mission to China, October to December, 1946* (London: HMSO, 1948) p. 18.

24. A. D. Kopkind, 'Moral and Political Considerations in the Debate in Britain on Recognition of the Peking Government', M.Sc. thesis (University of London, 1961) p. 5; and Department of State, *United States Relations with China, with special reference to the period 1944–49* (Washington: Government Printing Office, 1949) p. 300.

25. *Department of State Bulletin*, XXII (551), 23 Jan 1950, pp. 112–13.

26. *Manchester Guardian*, 13 Dec 1949.

27. United Nations, *Official Records of the General Assembly*, 4 (229), 26 Sep 1949, pp. 79–80.

28. China Association, *Annual Report 1949–50*, p. 2.

29. *The Economist*, 10 Dec 1949.

30. Guillain, *Manchester Guardian*, 20 Dec 1949.

31. *Christian Science Monitor*, 24 Dec 1949, interpreting official opinion in London.

32. G. G. Fitzmaurice, 'Chinese Representation in the United Nations', *Yearbook of World Affairs*, 6 (1952) p. 36.

33. Federation of Malaya, Department of Public Relations, *Broadcast by the Commissioner-General...*, no. 295 (1950).

34. *House of Commons Debates*, vol. 469, 17 Nov 1949, col. 2225.

35. *New York Times*, 20 Sep 1949.

36. *New York Times*, 13 Oct 1949.

37. *House of Commons Debates*, vol. 470, 14 Dec 1949, col. 2640.

38. *South China Morning Post*, 4 Nov 1949.

39. *The Times*, 20 Oct 1949.

40. Aneurin Bevan, *In Place of Fear* (London: Heinemann, 1952) p. 134.

41. *United Kingdom Trade Mission to China*, p. 40.

42. Quoted by O'Donovan in a report to the *Johannesburg Star*, 11 June 1949.

43. Hongkong and Shanghai Banking Corporation, *Annual Report 1949*, p. 19.

44. *Hearings before the Committee on Foreign Relations on the Japanese Peace Treaty . . .*, US Senate, 82nd Cong., 2nd session (Washington: Government Printing Office, 1952) p. 12.

45. 'Une Opinion Britannique', *Le Soir*, 5 Dec 1949.

46. *House of Commons Debates*, vol. 475, 24 May 1950 cols. 2186—7.

47. *The Times*, 8 Aug 1949.

Chapter 3

1. Rose, loc. cit.

2. Younger, loc. cit.

3. *South China Morning Post*, 23 July 1949.

4. *The Times*, 18 Aug 1949.

5. *House of Commons Debates*, vol. 475, 24 May 1950, col. 2086.

6. Bevin, *House of Commons Debates*, vol. 469, 16 Nov 1949, col. 2015.

7. *Manchester Guardian*, 4 Oct 1949.

8. *North China Daily News*, 24 Feb 1949; *South China Morning Post*, 17 June 1949.

9. *China Association Bulletin*, 41, 20 Oct 1949, p. 1.

10. *House of Commons Debates*, vol. 464, 5 May 1949, cols 1249—50.

11. *House of Lords Debates*, vol. 166, 7 Mar 1950, col. 88.

12. H. S. Albinski, *Australian Attitudes and Policies towards Communist China* (Princeton University Press, 1967) p. 31.

13. *The Times*, 14 Nov 1949.

14. *Winnipeg Free Press*, 16 Nov 1949.

15. *South China Morning Post*, 2 Sep 1949.

16. Tang Tsou, *America's Failure in China, 1941—50* (Chicago University Press, 1963) pp. 499—500.

17. Ibid., p. 514.

18. On this episode, see *The United States and Communist China in 1949 and 1950: The Question of Rapprochement and Recognition. A Staff Study prepared for the use of the Committee on Foreign Relations*, US Senate (Washington: Government Printing Office, 1973) pp. 7—12.

19. *United States Relations with China, with special reference to the period 1944—49* (Washington: Government Printing Office, 1949).

20. To which Bevin apparently replied that London could not delay recognition. See *Hearings on the Nomination of Philip C. Jessup to be United States Representative to the Sixth General Assembly of the United*

Nations, US Senate, Committee on Foreign Relations, 82nd Cong., 1st session (Washington: Government Printing Office, 1951) pp. 924, 928, 930.

21. *The United States and Communist China in 1949 and 1950*, pp. 12—13.

22. Ibid., p. 1.

23. *The Times*, 18 Nov 1949.

24. *Daily Telegraph* 14 Nov 1949; *South China Morning Post*, 16 Nov 1949.

25. *House of Commons Debates*, vol. 469, 16 Nov 1949, col. 2013.

26. *New York Times*, 20 Nov 1949.

27. *Military Situation in the Far East: Hearings before the Committee on Armed Services and the Committee on Foreign Relations*, US Senate, 82nd Cong., 1st Session (Washington: Government Printing Office, 1951) pp. 1778—9.

28. *House of Lords Debates*, vol. 166, 7 Mar 1950, col. 89.

29. Younger, op. cit., p. 16.

30. *The Times*, 7 Jan 1950.

31. *House of Commons Debates*, vol. 475, 24 May 1950, col. 2083.

32. *House of Lords Debates*, vol. 166, 7 Mar 1950, cols 90—1.

33. *Military Situation in the Far East*, pp. 1774, 1779.

34. H. Kubek, *How the Far East was Lost: American Policy and the Creation of Communist China, 1941—9* (Chicago: Regnery, 1963) pp. 415, 429; Tang Tsou, *America's Failure in China, 1941—50* (University of Chicago Press, 1963) p. 513.

35. *The United States and Communist China in 1949 and 1950*, p. 19.

36. Cited by Kubek, op. cit., pp. 423, 425—7.

37. *The United States and Communist China in 1949 and 1950*, p. 2.

38. *The Times*, 14 Nov 1949.

39. *New York Herald Tribune*, 23 June 1949.

40. *House of Commons Debates*, vol. 464, 26 Apr 1949, col. 26.

41. *The Times* 15 Sep 1949; *Manchester Guardian*, 21 Sep 1949.

42. Rose, op. cit., p. 218.

43. *Nomination of Jessup*, pp. 624—5, 907.

44. *North China Daily News*, 3 May 1949.

45. *New China News Agency*, 7 June 1949.

46. 'China will judge British Policy by Deeds, not Words', *New China News Agency*, 17 Jan 1950; *People's Daily*, 28 May 1950.

47. *New China News Agency*, 26 May 1950.

48. *The Times*, 5 Dec 1949.

49. Cited by Trygve Lie, *In the Cause of Peace: Seven Years with the United Nations* (New York: Macmillan, 1954) p. 255.

50. *South China Morning Post*, 14 Apr 1950.

51. *House of Commons Debates*, vol. 475, 24 May 1950, col. 2084.

52. *House of Commons Debates*, vol. 473, 31 Mar 1950, cols 790, 792.

53. Mott-Radclyffe, *House of Commons Debates*, vol. 475, 24 May 1950, cols 2149—50.

54. Ibid., col. 2071.

55. *The Times*, 26 Jan 1950.

56. *The Times*, 9 June 1950.
57. *The Times*, 25 May 1950.
58. Sir John Pratt, 'A Great American Blunder', *Manchester Guardian*, 14 Mar 1950.
59. *House of Commons Debates*, vol. 475, 24 May 1950, col. 2084.
60. *The Times*, 6 Apr 1950.
61. United Nations, *Official Records of the Security Council*, 5 (460), 12 Jan 1950, p. 6.
62. *Memorandum on Legal Aspects of the Problem of Representation in the United Nations, transmitted to the President of the Security Council by the Secretary-General*, 8 Mar 1950, UN Doc. S/1466, pp. 2—3.
63. *House of Commons Debates*, vol. 475, 24 May 1950, col. 2085.
64. Lie, op. cit., pp. 265—6.
65. *House of Commons Debates*, vol. 475, 24 May 1950, col. 2188.
66. *City Observer*, 2 June 1950; *China Association Bulletin*, 49, 20 June 1950, p. 2.
67. *New York Herald Tribune*, 11 July 1950.
68. *The Times*, 19 and 20 June 1950.
69. *South China Morning Post*, 14 June 1950.
70. *The Times*, 24 June 1950. Lie later, however, described his visit to Washington on 29 May as his last attempt to help resolve the issue of Chinese representation (op. cit., p. 271).

Chapter 4

1. *House of Commons Debates*, vol. 464, 5 May 1949, cols 1263—4. This was part of a broader argument on the popular nature of Mao's own party.
2. Ibid., col. 1233.
3. *House of Commons Debates*, vol. 473, 28 Mar 1950, cols 275—6.
4. *House of Commons Debates*, vol. 475, 24 May 1950, col. 2187.
5. Younger, *House of Commons Debates*, vol. 476, 21 June 1950, col. 1267.
6. *First Session, Parliament of India. Debates, Pt. II, Vol. II*, 17 Mar 1950, p. 1699.
7. N. Bhattacharya, 'Foreign Policy of the People's Republic of China', *Indian Yearbook of International Affairs*, I (1952) pp. 229—37.
8. *House of Commons Debates*, vol. 464, 5 May 1949, col. 1235.
9. *Department of State Bulletin*, XX (517), 29 May 1949, p. 696.
10. *House of Commons Debates*, vol. 473, 28 Mar 1950, cols 275—6.
11. D. E. McHenry and R. W. Rosecrance, 'The "exclusion" of the United Kingdom from the Anzus Pact', *International Organisation*, 12 (Summer 1958) pp. 320—9.
12. *New York Herald Tribune*, 2 Aug 1954.
13. *Sydney Morning Herald*, 17 May 1954.
14. *Sydney Morning Herald*, 18 May 1954.
15. (*sic*) *Hindu*, 8 Sep 1954.
16. *New York Times*, 3 Aug 1954.
17. *Hindu* 29 Aug 1954.

18. *House of Commons Debate*, vol. 526, 15 Apr 1954, col. *145*.
19. *Full Circle*, p. 93.
20. *House of Commons Debates*, vol. 532, 8 Nov 1954, cols 981–3.
21. *Manchester Guardian* in editorials on 2 and 6 July and 3, 17 and 20 Aug 1954.
22. *House of Commons Debates*, vol. 529, 23 June 1954, col. 444.
23. Ibid., col. 463.
24. Ibid., col. 531.
25. *Full Circle*, p. 109.
26. *House of Commons Debates*, vol. 529, 23 June 1954, col. 433.
27. *The Times*, 17 May 1954.
28. *Manchester Guardian*, 17 Aug 1954.
29. *Department of State Bulletin*, XXX (772), 12 Apr 1954, p. 540.
30. Dwight D. Eisenhower, *Mandate for Change, 1953–56* (London: Heinemann, 1963) pp. 346–7.
31. *Full Circle*, p. 93.
32. *The Times*, 14 Apr 1954.
33. *Full Circle*, p. 98.
34. Ibid., pp. 105–6.
35. *New York Herald Tribune*, 6 May 1954; and *Mandate for Change*, p. 364.
36. *House of Commons Debates*, vol. 527, 10 May 1954, cols 834–5.
37. *Christian Science Monitor*, 21 May 1954.
38. *House of Commons Debates*, vol. 528, 25 May 1954, col. 208.
39. *Mandate for Change*, p. 365.
40. *Full Circle*, p. 133.
41. *House of Commons Debates*, vol. 530, 12 July 1954, col. 44.
42. *Mandate for Change*, p. 349.
43. *Hindu*, 27 May 1954.
44. *The Times*, 4 Aug 1954.
45. *Department of State Bulletin*, XXXI (795), 20 Sep 1954, pp. 391–6.
46. *House of Commons Debates*, vol. 532, 8 Nov 1954, col. 940.
47. *Scotsman*, 9 Sep 1954.
48. *House of Commons Debates*, vol. 532, 8 Nov 1954, col. 932.
49. *Manchester Guardian*, 3 Sep 1954.
50. *House of Commons Debates*, vol. 532, 8 Nov 1954, cols 933–4.
51. Ibid., col. 970.
52. *Full Circle*, p. 141.
53. *People's Daily*, 6 Aug 1954.
54. *People's Daily*, 7 Sep 1954.
55. See for example the 'Report on the Draft Constitution of the People's Republic of China', *Documents of the First Session of the First National People's Congress of the People's Republic of China* (Peking: Foreign Languages Press, 1955) p. 123.

Chapter 5

1. References to the background of Anglo-Chinese trade are given in

the Bibliographical Note.

2. Michael Greenberg, *British Trade and the Opening of China, 1800—42* (Cambridge University Press, 1951) p. 152.

3. China Association, *Annual Report, 1949—50*, p. 4.

4. *United Kingdom Trade Mission to China*, p. 50.

5. *The Economist*, 23 July 1949.

6. *New York Times*, 24 June 1950.

7. *China Mail*, 21 Feb 1950; cited at *House of Commons Debates*, vol. 472, 7 Mar 1950, col. 216.

8. *Correspondence between the Government of the United Kingdom. . . and the Central People's Government of China on British Trade in China*, Cmd 8639, pp. 2—3.

9. *China Association Bulletin*, 46, 20 Mar 1950, p. 1.

10. Nutting, *House of Commons Debates*, vol. 505, 22 Oct 1952, cols. 1007—8.

11. China Engineers Ltd, *Quarterly Review*, (Nov 1951) and (Sep 1952); cited in the *China Association Bulletin*, 67, 20 Dec 1951, and 77, 20 Oct 1952.

12. China Association, *Annual Report 1950—51*, p. 2.

13. Hongkong and Shanghai Banking Corporation, *Annual Report 1952*, p. 13

14. Estimates drawn from the China Association *Annual Reports*; and *Sunday Times*, 18 May 1952.

15. Humphrey Trevelyan, *Worlds Apart: China 1953—5, Soviet Union 1962—5* (London: Macmillan, 1971) p. 59.

16. Cmd 8639, p. 4.

17. *The Times*, 20 May 1952.

18. *People's Daily*, 19 July 1952; Cmd 8639, pp. 5—6.

19. China Association, *Annual Report 1956—57*, p. 13.

20. *South China Morning Post*, 6 May 1952.

21. *New China News Agency*, 15 Apr 1952.

22. *House of Commons Debates*, vol. 495, 4 Feb 1955, col. 639.

23. Mutual Security Agency, *A Program for the Denial of Strategic Goods to the Soviet Bloc* (Washington: Government Printing Office, 1952) p. 27 (*First Battle Act Report*).

24. 'Fifteenth Anniversary of "Ice-breaker" mission', *China Trade and Economic Newsletter*, 153 (July 1968) pp. 1—2.

25. *Financial Times*, 16 Mar 1954.

26. *Financial Times*, 22 Apr 1954.

27. Wilson, *Manchester Guardian*, 2 and 3 June 1954.

28. *China Association Bulletin*, 99, 20 Aug 1954.

29. *Financial Times*, 10 July 1954. Traders' complaints persisted though: see 'Stalemate in China Trade', *Financial Times* 16 Dec 1955.

30. Hongkong and Shanghai Banking Corporation, *Annual Report 1955*, p. 4.

31. *China Association Bulletin*, 123, 15 Aug 1956, p. 4.

32. China Association, *Annual Report 1954—55*, p. 3.

33. Nutting, *House of Commons Debates*, vol. 551, 11 Apr 1956, col. 203.

34. Sir John Keswick, *Trade and Industry*, 10 (1973) pp. 262—3.

35. Hope, *House of Commons Debates*, vol. 546, 30 Nov 1955, cols 2291–2.

36. *Christian Science Monitor*, Hongkong, 13 Nov 1953.

Chapter 6

1. Mutual Security Agency, *The Strategic Trade Control System, 1948–56* (Washington: Government Printing Office, 1957) p. 32 (*Ninth Battle Act Report*).

2. Testimony of S. Weeks, in *East-West Trade. Hearings before the Permanent Subcommittee on Investigations of the Committee on Government Operations*, US Senate, 84th Cong., 2nd session (Washington: Government Printing Office, 1956) p. 404.

3. *Military Situation in the Far East*, p. 1726.

4. Shawcross, *House of Commons Debates*, vol. 487, 7 May 1951, col. 1589.

5. Eden, *House of Commons Debates*, vol. 512, 17 Mar 1953, cols 2072–3.

6. *First Battle Act Report*, pp. ii, 25–6.

7. Mutual Security Agency, *World-wide Enforcement of Strategic Controls* (Washington: Government Printing Office, 1953) p. 35 (*Third Battle Act Report*).

8. *Ninth Battle Act Report*, pp. 17–19, 31, 35. See further the studies cited in the Bibliographical Note.

9. Public Law 213, 82nd Cong., 1st session, Chapter 575, HR 4550; *First Battle Act Report*, Appendix A, pp. 31–4.

10. *House of Commons Debates*, vol. 632, 13 Dec 1960, cols 368 ff.

11. J. H. Dunning, 'United States Manufacturing Subsidiaries and Britain's Trade Balance', *District Bank Review* (Sep 1955) p. 22.

12. *House of Lords Debates*, vol. 182, 28 Apr 1953, col. 50.

13. *The Times*, 22 Apr 1957.

14. *House of Commons Debates*, vol. 487, 30 Apr 1951, cols *116–17*.

15. See for example *House of Commons Debates*, vol. 521, 8 Dec 1953, cols 1778–81.

16. *South China Morning Post*, 15 May 1956.

17. *The Times*, 9 Mar 1957.

18. Ibid.

19. *Manchester Guardian*, 16 Oct 1954.

20. *New York Times*, 23 May 1956.

21. *The Times*, 13 Feb 1956.

22. Hongkong and Shanghai Banking Corporation, *Annual Report 1954*, pp. 19–20.

23. *China Association Bulletin*, 92, 20 Jan 1954, Appendix, p. 2.

24. *House of Lords Debates*, vol. 195, 15 Feb 1956, cols 976–7.

25. 'The Economy of China', *The Statist*, 10 Dec 1949.

26. *Daily Worker*, 2 Dec 1949.

27. *China Association Bulletin*, 95, 20 Apr 1954.

28. *New York Herald Tribune*, Economic Supplement (Sep 1956).

29. *House of Commons Debates*, vol. 536, 27 Jan 1955, cols 416–17.

30. Williams, *House of Commons Debates*, vol. 562, 19 Dec 1956, cols 1263–4.

31. *Financial Times*, 16 Dec 1955.
32. *China Association Bulletin*, 95, 20 Jan 1954, 1.
33. Elibank, *House of Lords Debates*, vol. 184, 5 Nov 1953, col. 129.
34. *House of Commons Debates*, vol. 487, 10 May 1951, cols 2182—3.
35. Hongkong and Shanghai Banking Corporation, *Annual Report 1950*, pp. 17—18.
36. China Association, *Annual Report 1951—52*, p. 3.
37. Federation of Malaya, *Annual Report 1953* (London: HMSO, 1954) pp. 100—1.
38. *Full Circle*, p. 337.
39. *House of Commons Debates*, vol. 517, 16 July 1953, cols 2247—8.
40. *House of Commons Debates*, vol. 529, 6 July 1954, cols 1960—1.
41. Weeks, *East-West Trade*, p. 404; Amory, *House of Commons Debates*, vol. 529, 29 June 1954, col. 1084.
42. *China Association Bulletin*, 95, 20 Apr 1954.
43. *Fifth Battle Act Report*, pp. 16—17.
44. *The Times*, 2 Feb 1956.
45. Harold Macmillan, *Tides of Fortune, 1945—55* (London: Macmillan, 1969) p. 630.
46. *Ninth Battle Act Report*, p. 38.
47. Nutting, *House of Commons Debates*, vol. 552, 14 May 1956, cols 1631—2.
48. *Straits Times*, 4 June 1956.
49. *New York Times*, 20 Feb 1957.
50. *Department of State Bulletin*, XXXVI (933) 13 May 1957, pp. 772—3.
51. *The Times*, 22 Apr 1957.
52. Mutual Security Agency, *East-West Trade Developments, 1956—57* (Washington: Government Printing Office, 1958) p. 16 (*Tenth Battle Act Report*).
53. Ibid., pp. 16—17.
54. *People's Daily*, 28 Sep 1955.
55. *People's China*, 31 July 1954.
56. *People's Daily*, 1 Aug 1952.

Chapter 7

1. Department of State, *Foreign Relations of the United States: The Conferences at Cairo and Teheran, 1943*, (Washington: Government Printing Office, 1961); and *The Conference of Berlin, 1945*, (Washington: Government Printing Office, 1960).
2. Department of State, *Policy Information Paper: Formosa. Public Affairs Area: Policy Advisory Staff, Special Guidance No. 28*, 23 Dec 1949.
3. *Daily Telegraph*, 31 Dec 1949.
4. Statement by the Foreign Secretary, *House of Commons Debates*, vol. 462, 2 Mar 1949, cols 345—46.
5. *The Economist*, 23 July 1949.
6. *Report from the Committee on Foreign Affairs of the House of*

Representatives on United States Policy on China, Report 1618, 81st Cong., 2nd Session.

7. *The Times*, 13 Sep 1954, editorial.
8. *The Times*, 26 Feb 1955, correspondent in Bangkok.
9. *Statement on Defence, (1953–54)*, Cmd. 9075, p. 3.
10. Sir Roger Makins, 'The World Since the War: The Third Phase', *Foreign Affairs*, 33 (Oct 1954) p. 5.
11. *New York Times*, 13 Dec 1954.
12. *House of Commons Debates*, vol. 535, 20 Dec 1954, col. 2430.
13. *House of Commons Debates*, vol. 536, 26 Jan 1955, cols. 162–3.
14. *Daily Telegraph*, 7 Sep 1954; *Manchester Guardian*, 4 Sep 1954.
15. *Daily Herald*, 31 Jan 1955; *News Chronicle*, 16 Feb 1955.
16. *People's Daily*, 29 Jan 1955.
17. *People's Daily*, 4 Oct 1954.
18. *House of Commons Debates*, vol. 536, 26 Jan 1955, col. 160; 4 Feb 1955, cols. *159–60*.
19. Dwight D. Eisenhower, *Mandate for Change, 1953–56* (London: Heinemann, 1963) p. 609; Anthony Eden, *The Eden Memoirs* Vol 3: *Full Circle* (London: Cassell, 1960) p. 309.
20. *Mandate for Change*, pp. 471–2.
21. 'United States Policy on Defence of Formosa', *Department of State Bulletin*, xxxii, 7 Feb 1955, pp. 211–13, emphasis added.
22. *The Times*, 28 Jan 1955.
23. *House of Commons Debates*, vol. 536, 7 Feb 1955, col. 1540.
24. *Full Circle*, p. 309.
25. Harold Macmillan, *Tides of Fortune, 1945–55* (London: Macmillan, 1969) p. 553.
26. Ibid.
27. *House of Commons Debates*, vol. 540, 28 Apr 1955, col. 1103.
28. *Tides of Fortune*, p. 553.
29. Statement by Eden, *House of Commons Debates*, vol. 536, 7 Feb 1955, col. 1533.
30. United Nations, *Security Council, Official Records*, 10 (689) 31 Jan 1955, pp. 1–13.
31. *People's Daily*, 31 Jan 1955; *Kwangming Daily*, 1 Feb 1955.
32. *New China News Agency*, 4 Feb 1955.
33. *The Times*, 4 Feb 1955; *Observer*, 6 Feb 1955.
34. *House of Commons Debates*, vol. 537, 14 Feb 1955, cols. 28–9.
35. *Department of State Bulletin*, xxxii, 9 May 1955, p. 756.
36. *House of Commons Debates*, vol. 538, 8 Mar 1955, col. 160.
37. *Hindu*, 5 Mar 1955; *Scotsman*, 26 Mar 1955.
38. *House of Commons Debates*, vol. 538, 8 Mar 1955, cols. 160–1.
39. *Tides of Fortune*, p. 613. See Trevelyan, op. cit., pp. 129–50.
40. *Full Circle*, p. 310.
41. *Department of State Bulletin*, xxxiii, 8 Aug 1955, pp. 219–21; *Daily Telegraph*, 26 July 1955.
42. *Department of State Bulletin*, xxxix, 13 Oct 1958, p. 565.
43. *House of Commons Debates*, vol. 594, 30 Oct 1958, cols. 327–8.
44. Dwight D. Eisenhower, *The White House Years: Waging Peace*,

1956—61 (London: Heinemann, 1966) p. 300.
    45. *Manchester Guardian*, 13 Sep 1958.
    46. *House of Commons Debates*, vol. 594, 30 Oct 1958, col. 329.
    47. *The Times*, 6 Sep 1958.
    48. *New York Times*, 6 Sept 1958.
    49. *The Times*, 13 Sep 1958; *Daily Telegraph*, 29 Aug 1958.
    50. Speech to the Foreign Press Association reported in the *Manchester Guardian*, 17 Sep 1958.
    51. *People's Daily*, 12 Dec 1958.

Chapter 8

    1. Harold Wilson, *The Labour Government, 1964—1970: A Personal Record* (London: Weidenfeld and Nicolson/Michael Joseph, 1971) p. 425.
    2. Rodgers, *House of Commons Debates*, vol. 766, 13 June 1968, col. 578.
    3. *House of Commons Debates*, vol. 754, 13 Nov 1967, col. 19.
    4. *People's Daily*, 16 Mar 1968; *Hsinhua News Agency*, 13 Mar 1968.
    5. *Daily Telegraph*, 14 Mar 1968, 1 Aug 1968.
    6. *House of Commons Debates*, vol. 766, 13 June 1968, cols 571—4.
    7. *Daily Telegraph*, 15 Mar 1968. A similar line was taken by the *Daily Express* on 22 Mar and 8 Aug.
    8. *House of Commons Debates*, vol. 766, 13 June 1968, col. 581.
    9. *Financial Times*, 15 Aug 1968.
    10. *Daily Telegraph*, 6 May 1968, 7 Sep 1968.
    11. *House of Commons Debates*, vol. 773, 18 Nov 1968, col. 866.
    12. *Hsinhua News Agency*, 28 Dec 1968.
    13. *Daily Express*, 10 May 1969.
    14. *House of Commons Debates*, vol. 778, 17 Feb 1969, col. 34.
    15. *Sunday Times*, 16 Feb 1969.
    16. *House of Commons Debates*, vol. 788, 21 Oct 1969, col. *220*.
    17. *Hsinhua News Agency*, 5 Oct 1969.
    18. *Financial Times*, 23 Oct 1970.
    19. *The Labour Government, 1964—70*, p. 787.
    20. *Guardian*, 21 Mar 1970.
    21. *Daily Telegraph*, 20 Mar 71; *House of Commons Debates*, vol. 813, 19 Mar 1971, col. *411*.
    22. *Financial Times*, 2 Nov 1972.
    23. *Sunday Times*, 19 Mar 1972.
    24. Godber, *House of Commons Debates*, vol. 825, 4 Nov 1971, cols 481—2.
    25. *House of Commons Debates*, vol. 801, 5 May 1970, col. 266.
    26. *Sunday Times*, 29 Nov 1970.
    27. *House of Commons Debates*, vol. 825, 4 Nov 1971, cols 481—2. See further *Speeches welcoming the Delegation of the People's Republic of China. . . at the Plenary Meeting of the 26th Session of the United Nations General Assembly, November 15, 1971* (Peking: Foreign Languages Press, 1971).
    28. *House of Commons Debates*, vol. 822, 2 Aug 1971, col. 1069.
    29. *House of Commons Debates*, vol. 828, 14 Dec 1971, col. 256.
    30. *House of Commons Debates*, vol. 832, 6 Mar 1972, col. 1012.
    31. For the text see *The Times* and *Hsinhua News Agency*, 14 Mar 1972. The Foreign Secretary's remarks are at *House of Commons*

Debates, vol. 833, 13 Mar 1972, col. 32.

32. *Daily Telegraph*, 7 June 1972.

33. *House of Commons Debates*, vol. 822, 2 Aug 1971, cols 1068—9.

34. *Financial Times*, 26 Oct and 3 Nov 1972.

35. *Financial Times* 26 Oct 1972.

36. *The Times* and *Hsinhua News Agency*, 26 May 1974.

37. *Financial Times*, 11 Apr 1974.

38. *The Times* 5 Nov 1970.

39. *Sunday Times*, 28 Sep 1971; *Financial Times*, 18 Jan 1972.

40. *Agreement. . . covering the Exhibition of Archaeological Finds of the People's Republic of China, London, July 2, 1973*, Cmd. 5417 (1973).

41. *House of Commons Debates*, vol. 834, 27 Mar 1972, col. 16; and *The Great Britain — China Centre*, mimeo. (Feb 1975) p. 1.

42. *Britain — China*, 1 (Autumn 1974) pp. 1—2.

43. *The Great Britain — China Centre*, p. 2.

44. 'A Statement of Policy', *SACU News*, 2 (12) (Dec 1967) p. 3.

45. *Daily Telegraph*, 3 Oct 1967; *The Times*, 4 Oct 1967.

46. *Free China Gazette*, 104 (Feb 1968) p. 12.

47. *Britain — China*, 1 (Autumn 1974) p. 2; see the earlier letter from Roderick MacFarquhar in *The Times*, 17 Nov 1972.

48. 'Lu Hsu-chang's Statement to British Businessmen on Cultural Revolution', *China Trade and Economic Newsletter*, 139 (May 1967) pp. 8—9.

49. *The Times*, 1 May 1974.

50. *Daily Telegraph*, 15 Mar 1968.

51. J. D. Laughton, 'Chinese Market Merits a Fresh Look', *Board of Trade Journal* (1970) pp. 809—11.

52. Noble, *House of Commons Debates*, vol. 827, 6 Dec 1971, col. *209.*

53. *Daily Telegraph*, 16 Apr 1971.

54. *Financial Times*, 13 Apr 1973.

55. *House of Commons Debates*, vol. 854, 9 Apr 1973, col. 923.

56. *The Times*, 21 Mar 1973, special report.

57. *Notes on the Position of the United Kingdom's Trade with Formosa*, cited at *China Association Bulletin*, 125, 22 Oct 1956, p. 5. See further F. H. H. King, 'British trade with Nationalist China', *Far Eastern Economic Review*, 17 June 1954.

58. *House of Commons Debates*, vol. 757, 22 Jan 1968, col. 5.

59. Geoffrey Stewart-Smith, *Daily Telegraph*, 2 Aug 1971.

60. *Daily Telegraph*, 14 Mar 1972.

Bibliographical Note

This brief note lists chiefly secondary sources on Sino-British relations in the period since 1949. A number of general works have been written. Fuller references to the source material on which the present book has been largely based, with the exception of Chapter 8, can be found in the author's doctoral thesis, 'Britain and China: A Study of the Making of Foreign Policy in the United Kingdom, with special reference to relations with China since 1949' (University College London, 1969). Two valuable book-length studies are Evan Luard, *Britain and China* (Baltimore: Johns Hopkins, 1962), which throws light on the ways in which relations after 1949 had their roots in the earlier historical encounters, and B. E. Porter, *Britain and the Rise of Communist China: A Study of British Attitudes, 1945–54* (Oxford University Press, 1967). Richard Harris has contributed a general review entitled 'Britain and China: Coexistence at Low Pressure' to A. M. Halpern's edited volume, *Policies towards China* (New York: McGraw-Hill, 1965). We have the memoirs of one former British chargé d'affaires in Peking, which makes for good reading: Humphrey Trevelyan, *Worlds Apart: China 1953–5, Soviet Union 1962–5* (London: Macmillan, 1971). A short unpublished study by Pekka Laine assesses British and American policies on recognition of Peking, and on the question of Chinese representation, in the early 1950s: *Forenta Staternas och Storbritanniens Attityder till Erkannendet av Kina och till Kinas Representation i Forenta Nationera* (Meddelanden fran Institutet For Samhallsforskning up Pratthallet av Statsvetenskapliga Fakulteten vid Abo Akademi, nr 31, maj 1963).

There has been a large number of studies of the historical background to the period studied in this book. The classical source for the earliest encounters is H. B. Morse, *Chronicles of the East India Company Trading to China*, 5 vols (Oxford University Press, 1926–9), and *International Relations of the Chinese Empire*, 3 vols (London: Longmans, 1910–18). Other studies of the first trading contacts include J. B. Eames, *The English in China, 1600–1843* (London: Pitman and Son, 1909), Earl H. Pritchard, *Anglo-Chinese Relations during the Seventeenth and Eighteenth Centuries* (New York: Octagon Books, 1970; originally published in 1929), and Helen Robbins, *Our First Ambassador to China* (London: John Murray, 1908). The nineteenth century has been more intensively studied. See in particular the books by W. C. Costin, *Great Britain and China, 1833–60* (Oxford: Clarendon Press, 1937), Michael Greenberg, *British Trade and the Opening of China, 1800–42* (Cambridge University Press, 1951), E. Holt, *The Opium Wars in China* (London: Putnam, 1964), John Selby, *The Paper Dragon: An Account of the China Wars, 1840–1900* (London: Barker, 1968), James S. Gregory, *Great Britain and the Taipings* (London: Routledge and Kegan Paul, 1969), L. K. Young, *British Policy in China, 1895–1902* (Oxford University Press, 1970), Francis E. Hyde, *Far Eastern Trade, 1860–1914* (London: Adam and Charles Black, 1973), and E. V. G. Kiernan, *British Diplomacy in China, 1880 to 1885* (Cambridge University Press, 1939). Extraterritoriality in China is discussed more specifically also in W. R. Fishel, *The End of Extraterritoriality in China* (University of California Press, 1962), and in W. W. Willoughby, *Foreign Rights and Interests in China*, 2 vols (Baltimore: Johns Hopkins, 1927).

British and Chinese attitudes during these periods are discussed in the first chapters of Luard's study. They are set in a broader perspective in two valuable works: R. Iyer, ed., *The Glass Curtain between Asia and Europe: A Symposium on the Historical Encounters and the Changing Attitudes of the Peoples of the East and West* (London: Oxford University Press, 1965), and Raymond Dawson, *The Chinese Chameleon: An Analysis of European Conceptions of Chinese Civilisation* (London: Oxford University Press, 1967). The impact of the two cultures on each other is the subject of Sir John T. Pratt's *China and Britain* (London: Collins, 1946). See also in this connection N. A. Pelcovits, *Old China Hands and the Foreign Office* (New York, 1948). Studies of British and European attitudes can with profit be compared with those of the

Americans, notably in H. R. Isaacs, *Scratches on Our Minds: American Images of China and India* (New York: Day, 1958), and in the beginning sections of A. T. Steele, *The American People and China* (New York: McGraw-Hill, 1966).

As documents have become available, scholars have increasingly turned their attention to the 1920s and 1930s. One book published in the United States nearer the time is Irving S. Friedman, *British Relations with China: 1931—39* (New York: Institute of Pacific Relations, 1940). More recent works include Ann Trotter, *Britain and East Asia, 1933—37* (Cambridge University Press, 1975), and Bradford A. Lee, *Britain and the Sino-Japanese War, 1937—1939: A Study in the Dilemmas of British Decline* (Stanford University Press, 1973).

The present book has devoted considerable attention at times to the ways in which post-1949 British policy towards China formed part of a wider Anglo-American approach to the problems posed by the establishment of the People's Republic. There is not the space here to list the studies that have been produced of various aspects of United States policy during this period. However, a number of Congressional documents contain much of value for an understanding of Washington's policy, and also of Anglo-American official exchanges on China policy. Some of the more useful in this respect (all published by the Government Printing Office, Washington, D.C.) are: *Military Situation in the Far East: Hearings before the Committee on Armed Services and the Committee on Foreign Relations*, US Senate (82nd Cong., 1st session, 1951), *Investigations on Shipments to Communist China: Hearings before a Committee on Interstate and Foreign Commerce*, US Senate (81st Cong., 2nd session, 1950), *Hearings before the Committee on Foreign Relations on the Japanese Peace Treaty . . .*, US Senate (82nd Cong., 2nd session, 1952), *Hearings on the Institute of Pacific Relations, Committee on the Judiciary*, US Senate (82nd Cong., 1st session, 1951), *Hearings on the Nomination of Philip C. Jessup to be United States Representative to the Sixth General Assembly of the United Nations, Committee on Foreign Relations*, US Senate (82nd Cong., 1st session, 1951), *The United States and Communist China in 1949 and 1950: The Question of Rapprochement and Recognition. A Staff Study prepared for the use of the Committee on Foreign Relations*, US Senate (93rd Cong., 1st session, 1973), *Economic*

Assistance to China and Korea: 1949—50. Hearings held in Executive Session before the Committee on Foreign Relations. US Senate (81st Cong., 1st and 2nd sessions, 1949 and 1950; published 1974), *Report from the Committee on Foreign Affairs of the House of Representatives on United States Policy on China, Report 1618* (81st Cong., 2nd session, 1950), *East-West Trade: Hearings before the Permanent Subcommittee on Investigations of the Committee on Government Operations*, US Senate (84th Cong., 2nd session, 1956), *United States Policy with respect to Mainland China. Hearings before the Committee on Foreign Relations*, US Senate (89th Cong., 2nd session, 1966), and *United States Relations with the People's Republic of China. Hearings before the Committee on Foreign Relations*, US Senate (92nd Cong., 1st session, 1971). The Truman Administration's 1949 White Paper is published as *United States Relations with China, with special reference to the period 1944—49* (1949).

Studies include Tang Tsou, *America's Failure in China, 1941—50* (University of Chicago Press, 1963), H. Kubek, *How the Far East was Lost: American Policy and the Creation of Communist China, 1941—9* (Chicago: Regnery, 1963), which approaches the period from an anti-appeasement viewpoint, and Roderick MacFarquhar, ed., *Sino-American Relations, 1949—71* (New York: Praeger, 1972). R. P. Newman's book, *Recognition of Communist China? A Study in Argument* (New York: Macmillan, 1961) is useful for enumerating the various aspects of the recognition debate as they have arisen in Congress and the press. There have been many articles of a more technical nature in the American law journals on questions of recognition. For a broader discussion see S. K. Hornbeck, 'Which Chinese: diplomatic recognition and official representation', *Foreign Affairs*, 34, 1 (Oct 1955).

Two articles which focus specifically on Anglo-American relations in the context of Far Eastern policy are the thoughts of the former Labour Prime Minister in C. R. Attlee, 'Britain and America: Common Aims, Different Opinions', *Foreign Affairs*, 32, 2 (Jan 1954), and G. F. Hudson, 'Will Britain and America split in Asia?', ibid., 31, 4 (July 1953).

Other powers regarded by Britain as legitimate contributors to British thinking on Asian problems have been India, Australia and Canada. The approaches of several countries to China are reviewed in Halpern's book cited above. On India, a former ambassador has written *In Two Chinas: Memoirs of a Diplomat* (by K. M. Panikkar; London: Allen and Unwin, 1955). There is a short general review, published at a period of later conflict between New Delhi and Peking: P. C. Chakravarti, *India's China Policy* (Bloomington: Indiana University Press, 1962). Further Commonwealth perspectives can be found in H. S. Albinski, *Australian Attitudes and Policies towards Communist China* (Princeton University Press, 1967), W. Levi, *Australia's Outlook on Asia* (Sydney: Angus and Robertson, 1958), and H. F. Angus, *Canada and the Far East, 1940—53* (Toronto University Press, 1953).

The period 1949—50, which embraced the first British reactions to the prospects of Communist rule in China, the establishment of the People's Republic, British diplomatic recognition, and the Sino-British official exchanges which followed, is discussed in each of the general surveys listed at the beginning of this note. In addition, a number of shorter pieces have discussed the encounters. One useful but unpublished study in this respect is A. D. Kopkind, 'Moral and Political Considerations in the Debate in Britain on Recognition of the Peking Government' (M.Sc. thesis, University of London, 1961). See further J. P. Jain, 'Chinese Reaction to British Recognition of the People's Republic of China', *International Studies*, IV, 1 (July 1952), and Hsi-en T. Chen, 'Relations between Britain and Communist China', *Current History*, 23, 135 (Nov 1952). Two discussions from a legal point of view are R. Gherson, 'British Recognition of China: Some Issues Examined', *The New Commonwealth* (Mar 1950), and G. W. Keeton, 'International Law in the Far Eastern War', *Twentieth Century* (Feb 1951). A Legal Adviser to the Foreign Office has summarised his views on the UN question in G. G. Fitzmaurice, 'Chinese Representation in the United Nations', *Yearbook of World Affairs*, 6 (1952). For the general background, see further H. Lauterpacht, *Recognition in International Law* (Cambridge University Press, 1947). N. V. K. Murthy has written a short comparative study: 'Recognition of Communist China under International Law, with special reference to the policies of Great Britain, the United States and India', *Indian Journal of Political Science*, 20, 2 (Apr—June 1959). Some indication of left-of-centre thinking at the time can be gained from the contributions to Otto B. van der Sprenkel, ed., *New China: Three Views* (London: Turnstile Press, 1950); see also the views of a former minister in K. G. Younger, 'The Far East', in T. E. M. McKitterick and K. G. Younger, ed., *Fabian International Essays* (London: Hogarth Press, 1957), and Bertrand Russell's *The Problem of China* (London: Allen and Unwin, 1966, 2nd impression).

Many books and articles have been written on the development of China's foreign policy during this period; these are useful for setting in perspective the Chinese response to British recognition, since this step was taken at the commencement of formal Sino-Soviet talks on the signing of an alliance between the two Communist powers. The Chinese view on the establishment of diplomatic relations in general terms can be found in *China. The Important Documents of the First Plenary Session of the Chinese People's Political Consultative Conference* (Peking: Foreign Languages Press, 1949), especially Chapter VII pp. 19–20. On the representation issue in the United Nations, see B. S. Weng, 'Communist China's Changing Attitudes towards the United Nations', *International Organisation*, XX, 4 (Autumn 1966), H. W. Briggs, 'Chinese Representation in the United Nations', *International Organisation*, VI, 2 (May 1952), and a more recent work, L.–C. Chen and Harold D. Lasswell, *Formosa, China and the United Nations: Formosa in the World Community* (New York: St Martin's Press, 1967), which discusses the merits of the various two-Chinas solutions to the question in the context of possible shifts of Western policies.

The evolution of Sino-British trade relations is discussed in the various studies of the background from the seventeenth century noted above. A major study here is G. C. Allen and A. G. Donnithorne, *Western Enterprise in Far Eastern Economic Development: China and Japan* (London: Allen and Unwin, 1954). Sir Compton Mackenzie has written up the history of one of the major banks: *Realms of Silver: One Hundred Years of Banking in the Far East* (London: Routledge and Kegan Paul, 1954). The Board of Trade's mission of 1946 reported on many aspects of Chinese commercial, financial and political life, and played some part in shaping the government's response to China during the civil war period and after: see its *Report of the United Kingdom Trade Mission to China, October to December, 1946* (London: HMSO, 1948). See also H. J. Collar, 'British Commercial Relations with China', *International Affairs*, 29, 4 (Oct 1953).

The best guides to developments in connection with strategic regulation of the China trade are often the publications of the United States Mutual Security Agency: *Battle Act Reports* (annually from 1952, various titles). See further Susan Strange, 'Strategic embargoes', *Yearbook of World Affairs* (1958), J. Wilczynski, *The Economics and Politics of East-West Trade* (London: Macmillan, 1969; New York: Praeger), and J. R. Garson, 'The American Trade Embargo against China', in Alexander Eckstein, ed., *China Trade Prospects and United States Policy* (New York: Praeger, 1971), which reviews the evolution of the NATO control system.

Anglo-American exchanges on SEATO are evaluated in L. O. Lerche, 'United States, Great Britain, and SEATO: A Case Study in the Fait Accompli', *Journal of Politics*, 18, 3 (Aug 1956). For a later appreciation, see Peter Lyon, 'SEATO in perspective', *Yearbook of World Affairs* (1965). On one of the factors lying behind the 1954 exchanges, see D. E. McHenry and R. W. Rosecrance, 'The "exclusion" of the United Kingdom from the ANZUS Pact', *International Organisation*, 12, 3 (Summer 1958).

Two short studies of the offshore islands problem in the light of United States policy are O. E. Clubb, 'Formosa and the Offshore Islands in American policy, 1950–5', *Political Science Quarterly*, 74, 4 (Dec 1959), and Tang Tsou, 'The Quemoy Imbroglio: Chiang Kai-shek and the United States', *Western Political Quarterly*, XII (Dec 1959). The situation seen from a British perspective is discussed in G. F. Hudson, 'Typhoon Coast', *Twentieth Century* (Apr 1958).

Index